T0291519

THE COMING
NEW INDUSTRIAL
STATE:
RELOADED

THE COMING NEW INDUSTRIAL STATE: RELOADED

SERGEY BODRUNOV

Translated by
Tomi Haxhi

BOSTON
2023

Library of Congress Cataloging-in-Publication Data

Names: Bodrunov, S. D. (Sergeĭ Dmitrievich), 1958-, author. | Haxhi, Tomi,
    translator.
Title: The coming new industrial state : reloaded / Sergei Bodrunov.
Other titles: Grĩadushchee. English
Description: Boston : Academic Studies Press, 2023. | Originally published
    as Grĩadushchee : novoe industrial'noe obshchestvo : perezagruzka,
    INIR im. S.ĨU. Vitte, Sankt-Peterburg, 2016. | Includes
    bibliographical references. | In English, translated from the original
    Russian.
Identifiers: LCCN 2023023131 (print) | LCCN 2023023132 (ebook) | ISBN
    9798887192864 (hardback) | ISBN 9798887192888 (adobe pdf) | ISBN
    9798887192895 (epub)
Subjects: LCSH: Industrial policy–Russia (Federation) | Industrial
    management–Russia (Federation) | Russia (Federation)–Economic
    conditions–1991- | Russia (Federation)–Economic policy–1991-
Classification: LCC HD3616.R83 B63 2023 (print) | LCC HD3616.R83 (ebook)
    | DDC 322/.30947–dc23/eng/20230616
LC record available at https://lccn.loc.gov/2023023131
LC ebook record available at https://lccn.loc.gov/2023023132

ISBN 9798887192864 (hardback)
ISBN 9798887192888 (adobe pdf)
ISBN 9798887192895 (epub)

Book design by Lapiz Digital Services
Cover design by Ivan Grave

Published by Academic Studies Press.
1577 Beacon Street
Brookline, MA 02446, USA
press@academicstudiespress.com
www.academicstudiespress.com

Contents

Introduction

The successive crises of the late twentieth and early twenty-first centuries have made one thing clear: the world has changed. The increased instability of our social systems, the turbulent waters of global finance, and the tectonic shifts underway in the global economy are all harbingers of our civilization's transition to a new state, which our accepted economic-philosophical constructs and socioeconomic models cannot adequately describe.

What, then, is the driving force of this change? And where are we going?

Karl Marx deemed modern society a "realm of necessity," and dreamed of a "realm of freedom." "Just as the savage must wrestle with Nature to satisfy his wants, to maintain and reproduce life, so must civilized man, and he must do so in all social formations and under all possible modes of production. With his development this realm of physical necessity expands as a result of his wants; but, at the same time, the forces of production which satisfy these wants also increase."[1]

Human *needs* are those same "necessities" that require conscious human activity to satisfy them. Since the beginning of human history, humanity has been satisfying its needs by creating material goods, things, products, through an activity called material production. In this sense, the history of humanity is the

---

1 Karl Marx, *Capital*, vol. 3 (New York: International Publishers, 1959), 593.

history of material production and its development to meet increasing human needs. Marx terms this history "the expansion of the forces of production," that is, the steady increase in the capacity of material production to meet the various—not only material—needs of society. Moreover, the state of material production largely determines the type of social order of any given epoch. The development of technology brings us closer to Marx's "realm of freedom," to freedom from want. It allows us to reduce the necessity of devoting the majority of our time, resources, and energy to the production of material products.

This development raises a legitimate question: what caused the changes in material production itself? Why and how did these changes come about? And what are the patterns of their development?

The concept of *social production* [obshchestvennoe proizvodstvo] brings together and puts into focus some of these fundamental questions: on the one hand, on the relationship between material production and public services, the structure of the economic system and the developmental patterns of its material foundations, and the relationship between industrial and postindustrial tendencies; and on the other hand, on the most important practical issues of reindustrialization, import substitution, and the revival or integration of high-tech production, science, education, industrial policy, etc. The present book is devoted to this complex of problems, and its somewhat provocative title makes clear the author's position. This book goes beyond the widespread (and author-supported) imperative of reindustrializing the economy on a new technological basis. Not only does it criticize the ideas of post-industrialism and assert the importance of material production, without, however, reproducing the work of John Kenneth Galbraith on the "new industrial state"—it goes much deeper than that. Among the concepts discussed within are, firstly, the "negation of the negation" of Galbraith's "new industrial state" of fifty years ago, which allows us to synergize the achievements of modern technological and organizational production on the basis of new technologies and in new economic and institutional forms; and secondly, the dialectical negation of postindustrial trends and achievements (such as the elevated role of the individual, the growing importance of the environmental and social problems of industrial activity, the growth of the knowledge-intensity of social production, etc.), and simultaneously the rejection of its vices. In the end, this book is about the inevitability of society's transition to a new stage of development, the next generation of industrial society, which I have named the second generation of the new industrial state: NIS.2.

Despite its relatively short length, this book was written over a long period of time. I came up with some parts more than twenty years ago, and others in more recent years, using research on the technological development of modern material production, which my colleagues and I have carried out at the S. Y. Witte Institute for New Industrial Development (INID). I have put forward many of the book's tentative theses at various scientific forums and conferences, in scientific journals, public speeches, in my own or collectively authored monographs, and the works of the INID. Until now, however, my ideas on the development of modern society and the basis of this development—material production—have not been published in full. What has been published of my ideas on the coming civilizational changes, which are not all that contradictory to existing conceptual frameworks, has not elicited any particular objections. Presented in full and arranged in a certain sequence, however, my ideas offer a vision of the future that differs significantly from accepted opinion. Nevertheless, I look forward to my readers' careful analysis of the book and your thoughtful criticism.

Part One

MATERIAL PRODUCTION AND INDUSTRY: TECHNOLOGY, LABOR, AND PRODUCT

Since the second half of the twentieth century, the economies of developed countries have seen their service industries grow and their industries of material production shrink, both in number of employees and in share of the GDP. Similar structural shifts are now taking place in the economies of newly industrialized countries. Most scholars saw these shifts as clear evidence of the transition to a postindustrial stage of development, and, indeed, as progress, though there were also critics who championed deindustrialization and spoke of the decline of capitalist civilization.[1]

Does the growth of the service industry necessarily mean the decline of material production, its role and importance in a society? Is the growing importance of the service industry always a good thing, a sign of progress? And is the industrial mode of production now a thing of the past? Such questions come naturally when we analyze the ongoing structural shifts in the economies of developed countries and force us to examine the core concepts of the process of production and its results.

---

1 See, for example: Robert Heilbroner, *An Inquiry into the Human Prospect* (New York: Norton, 1974); Robert Heilbroner, *Business Civilization in Decline* (New York: Norton, 1976); Robert Heilbroner, "Economic Problems of 'Postindustrial' Society," in *Dimensions of Society*, ed. D. Potter and P. Sarre (London: Hodder & Stoughton Educational Division, 1974), 234.

Chapter 1

Production and Its Process: The Industrial Mode of Production

---

1.1 The product and the production process

A product is an external object, a thing that is obtained by transforming natural material and adapting it to meet human needs. It is the materialized [materializovannym] result of the application of human knowledge for human needs, primarily through the production of material goods or the provision of services based on the use of said goods. Products (things) created by humankind do not necessarily take physical form, as some needs are met by products that have an intangible, immaterial nature. In this case, there are two circumstances that we must always take into account.

The first is that all services (with very few exceptions) are rendered only by means of this or that material product. Without the production of material products, one cannot render services.

The second is that it is only through material production that people can satisfy their basic needs for food, clothing, shelter, transportation, communication, etc. Many of those engaged in the provision of services can only exist and go about their business because there are others providing them with the necessary material products.

As the production process develops, natural matter plays less and less of a role in each man-made product, and the technosphere [tekhnosfera] plays more and more of one. And when it comes to the technosphere, it is not the physical power of tools or the skills to use them that matters, but the power of knowledge embodied in those tools, which determines a person's ability to use them and increases his efficiency in achieving his goals. This dynamic also informs the evolution of the product itself. To determine the extent of this evolution, I will introduce the concept of the level (or complexity) of the product. This concept may be expressed purely quantitatively, by determining how many steps the raw materials have gone through in the process of production, to arrive as a finished product that satisfies certain needs. However, a qualitative assessment of the complexity of the product is much more important.

Philosophically speaking, any product is objectified human knowledge, embodied in a thing, an object, created with the help of this knowledge. The general trend as the production process develops is a significant reduction in the use of natural matter, natural energy, and natural power to make a product. As a result, there is a decrease in the consumption of raw materials and supplies. At the same time, the role of increasingly complex tools and, most importantly, the amount of knowledge needed to produce a higher-level product increase dramatically.

The process of making a product, i.e., the transformation of a natural substance to meet human needs, is the production process. The most essential elements of the production process are human labor, source and raw materials, technology, and the organization of production. But it is the interaction of these elements that is the most important.

Thus, it is possible to identify three essential elements of human activity in the production process: labor, technology, and the coordination of labor and necessary technologies. To obtain in the product the necessary quality, quantity, and other such criteria, it is necessary to manage the production process, to organize it. From this point of view, the product is the result of the interaction of the three aforementioned components of the production process.

1.2 The industrial mode of production

The question of the mode of production, or the type of production process, is of fundamental importance, because it is one of the determining factors of the structure of the social order. Historically, we can identify two stages in the development of the process of social production. The first is a mode of production based on the use of simple (manual) tools and a number of simple mechanisms, operated by human or animal muscle power, or less often by other purely natural forces (such as wind or water). The complexity of the necessary tools of labor is low, the product is made primarily by natural energy, and the amount of knowledge required to activate the correct combination of components in the production process is small and changes little over time.

The second stage is the industrial mode of production, in which most of the work is carried out with the help of machines (complex tools of labor that include a motor, a transmission mechanism, and an operating instrument). The energy required to perform the work is generated and/or converted into the necessary form by machines. The amount of knowledge necessary to make the various components work together is considerably higher. And improving the various components of the production process requires that that knowledge be constantly updated. Simple, traditional skills are no longer sufficient; rather, a broad scientific knowledge and its proper application become necessary. The organization of the production process also becomes more and more complex.

The industrial mode of production could not, of course, have emerged without the previous mode of production based on manual labor and manual tools.

At first, ancient human societies knew no machinery at all. The products and goods produced by ancient people were created with human or animal energy, in labor-intensive production activities such as plowing, transporting, etc. As labor knowledge and experienced developed, humankind began to make active use of other natural forces from the realm of inanimate nature. Creating heat by chemical reaction, combustion via oxidation of organic substances, found wide and various uses: in pottery (kilning), metallurgy (smelting), metal processing (forging, casting), and cooking (boiling, frying, smoking). Wind power was now used to propel ships and power windmills and water-lifting mechanisms. Flowing water was also used to power mills and water-lifting mechanisms.

It is worth noting that the various types of mills were the first type of machine to be widely used in the preindustrial era.

The development of manufacturing, which divided previously unified production processes into specialized operations, represented another step toward a new mode of production. Dividing the production process into more simplified components created the opportunity to carry out these simplified operations with mechanical tools rather than manual labor.

Around the end of the seventeenth century, a different situation emerges in production. The amount of knowledge accumulated, the use and transformation of natural energy, the laws of mechanics, and yet other factors led to a new stage in the development of production: the transition to a mechanical method of production. The invention of the steam engine, the study of electricity, methods of its conversion and storage, the development of mechanical and electrical power transmission, all led to the mass use of devices which allowed for a qualitatively different type of production.

Previously the use of complex machines was dependent on natural power like wind or water, and the machinery was placed only where such power could be accessed and harnessed. With the invention of the steam engine and internal combustion engine, it became possible to produce food products almost anywhere where fuel could be transported, or electrical power could be transmitted. This development also allowed for an unprecedented level of security and reliability in the production process, now free from the vagaries of natural forces.

Moreover, more complex machines powered by new energy sources enabled the mass production of uniform products with the same approximate characteristics (size, quality, etc.). There was a sharp increase in the volume of production and in the range and quality of products available. Machine technology allowed for the standardization of manufacturing processes. The potential for the further automation of the production process was evident, as more and more human skills were replaced with increasingly sophisticated machines.

This new mode of production greatly reduced the necessity for natural energy sources. While the specific consumption of materials fell, the use of complex machines increased considerably. This development entailed an increase in in the amount of knowledge used in the production of industrial goods.

The *technological application of knowledge*, or *technology* itself as part of the production process, is bipartite: there is the tangible part (workers of appropriate qualifications, equipment, appliances, raw materials) and the intangible part, the knowledge of how best to use the physical technology. It is specifically the knowledge that goes into the product that defines the product's quality, its consumer features and characteristics, or its ability to satisfy the growing needs of its users.

As of yet, there are no modes of production other than the industrial and the preindustrial. Thus, depending on its mode of production, a product can be either industrial or nonindustrial. Nonmachine technologies (such as biotechnology) have emerged and are already in use, but they are still far from becoming the basis for a fundamentally new mode of social production.

As noted above, a product can be both tangible and intangible (a service). This principle applies also to products of industrial production. A service can be industrial in nature if, for example, in the process of its provision an industrial product is used, or if the service is aimed at maintaining the process of industrial production. In this case, this sort of service would be impossible in a nonindustrial mode of production. Both the industrial product and the industrial service are aimed at satisfying those human needs that arise at a certain stage of societal development, when the industrial mode of production becomes dominant. From this point of view, an industrial service is not inherently different from an industrial product.

1.3 Industrial labor

The active force that unites all the components of production into a single process is human labor. "Labor is, in the first place, a process in which both man and Nature participate, and in which man of his own accord starts, regulates, and controls the material re-actions between himself and Nature. He opposes himself to Nature as one of her own forces, setting in motion arms and legs, head and hands, the natural forces of his body, in order to appropriate Nature's productions in a form adapted to his own wants. By thus acting on the external world and changing it, he at the same time changes his own nature."[1]

For this reason, labor is first of all a purposeful activity: the person engaged in the labor process pursues a certain goal, directs his efforts to achieve a certain end result. Toward this end, the worker must know exactly what he wants to achieve, i.e., he must have an image in his head of the final product. Additionally, he must be able to imagine which technologies could help him achieve his desired result, which requires a certain knowledge. In addition to that knowledge, the worker should have the skills to translate his ideal plan into practice. The labor process also requires that the worker subordinate his will to his desired goal, to concentrate and mobilize his knowledge, skills, and energy to obtain the final result: the product of labor.

The labor process also depends on the material conditions under which the worker works, on the availability of raw materials and tools. Industrial labor is based on the use of machinery and aims to create an industrial product, i.e., a product of high complexity with standardized characteristics, adapted for mass production in order to obtain a multiplicity of homogenous products. Industrial labor differs from nonindustrial labor in the volume of applied knowledge. This knowledge may be unequally distributed among the workers in the labor process, who possess the full volume of necessary knowledge only as a unit.

---

1   Karl Marx, *Capital*, Vol 1. (Moscow: Progress Publishers, 1977).

An industrial worker's qualifications depend not only on his experience, but also on his training, special skills, and acquired knowledge. As a general rule, industrial labor is the activity of a person who has undergone the appropriate training, through which he gained the necessary knowledge to produce an industrial product. The industrial worker should know and understand the characteristics of the applied technologies and equipment, their limits and how best to use them, as well as the characteristics of the raw materials and the methods of their processing toward the final result. The efficiency of industrial labor thus depends significantly on the level of the worker's knowledge.

1.4 Technologies

To give the simplest definition, technology is a set of production methods and processes that enables the processing of raw materials into a final product. A more detailed definition suggests that "technology (from the Greek *techne* [art] and *logos* [word, instruction]) is a method of transforming matter, energy, and information in the process of manufacturing, processing, and recycling materials, assembling a finished product, quality control, and management. Technology is the realization of methods, techniques, a mode of work, and sequence of operations. It is closely linked with the means used, the equipment, tools, and materials. A set of technological operations constitutes a manufacturing process."[2]

Without knowledge of technology, and without the knowledge needed to develop and apply technology, it is impossible to ensure a normal production process that achieves its purpose. "Natural science *informs* us more or less adequately about objective natural processes, while technology more or less effectively *controls* these processes on the basis of this information, transforming them into *purposeful* processes, i.e., technological ones."[3]

Since its inception, industrial technology has demanded a greater and greater application of scientific knowledge. Whereas the first machines could be the product of amateur and self-taught inventors, more recent machinery, its systematic development, and the industrial mode of production as a whole could not take place without a deep scientific knowledge of technological

---

2   B. A. Raizberg, L. Sh. Lozovsky, and E. V. Starodubtseva, eds., *Modern Economics Dictionary*, 2nd ed. (Moscow: Infra-M, 1999), 479. (in Russ.)

3   S. K. Abachiev, "Machine and Non-Machine Technology: Essence, History, Prospects," *Naukovedenie* 3, no. 4 (2012): 4. http://naukove-denie.ru/sbornik12/12-34.pdf. (in Russ.)

processes. The evolution of theoretical mechanics, physics, and chemistry in the seventeenth and eighteenth centuries created the scientific basis for the subsequent breakthroughs that allowed for an industrial mode of production. By the nineteenth century, a special theory of machines began to develop. The rapid growth in the use of machinery required further development of scientific knowledge in a wide range of disciplines.

The increasing complexity of all the components of the industrial production process determined this development. It became necessary to study the properties of different materials, how to process them and create new materials, and the properties of different kinds of energy (mechanical, thermal, electric), how to produce, convert, transmit, and use it in the production process. Extensive research was necessary to create and use complex machines, to understand complex physical and chemical processes that occur during the processing of raw materials with different tools. Finally, the labor process itself became the subject of scientific research with the aim of a more effective use of human labor. Technology, as a necessary element of the production process, has a complex structure. It has tangible content: the equipment, devices, appliances, and materials that are put into action by technology and in which technology is substantively realized. It also has intangible content, no less important: the knowledge of how to use the material component of technology. It is no coincidence that the word *technology* itself is used to refer not only to technological processes as such, but also to the branch of knowledge that studies technological processes.

It can be said that the level of a technology depends directly on the amount of knowledge that has been incorporated in it. The widely used term *high tech* refers precisely to technologies based on the application of the latest scientific knowledge.

The complexity and infinite variety of industrial technology has predetermined an extreme development in specialization and division of labor. As a result, most workers no longer possess the full technology for the production of a certain product but perform only one partial function within the framework of this technology.

1.5 The organization of production

In the industrial mode, the organization of production is especially important due to two main circumstances. I have already discussed the first at length: the increasing complexity of the production process, the sound combination and interaction of all its components, requires specialized knowledge. The second is the transformation of the production process from a predominantly individual to a predominantly collective process based on the interaction of many workers. The management of human interaction becomes a necessary element in the production process due to a newfound specialization and division of labor.

For this reason, the organization of production addresses two of the most important challenges in the industrial production process: the organization of technological processes and the organization of people, both in the most rational way. The results of both must fit together so that there is no conflict between the interests of the efficiency of the technological process and the interests of the workers.

Development in the methods of organization lagged slightly behind the other elements of industrial production. As early as the nineteenth century, methods of organizing flow production were evolving somewhat spontaneously, based on the physical placement of the machines in the form of the production line, allowing for consistent activity. It was only at the beginning of the twentieth century that we see the first conscious methods of production organization arise; Taylorism, Fordism, the conveyor method in assembly-line production.

The conveyor method, derived from the principle of flow production (an assembly of workers performing sequential operations along a conveyor line, along which the assembled product moves), needed a big upgrade in its organization. The method necessitates the timely delivery of parts and components in the right quantity to each assembly point. This required an upgrade in the logistics of production, as well as the continuous and rhythmic flow of required parts and components. The *just-in-time* [strogo vovremia] delivery method was another step in the development of flow production and its organization. It allowed workers to make do without large stocks of parts and raw materials.

However, the conveyor production failed to address the conflict between the maximum efficiency of the technological production process and the personal interests of the workers. Conveyor work was, with good reason, seen as boring and monotonous. Workers were also displeased with the rigid hierarchy of production management inherent in the conveyor method. Different methods of organizing production developed to respond to these problems. In some cases, instead of the conveyor method with its extreme division of labor, the brigade method was used instead. An ethos of "human relations in the workplace" supplemented the hierarchical management system, better addressing how to motivate workers.

As technology, labor, and product continually become more and more complicated, the organization of production plays an ever-greater role in increasing its efficiency. With each new improvement of technology, there must be a corresponding improvement of the organization of production, aimed at a greater efficiency in providing industrial products and services. The complexity of the organizational system depends most critically on the amount of knowledge necessary to develop its methods and to carry them out.

1.6 Knowledge

The nature of the knowledge that goes into a product ultimately determines the product's level. This knowledge determines the utilitarian properties of a product, how it will perform in the hands of the consumer. It increases the product's capacity to answer increasingly more diverse human needs.

When you increase or decrease the amount of knowledge that goes into a product, you complicate or simplify the product, respectively. In much the same way, an increase in the knowledge that goes into a technology leads to its improvement, and a decrease to its primitivization. An increase in the worker's knowledge leads to better qualifications, and a decrease to worse qualifications.

The enormous amount of knowledge that goes into the industrial mode of production has led, since the late nineteenth century, to a new trend in production: a new kind of production where we see a large transfer of knowledge and its technological application into more specialized branches of social production. Science, education, and research and production (R&D) continue to gain a larger and larger share in state budgets and in their GDP. The interaction and transfer between knowledge production and direct production is growing closer. This trend leads us to think that the future society will be—or already is—a society based primarily on knowledge production, rather than one based on the production of material goods. Allow me to probe this question further.

Having first considered the building blocks of the production process and having then demonstrated the characteristics of the industrial mode of production, I will now move on to the historical evolution of this mode and I will examine the problems that arise in the course of this evolution in different countries. Although I will primarily focus on the Russian example, it is important to consider it in the global context, which influences Russia's economic situation and perspectives.

I will now return to the questions posed at the beginning of the book. One of the most obvious trends in industrial production over the last half century, and a symptom of many other changes, is the profound structural shift away from material production and toward services. These changes have been interpreted variously, and their interpretations have a major influence on economic policymaking, and by extension, on the future of the states that adopt those policies. For this reason, the concern of this book is to understand the nature of the ongoing structural shifts and their importance in the present day.

Chapter 2

The Service Industry, Material Production, and Their Correlation in the Modern Economy[1]

Today's Russian economy is characterized by the clear deterioration—or at the very least, the stagnation—of a majority of the sectors of material production. The situation demands that we take a closer look at the correlation between the service industry and industries of material production. To what extent does growth in the service sector determine trends of technological and social progress? Is a decrease in the share of material production always a good thing for an economy? To tackle these questions, we need to establish clear criteria. This will provide a solid scientific basis for any structural policy guidelines.

2.1. How to distinguish between services and material production

The French economist Jean-Baptiste Say was the first to introduce the category of "service" in economic theory. In his 1803 "Treatise on Political Economy," he

---

1 The first four paragraphs of this chapter are from: S. D. Bodrunov and A. I. Kolganov, "The Sphere of Services and Material Production: Problems of Correlation in Modern Economy," *Economic Revival of Russia* 1 (2016): 9–30. (in Russ.)

discussed machine services (chapter 4)[2] and capital services (chapter 7).[3] Adam Smith and David Ricardo, whom Say considered his teachers, had, however, written about services in an economic sense before him. It is more accurate, then, to call Say the originator of a more modern, broader interpretation of the concept of "service."

Unlike the titans of classical political economy, Say singled out three factors of production— labor, capital, and land. In this, he became the founder of the theory of the three factors of production. These factors constitute the total "productive funds." The three factors directly contribute to the creation of all the goods of a nation, and their sum total constitutes the basic national wealth. Each fund provides a "productive service" through which real products are made.[4]

Man, capital, and land thus constitute what Say calls productive services. The law of supply and demand regulates the price of services—the cost of rent, interest, and wages—as well as the price of products. Thanks to the entrepreneur, the value of products is distributed among "various productive services," and services are distributed among industries according to the needs of the latter. The theory of the distribution of wealth is thus in harmony with the theory of exchange and production.[5]

A later French economist, Frédéric Bastiat (1801–1850), built on Say's theory of services but focused more on personal services and their role in the harmonization of interests. By "service" Bastiat meant not only the real input of labor in the production process, but also any effort someone makes, or effort from which someone is relieved by using the service (thus the idea of social services).[6] In Bastiat's view, the market economy is a real realm of freedom and harmony because all the members of a market society "are compelled to render each other mutual services and assistance toward a common goal."[7]

Despite the difference between Say's and Bastiat's view on services, they share a common approach, which suggests that capitalist society is a society of a mutual and mutually beneficial exchange of services, and the beneficial effects of

---

2 Jean-Baptiste Say, *Treatise on Political Economy*. http://ek-lit.narod.ru/saysod.htm
3 Ibid.
4 See O. von Böhm-Bawerk, *Capital and Interest, 1884–1889*, in *Selected Works on Value, Interest, and Capital* (Moscow: Eksmo, 2009), 373. (in Russ.)
5 See S. Gide and S. Rist, *History of Economic Doctrines* (Moscow: Ekonomika, 1995), 3. (in Russ.)
6 See T. D. Burmenko, *The Sphere of Services in Modern Society: Economics, Management, Marketing; A Course of Lectures*, ed. T. D. Burmenko, N. N. Danilenko, and T. A. Turenko (Irkutsk: BGU-EP, 2004). (in Russ.)
7 N. E. Titova, *History of Economic Studies: A Course of Lectures* (Moscow: Humanities Publishing Center "VLADOS," 1997), 288. http://www.gumer.info/bibliotek_Buks/Econom/Titova/10.php. (in Russ.)

human activity may be broadly classified as "services" (for Say, this also includes the use of things). In the same way, any economic relations between people can be interpreted as mutual services.

Meanwhile, the modern conceptualization of services goes back to Adam Smith. He divided the results of human activity into those that are embodied in goods, and those that disappear the moment their useful effect takes place. Services belongs to the latter category.[8]

Marx adopted and developed Smith's take on services. Some of Smith's positions on the concept of services also entered into modern academic discourse. Though he devoted much of his attention to the concept of services, Marx was sharply opposed to Say's and Bastiat's positions on the topic. From his point of view, the notion of capitalist industrial relations as a system of the mutual and harmonious exchange of services not only obscures the real nature of economic relations in capitalist society but makes the very concept of "service" empty and meaningless, since anything can be fitted under this concept.

Describing the concept of services as a result of the production process, Marx wrote: "*Service*, [...] is nothing but a term for the particular use-value which the labor provides, like any other commodity; it is however a specific term for the particular use-value of labor in so far as it does not render service in the form of a *thing*, but in the form of an *activity*."[9]

Marx's distinction between services whose effects are embodied in goods and services with no tangible results is the basis for the modern division of services into tangible and intangible. "Certain *services*, or the *use-values*, resulting from certain forms of activity or labor are embodied in *commodities*; others on the contrary leave no tangible result *existing apart* from the persons themselves who perform them; in other words, their result is not a *vendible commodity*."[10]

From Marx's point of view, social production must be structured such that material production provides sufficient funds to pay for nonproductive services. It is the workers engaged in material production who hold up the rest of society. "All productive workers, when all is said and done, produce firstly the means for the payment of unproductive workers, and secondly, products which are consumed by those who *do not perform any labor*."[11]

There are services that play a different role from all the others because they are part of the process of the reproduction of the labor force. Marx interprets

---

8 See Adam Smith, *An Inquiry into the Nature and Causes of the Wealth of Nations* (Moscow: Sotsekgiz, 1962), 244. (in Russ.)
9 Karl Marx, *Theories of Surplus Value* (Moscow: Progress Publishers, 1969), 1326.
10 Ibid., 1327.
11 Ibid., 348.

this distinction as follows: "The whole world of 'commodities' can be divided into two great parts. First, labor- power; second, commodities as distinct from labor-power itself. As to the purchase of such services as those which train labor-power, maintain or modify it, etc., in a word, give it a specialized form or even only maintain it—thus for example the schoolmaster's service, in so far as it is 'industrially necessary' or useful; the doctor's service in so far as he maintains health and so conserves the source of all values, labor-power itself—these are services which yield in return 'a vendible commodity, etc.,' namely labor-power itself, into whose costs of production or reproduction these services enter."[12] In Marx's time, the share of this kind of labor in the total cost of the reproduction of the labor force was insignificant. Today, however, the importance of such services in the reproduction of the labor force (specially the most qualified part of it) has increased significantly. Economists have taken note, and the modern concept of "human capital" reflects this increase in importance.

According to Marx, from the capitalist point of view all labor, regardless of its characteristics, is productive if it is exchanged for capital. "An actor, for example, or even a clown, according to this definition, is a productive worker if he works in the service of a capitalist (an entrepreneur) to whom he returns more labor than he receives from him in the form of wages; while a jobbing tailor who comes to the capitalist's house and patches his trousers for him, producing a mere use-value for him, is an unproductive worker."[13]

Marx thus clearly distinguishes between economic and productive approaches to the interpretation of services. According to Marx, economically, a service is something that is exchanged not for capital, but for income.

Personal services are unproductive from the point of view of value creation (they can influence the productivity of labor that does create value but are not themselves part of the process of value creation), and the same goes for their consumer (net expenses). But if the provision of services is organized as capitalist entrepreneurship, it becomes productive for the entrepreneur (because it brings him a return on capital).

The situation is more complicated with services directly related to the process of production, such as bookkeeping. Marx approaches these services as he does personal services: they may contribute, in one way or another, to the productivity of labor that creates value (or saves on production costs), but they do not themselves create value. Marx does not, however, draw a clear line between the types of service activities included in this category.

---

12 Ibid., 310.
13 Ibid., 303.

Nevertheless, this question is very relevant when it comes to the transformation of science into a direct productive force, and to the modern-day "information revolution."

Economic theory currently provides only some general ideas about how a service differs from a material product. There is as of yet no consensus between economists, or between legal scholars, on the issue, and many in these fields complain that the concept of "service" remains ill-defined for academic use. Thus, Vladislav A. Perepelkin notes that even in economic dictionaries there are conflicting definitions,[14] and lists some of them.[15]

There is likewise no uniform interpretation of a service in international practice.[16] According to Kh. Vorachek, there exists no unified concept of services that could encompass the diversity of the phenomenon—though many varied opinions exist on the topic.[17]

A service is most commonly defined in opposition to the material product of production, as another kind of result of production. This is essentially a negative definition. "The decades-long academic debate over what should be understood as a service has up to now led only to negative definitions, determined by separating services from material goods (commodities), instead of forging a positive definition that reveals the deep essence of that economic category we call 'services.'"[18]

The existing approach to distinguishing between different services dates back to Marx. According to this approach, there are two types of services: tangible (productive) services are those that result in material goods; intangible (nonproductive) services are those with no tangible result.[19] As a rule, the latter set, so-called personal services, aims to meet the personal needs of the populace.[20]

---

14 V. A. Perepelkin, "The Concept of 'Service' in Economic Theory," in *Vestnik of Samara State University* 69 (2009): 38. http://cyberleninka.ru/article/n/ponyatie-usluga-v-ekonomicheskoy-teorii. (in Russ.)

15 L. I. Lopatnikov, *Economic and Mathematical Dictionary* (Moscow: Nauka, 1993), 448; I. Bernard, *Explanatory Dictionary of Economics*, Vol. 2, ed. I. Bernard and J.-C. Collie (Moscow: International Relations, 1994), 720; A. Woll et al., *Wirtschaftslexikon* (Munich: Oldenbourg, 1994), 770.

16 A. N. Korol and S. A. Khlynov, "Services: Definition and Classification," in *Scientific Notes of Taganrog State University* 5, no. 4 (2014): 1323–28. http://pnu.edu.ru/media/ejournal/articlec/2014/TGU_5_357.pdf.

17 Kh. O. Vorachek, "On the State of the 'Theory of Services Marketing,'" *Problems of the Theory and Practice of Management* 1 (2002): 99–103.

18 Perepelkin, 38.

19 M. V. Solodkov, T. D. Polyakova and L. N. Ovsyannikov, *Theoretical Problems of Services in the Non-Productive Sphere under Socialism* (Moscow: Moscow University Press, 1972), 107–8; V. S. Semionov, *The Service Sphere and Its Employees* (Moscow: Politizdat, 1966), 4.

20 L. B. Sitdikova, "Theoretical Bases of Service under Russian Federation Legislation," *Law Education and Science* 1 (2008): 28–32.

Theoretical interest in the concept of "services" peaked in the 1970s, when there was a rapid increase in the service industry's share in the economy. Since then, the study of the concept has focused more on its applied aspects, in order to identify problems related to the growing importance of new types of services, like information services. For this reason, a number of researchers argue that the general theoretical description of "services" remains vague and ambiguous and cannot be applied with precision to all types of services.

The current situation, I argue, is related to the haphazard application of both industrial and economic approaches to the concept of services, and sometimes to the outright rejection of economic approaches. For a long time, any activity provided as personal services (in the economic sense), whether its result was tangible or intangible, was categorized under the large umbrella term "services." All such activities have retained the traditional designation of "services" whether they are personal services or entrepreneurial services, like repair work, cooking, sewing clothes, etc. In the case of the latter, it would be more correct to consider them as a continuation of material production, albeit in another sphere, that of consumption.

This interpenetration of services and material products makes the distinction between the *spheres* of services and material production even more difficult than that between the categories of "service" and "material product."

The spheres of services and material production are sectors of the economy: the former supplies services, and the latter produces material products. At the same time, the processes of supplying a service and producing a material product may be closely intertwined in the same industry. Catering, for example, combines food preparation, which results in a material product, with food service, which, as the name suggests, is a service. Moreover, the process of the production of any material product is mediated by the provision of services like, for example, equipment maintenance or accounting. These days, information and telecommunication services play an important role in most material production processes.

For all these reasons, the traditional division between service industry and material production seems outdated if not downright problematic.

2.2. Changes in the relative importance of services and material production in economic development

Several factors had a hand in changing the relative importance that services and material production play in the economy: technological progress, a better educated populace, more qualified workers, economic shifts (globalization, financialization, shifts in consumption patterns, and more. By the late 1950s, the service sector was steadily growing to occupy a larger share of the economy. As Marx predicted, the development of technology led to a growth in productivity, displacing the role of the human worker in the process of material production. Moreover, globalization made it possible to move a number of industrial sectors from developed to developing countries, ensuring lower production costs and product prices. By importing rather than producing certain goods, those developed countries saw their costs of production and labor decrease accordingly.

The *Economist* noted that, "the slide in manufacturing's share of GDP largely reflects a fall in the prices of goods relative to services. Measured in constant prices, the share of manufacturing in GDP has been broadly unchanged in America, and in developed countries as a whole, since 1980."[21]

According to Vladislav L. Inozemtsev, theorists of postindustrial societies tend to see the structural shift toward a greater share of services in an economy as the most important sign of the transition to the postindustrial stage.[22] But the service industry, he goes on to say, has always played an important role in European societies. Even in the late nineteenth century, domestic workers in Britain were the largest group of workers, and in France the second largest, second only to agricultural workers.[23] In the United States, meanwhile, industrial workers have never outnumbered service workers.[24]

Different services sectors play different roles in the modern economy. The economy is traditionally divided into three sectors, based on Alan Fisher and Colin Clark's model of social production. According to this model, the primary sector is the extractive and agricultural industries, the secondary sector is manufacturing, and the tertiary sector is the service industry.[25] According

---

21 *The Economist*, "Industrial Metamorphosis: Factory Jobs Are Becoming Scarce. It's Nothing to Worry about," Septmeber 29, 2005. https://www.economist.com/finance-and-economics/2005/09/29/industrial-metamorphosis.

22 See Daniel Bell, *The Coming of Post-Industrial Society: A Venture of Social Forecasting* (New York: Basic Books, 1973).; Zbigniew Brzezinski, *Between Two Ages: America's Role in the Technetronic Era* (New York: The Viking Press, 1970), 9–10.; M. J. Naisbitt, *Megatrends: The New Directions Shaping Our Lives* (New York, 1984), 7–9; R. W. Judy and C. D'amico, *Workforce 2020: Work and Workers in the 21st Century* (Indianapolis: Hudson Institute, 1997) 44.

23 See Jean-Claude Delaunay and Jean Gadrey, *Services in Economic Thought: Three Centuries of Debate* (New York: Springer, 1992), 13, 66.

24 N. Spulber, *The American Economy: The Struggle for Supremacy in the 21st Century* (Cambridge: Cambridge University Press, 1995), 156.

25 A. Fisher, "Production, primary, secondary and tertiary," *Economic Record* 15, no. 1 (1939): 24–38; A. Fisher, *The Clash of Progress and Security* (London: Macmillan, 1935); C. Clark, *The Conditions of Economic Progress* (London: Macmillan, 1940).

to Clark, every country goes through three stages of development: agrarian, wherein production grows slowly; industrial, wherein production reaches its peak; and service-oriented, wherein production stalls. In terms of employment, the labor share of the agricultural sector decreases steadily, the share of the industrial sector grows initially but decreases in the long term, and the share of the service sector grows constantly.[26]

With the many differences in the various service sectors of today, it is impossible group them all together. David Bell proposed a five-sectoral model, which supplements the three-sectoral model with a fourth and fifth stage that reflect the transition from industrial to postindustrial. According to this model, services comprise the third, fourth, and fifth sectors. The third includes transportation and utilities, the fourth includes trade, insurance, and real estate, and the fifth includes health care, education, research, public administration, and recreational activities.[27] However, Bell does not have clear criteria for assigning a particular service industry to one of these three sectors. Typically, the most importance services are considered to be information and telecommunication services, research and development, education, health care, financial and business services, and management, i.e., those activities that ensure the progress of modern society.[28]

In the last few years, there have been signs that the relative share of various sectors in the economies of developed countries is stabilizing: the decades-long, uninterrupted growth of the service industry is slowing down. In the US, for example, the share of services and that of material production in the GDP are growing closer (table 1), though employment numbers in material production continue to decline (figs. 1 and 2). This trend contributes to the concern, among the American political and business class, that moving manufacturing abroad may have significant repercussions in the long term, potentially threatening the country's economic security. This trend also makes the US economy less diversified, and therefore more susceptible to cyclical downturns in production.

---

26 *Political Economy: Economic Encyclopedia*, Vol. 4 (Moscow: Soviet Encyclopedia, 1980), 176–178. (in Russ.)

27 See Bell, 158.

28 An article by Eivaz Hasanov covers the confusing issue of foreign modern approaches to the structure of the service sector and the definition of the role of its various sectors. See E. Hasanov, "Structure of the Information Economy and its Main Functions," *Bulletin of Khabarovsk State Academy of Economics and Law* 1 (2005):14–29. (in Russ.)

TABLE 1. Value added by industry as a percentage of GDP (Release Date: November 5, 2015)

No.	Industry	2008	2009	2010	2011	2012	2013	2014
	Gross domestic product	100.0	100.0	100.0	100.0	100.0	100.0	100.0
	Private industrial sector	86.4	85.7	85.7	86.0	86.4	86.6	86.9
	Agriculture, forestry, fishing, hunting	1.0	1.0	1.1	1.3	1.2	1.4	1.2
	Mining	2.7	2.0	2.2	2.6	2.5	2.6	2.6
	Construction	4.4	4.0	3.6	3.5	3.6	3.7	3.8
	Production	12.3	12.0	12.2	12.3	12.3	12.2	12.1
	Transportation and warehousing activities	2.9	2.8	2.8	2.9	2.9	2.9	2.9
	Information	5.0	4.9	4.9	4.7	4.6	4.8	4.8
	Financial transactions, insurance, real estate transactions, leasing and renting	19.1	19.9	19.7	19.7	20.0	19.8	20.0
	Financial transactions and insurance	6.2	6.7	6.7	6.7	7.1	6.9	7.0
	Real estate, rental, and leasing	12.9	13.2	13.0	13.0	12.9	12.9	13.0
	Professional and business services	11.9	11.5	11.6	11.7	11.8	11.7	11.9
	Education, health care, and social security	7.8	8.4	8.3	8.3	8.3	8.2	8.2
	Education	1.0	1.1	1.1	1.1	1.1	1.1	1.1
	Healthcare and welfare services	6.8	7.3	7.2	7.2	7.1	7.1	7.1
	Cultural events, entertainment, leisure, hospitality, and restaurants	3.6	3.6	3.6	3.6	3.7	3.8	3.8
	Government	13.6	14.3	14.3	14.0	13.6	13.4	13.1
	Private production	20.5	18.9	19.1	19.7	19.6	19.9	19.8
	Private services	65.9	66.7	66.6	66.4	66.8	66.8	67.1
	Production of information and communication technologies	6.0	5.9	5.9	5.8	5.7	5.9	5.9

Source: http://www.bea.gov/iTable/iTable.cfm?ReqID=51&step=1#reqid=51&step=51&isuri=1&5114=a&5102=5

FIGURE 1. US industrial employment (1963–2013)

Source: Cardiff Garcia, "Manufacturing vs. construction, revisited," *Financial Times*, February 15, 2023. https://www.ft.com/content/5815395f-4599-34a2-a627-20bacfd9dbbc

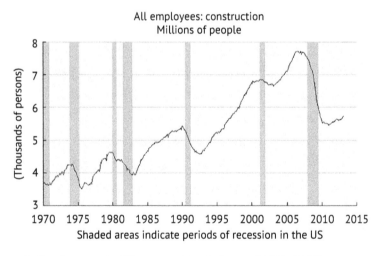

FIGURE 2. Employment in US construction industry (1970–2015)

Source: Cardiff Garcia, "Manufacturing vs. construction, revisited," *Financial Times*, February 15, 2023. https://www.ft.com/content/5815395f-4599-34a2-a627-20bacfd9dbbc

As a rule, industries with high growth in productivity saw the greatest reduction in number of workers (table 2). This trend makes sense: an increase in productivity in material production sectors allows for a portion of that labor force to move the service sectors, where such productivity growth, as a rule, did not take place.

Table 2. Indicators of productivity growth and employment growth by industry, in %

goods	Industry	Share as of 2008		Contribution to employment growth		Efficiency growth[29]	
		Employment	GDP	1990–2000	2000–2008	1990–2000	2000–2008
	manufacturing	8.8	10.0	-4.5	-66.5	36.7	19.2
	Construction	6.5	4.3	6.9	12.4	-0.5	-11.0
	Natural resources	1.9	3.3	-2.5	-0.5	1.6	0.2
	Computer products and electronic devices	0.9	1.4	-1.0	-11.1	n/a	22.5
	Real estate, rental, and leasing	1.8	13.0	1.9	4.1	19.8	18.4
	Wholesale	4.3	5.7	2.7	4.2	17.5	11.2
	Information	2.1	4.5	4.2	-12.5	7.4	21.6
	Transportation and warehousing	3.4	2.9	4.2	3.3	3.8	3.9
	Retail	10.4	5.8	9.0	7.5	9.8	1.5
	Administration and other services	6.0	2.9	18.1	-1.7	-4.7	5.6
	Hospitality and restaurant services	7.0	2.8	8.5	18.7	-2.8	-3.2

(continued)

29 Source: US Bureau of Economic Analysis; Moody's Economy.com; McKinsey Global Institute Sunrise Productivity Model.

Industry	Share as of 2008		Contribution to job growth		Productivity growth[29]	
	Employment	GDP	1990–2000	2000–2008	1990–2000	2000–2008
Other services (except for government services authorities)	5.1	2.4	5.5	7.6	-1.7	-4.8
Cultural events, entertainment, and recreation	1.5	0.9	3.5	5.4	-0.7	-0.8
Financial operations and insurance	4.4	7.7	1.9	8.5	16.9	9.9
Professional, research, and engineering services	6.3	7.6	11.1	22.2	7.3	9.7
Company management	1.3	1.8	0.4	3.9	0.7	-0.6
Government	14.8	12.9	9.5		-4.1	1.0
Services healthcare and social services	11.0	7.0	17.6	13.2	-8.1	-1.7
Education	2.2	1.0	3.4		-1.5	-3.1
Government and public sectors[30] utilities	0.4	1.8	-0.6	-0.8	2.5	0.5

Source: ftalphaville.ft.com/2013/02/15/1387262/manufacturing-vs-construction-revisited/mckinseyprodchart2/

[1]Source: U.S. Bureau of Economic Analysis; Moody's Economy.com; McKinsey Global Institute Sunrise Productivity Model. 2 Government and public sectors

Note: ■ – upper quartile; ■ – values between 25...50; ■ – lower quartile.

30 Government and public

I should note that, after the 2008 economic crisis, the share of manufacturing in the GDP stabilized not only in the US, but also in Italy, France, and the UK. Meanwhile, in Germany and China, there has been an upward trend since as early as the 1990s (fig. 3). Nevertheless, this stabilization of the manufacturing share is limited to a very short period of time.

At the same time, on a global scale there has not been the same trend of consistent decline in industry over the last thirty years. Though it did take place in most developed countries, many others continued to develop industrial production intensively (fig. 4).

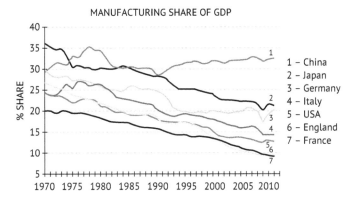

FIGURE 3. Share of manufacturing in GDP of different countries, in %
Source: Kate Mackenzie, "Productivity, "reindustrialisation" and the US profit share," *Financial Times*, April 8, 2013, https://www.ft.com/content/3d87b602-0988-399f-a1ea-b1dc53be9fde.

Rank	1980	1990	2000	2010
1	USA	USA	USA	USA
2	Germany	Japan	Japan	China
3	Japan	Germany	Germany	Japan
4	UK	Italy	China	Germany
5	France	UK	UK	Italy
6	Italy	France	Italy	Brazil
7	China	China	France	South Korea
8	Brazil	Brazil	South Korea	France
9	Spain	Spain	Canada	UK
10	Canada	Canada	Mexico	India
11	Mexico	South Korea	Spain	Russia
12	Australia	Mexico	Brazil	Mexico
13	Netherlands	Turkey	Taiwan	Indonesia
14	Argentina	India	India	Spain
15	India	Taiwan	Turkey	Canada

FIGURE 4. Industrial development in different countries
Source: http://topforeignstocks.com/wp-content/uploads/2013/01/Top-manufacturing-countries-by-decade.gif

2.3. Contradictions in the contemporary development of services and material production, and how to resolve them

When we analyze the structure of the modern global economy, we should pay special attention to the fact that the methods used to estimate the contribution of various sectors to a national GDP may in fact distort the real structure of production. These estimates reflect the distribution of revenue among different sectors, but not their contribution to production itself. There is still much ambiguity in estimating the contribution of financial services to the GDP. A simple increase in speculative turnover in the financial markets, for example, automatically increases the financial sector's contribution to the GDP.

As the relative growth of employment demonstrates, productivity in the industrial sectors is growing faster than in the more technologically primitive service sectors: the restaurant and hotel business, the entertainment industry, the trade industry, etc. are all based on manual labor, or on technologies only as sophisticated as industrial technologies. For this reason, though modern society may be rightly called a *service society*, it can hardly claim to be a *postindustrial society*.

Vladislav L. Inozemtsev, a respected Russian authority on postindustrial society, interviewed several major American sociologists and economists—Peter Ferdinand Drucker, Lester Karl Thurow, John Kenneth Galbraith, Marshall Goldman, Francis Fukuyama—in 1998 to gather their thoughts on the concept. Their attitudes toward the concept were roundly negative. This group of scholars insisted that we still live in an industrial society, though its characteristics have changed in recent years. Goldman, for example, has stated quite explicitly: "I think the use of the term 'post-' has become something of an anachronism . . . I don't think we're really in the postindustrial era. The reason is that industrial production not only remains very important, but in a way is even more important than ever before, even though its technological basis is changing. We shouldn't forget that even software production, though very different from the production of machinery or cars, remains an industry."[31]

Even though the information and telecommunication revolution has introduced unforeseen innovations, the fact remains that there is as yet no technology capable of moving past the industrial mode of production. Emerging nonindustrial technologies like biotech occupy a still-small share of production.

---

31 See "Rethinking the Future: Major American Economists and Sociologists on the Prospects and Contradictions of Modern Development," *MEMO* 11 (1998). (in Russ.)

And hybrid industrial-information technologies, like 3D printers, only demonstrate the further development of the industrial mode of production, not its replacement by nonindustrial technologies. (Goldman also considers these hybrids another form of industrial tech.) Service sectors like R&D, IT, and telecommunications, expected to be the harbinger of a fundamentally new stage of production, have indeed made impressive progress, but they have not made that leap into the future.

Another problem to consider is the hypertrophy of the financial sector, and its ambiguous influence on the development of the real economy. At first, the financial sector allowed for the accumulation of temporarily free funds, and for the redistribution of monetary capital to the most effective sectors of the economy. (Though it is true that, alongside this function, the financial sector has always had a purely speculative function.)

Up to a certain point, speculative transactions could be seen as a way of identifying the most profitable uses of capital (and "economics" textbooks still treat them as such).

But when property titles and titles on future income (in the form of stock instruments) were detached from the real capital that they represent, serious problems came to light: pyramid schemes, creating fictitious demand for goods and services; the high volatility of the stock market, confusing guidelines for investing; the diversion of investments from the real sector to the financial sector. All these factors combined, under conditions of economic crisis, can lead to devastation in the real economy.

2.4. Specifics of the Russian situation

As I have already discussed, in developed and newly industrialized countries, the outsize growth of the service sector is linked to the growth of productivity in material production (agriculture, mining, manufacturing, construction). Workers who had to leave industries of material production moved to the service industry, while material production itself continued to grow and develop.

But the situation in Russia and other post-Soviet states during the market reforms of the 1990s was different. In those countries, the growth of the service industry accompanied a total decline of productivity in material production. Moreover, the insufficient development, or downright underdevelopment, of the financial market, real estate market, wholesaling and retailing, management services, consulting, and more, predetermined the redistribution of a significant part of the economy's revenue toward these underdeveloped infrastructures.

As a result, the share of trade in Russia's GDP has long outweighed its value in developed countries, and the rate of profit in Russian retail networks is still much higher.

As a result of the disproportionate prices of goods and services, the profitability of the service sector is much higher than that of industry and agriculture (except for monopolies on natural resources and extractive industries like oil and gas). Under these circumstances, wherein some manufacturing industries are not at all profitable, investors turn to restaurant or hotel development, or to the real estate market. Such a situation makes it impossible to overcome the imbalance between services and material production. Moreover, the long-lasting investment drought of the 1990s led to the progressive obsolescence of fixed capital (the average age of equipment has almost doubled). Though the situation has stabilized, there are no signs that it will improve, as the competitiveness of most manufacturing industries continues to wane.

The isolation and self-sufficiency of the financial market, its unconcern for the needs of material production, poses yet another problem, as it shifts credit operations away from the interests of the real economy. The low profitability and competitiveness of business in material production is partly to blame for this gap between the two, leading to a dearth of economically attractive investment projects. Liberal-conservative policymaking on the part of the financial authorities further exacerbates the problem, as they make little effort to channel easy money into the technological modernization of manufacturing and agriculture.

With such deep structural imbalances in place, the road ahead will be slow and tenuous unless extraordinary measures are put into place to mobilize economic resources for industrial development.

2.5. Manufacturing (industrial) services

The importance of industrial services in increasing the efficiency of production processes is currently growing. "After decades in which traditional product-oriented strategies could be successfully pursued, major players in the capital goods industries are now being forced to shift their attentions to the service business as an opportunity for growth and profitability," states research from the Monitor Group.[32] Christian Kowalkowski suggests that the factors that improve

---

32 Research Study Monitor Group, *Industrial Services Strategies. The Quest for Faster Growth and Higher Margins* (Zürich, 2004), 7. http://skyadvisory.ch/wp-content/uploads/2015/03/2004-Monitor-Group_Industrial-Services-Strategies.pdf.

the role of industrial services are: competitive advantages, a stable connection between supplier and consumer, increased chances of repeat orders, steady technological leadership, high profitability, low dependence on the state of the business cycle, the ability for industrial companies with advanced technological knowledge and production techniques to turn them into marketable services, etc.[33]

The industrial services market is a large and growing sector. In the UK, for example, the total market for business services in 2009 was 329 billion dollars—and industrial services were the largest sector of this market (18 percent).[34] That same year in Germany, the expenditures for industrial equipment maintenance alone were 31.14 billion euros.[35]

Academics have yet to develop this topic satisfactorily. In the majority of works on industrial services, both in Russia and abroad, academics have attempted to explain their economic nature by separating them from the process of material production, on the one hand, and from other types of services, on the other. Their task is mainly to distinguish between industrial services and other activities, which is necessary for proper taxing and accounting. Take, for example, the following definition: *"Labor (services) of an industrial nature* are individual operations for production (manufacturing) of goods, the performance of labor, provision of services, processing of raw materials, compliance with established technological processes, maintenance of fixed assets *and other similar labor* (emphasis added), as well as transportation services provided by third-party organizations (including individual entrepreneurs) and (or) structural subdivisions of the organization for the transportation of goods within it, in particular the movement of raw materials, tools, parts, blanks, and other types of goods from the base (central) warehouse to the workshops (departments), and the delivery of finished products in accordance with the

33 Ch. Kowalkowski, "Enhancing the Industrial Service Offering: New Requirements on Content and Processes," (PhD diss., International Graduate School of Management and Industrial Engineering, Linköping University, 2006), 2. http://www. diva-portal.org/smash/get/diva2:22258/FULLTEXT01.pdf.

34 R. Herbert and C. Paraskevas, *The Business Services Sector: Calculating the Market Size*, Report, Lloyds Bank, 2012, 4, 6. http://www.lloydsbankcommercial.com/Business-Services-Calculating-the-market-size.

35 Christoph, Eick, Jens Reichel, and Paul Schmidt, *Instandhaltung des Kapitalstocks in Deutschland: Rolle und volkswirtschaftliche Bedeutung.* (Frankfurt am Main: VDI Forum IH, 2011), 5. http://www.fokus-instandhaltung.de/fileadmin/betriebsrat_vdi_ev/redakteur/ringelmann/Dateien/20110309_ Instandhaltungsvolumen_ in_ der_BRDx.pdf

terms of the agreements (contracts)."[36] Or this definition, with reference to the Tax Code [Nalogovyi kodeks]:

Labor and services of an industrial nature

- The notion set forth in pp. 6 p. 1 art. 254 Tax Code. Labor (services) of an industrial nature includes:
- Individual operations for production (manufacturing) of goods, the performance of labor, provision of services, processing of raw materials, compliance with established technological processes, maintenance of fixed assets *and other similar labor* (emphasis added)
- Transportation services provided by third-party organizations (including individual entrepreneurs) and (or) structural subdivisions of the organization for the transportation of goods within it, in particular the movement of raw materials, tools, parts, blanks, and other types of goods from the base (central) warehouse to the workshops (departments), and the delivery of finished products in accordance with the terms of the agreements (contracts). Expenses for the payment of labor and services of an industrial nature are classified as material expenses and included in production and sales expenses.[37]

Note that for accounting and taxing, these definitions are of little use. The addendum "and other similar labor" makes this definition of production-related labor and services ambiguous and open to arbitrary interpretation.

Meanwhile, other scholars are hard at work trying to distinguish industrial services from other types of services. Multiple classifications based on several different criteria can be found in the academic literature. According to one, industrial services include "engineering, leasing, maintenance, and equipment repair."[38] A few paragraphs down, the author includes transportation services under production services, as is often the case. But it is unclear why leasing is included in production services, and not in professional financial services, which,

---

36 Y. A. Lukash, "Works (Services) of Industrial Character," in *Encyclopedic Dictionary-Handbook of the Head of the Enterprise* (Moscow: Book World, 2004), 1504. (in Russ.)

37 A. V. Tolkushkin, "Production works and services," in *Encyclopedia of Russian and International Taxation* (Moscow: Iurist, 2003).

38 T. A. Frolova, "Economics and Management in the Sphere of Social and Cultural Service and Tourism" (Lecture at TTI SFU, Taganrog, 2010). http://www. aup.ru/books/m204/1_2.htm (in Russ.)

according to the author, includes "banking, insurance, financial, consulting, and advertising" services.

Ralf Gitzel, of the ABB Corporate Research Group,[39] singles out approaches based on: 1) the specific equipment used (industrial equipment maintenance);[40] 2) the type of company (industrial company services);[41] and 3) the technology used (industrial technology).[42]

Many official classifications of services exist with purely practical purposes. These classifications[43] suffer from a poor academic understanding of the definition of industrial services, as well as a lack of clear criteria for their separation from business (professional) services.

At first, several possible approaches existed in the theoretical description of industrial services as an economic phenomenon. These definitions were motivated by the objectives of industrial marketing. From this point of view, industrial services include everything an "industrial" client may need: "liability and property insurance, banking and other financial services, construction support services, auditing, data processing, as well as consulting services of all kinds (including architectural and engineering), transport services, advertising and marketing services."[44]

This approach is developed by looking at industrial services from the perspective of the relationship between the customer and the service provider. From this point of view, any services provided by enterprises and organizations (commercial, noncommercial, state, municipal, etc.) can be referred to as

---

39 Ralf Gitzel, "Industrial Service as a Research Discipline." *ABB Corporate Research Service Solutions*, slide 7, June 6, 2014. http://cbi2014.unige.ch/Documents/CBI2014. IndustrialServiceAs AResearchDiscipline. RalfGitzel.Pdf.

40 See O. Rogelio and R. Kallenberg, "Managing the Transition from Products to Services," *International Journal of Service Industry Management* 14, no. 2 (2003): 160–172.

41 See C. Homburg and B. Garbe, "Towards an Improved Understanding of Industrial Services: Quality Dimensions and Their Impact on Buyer-Seller Relationships," *Journal of Business-to-Business Marketing* 6, no. 2 (1999), 39–71; P. D. Cooper and R. W. Jackson, "Applying a Services Marketing Orientation to the Industrial Services Sector," *Journal of Business & Industrial Marketing* 3, no. 2 (1988): 51–54; J. B. Quinn, T. L. Doorley and P. C. Paquette, "Beyond Products: Services-based Strategy," *Harvard Business Review* 68, no. 2 (1990): 58–60.

42 See Arch. G. Woodside and William G. Pearce, "Testing Market Segment Acceptance of New Designs of Industrial Services," *Journal of Product Innovation Management* 6, no. 3 (1989): 185–201; Ch. Kowalkowski, 42.

43 For an overview of such classifications see E. V. Povorina, "Approaches to Determining the Place and Structure of the Market of Services to Enterprises and Organizations," *Service Plus* 2 (2011): 9–10. http://cyberleninka.ru/article/n/podhody-k-opredeleniyu-mesta-i-struktury-rynka-uslug-predpriyatiyam-i-organizatsiyam# ixzz3wHscKtKJ. (in Russ.)

44 "Industrial Marketing: Marketing and marketing research," http://www.raskruting.ru/nature/nature3.html. (in Russ.)

industrial services. Any services of B2B (business-to-business) relations also falls under such a definition. In this case, the list of industrial services includes not only the technical, technological, and transport services traditionally included in this category, but also a significant number of business and professional services (accounting, auditing, financial analysis, consulting, etc.), as well as some "cognitive" services (industrial information services, applied industrial research and development).[45]

Another approach is based on the historical definition of industrial services as after-sales services of industrial equipment (supply of spare parts, adjustment, repair, training of personnel, technical update of equipment, technological control, etc.). This approach, stemming from industrial marketing, significantly narrows down the field of industrial services. "Industrial services are all business transactions which, subsequent to the sale/installation of a physical product, are intended to maintain and/or optimize the operational process, upgrade performance and cover its resource needs throughout the entire life cycle."[46] Based on this definition, industrial services include: supply of spare parts, repairs, performance improvement (upgrades), refurbishment, technical inspection and testing, serviceability, technical support, technical advice, user training, equipment management, and financial support.[47]

When looking at the specifics of industrial production and its product, industrial services include only those rendered in the process of industrial production, like maintenance or technological support. This approach also tends to include in under the category of industrial services those that affect the process of industrial production: "repair and maintenance, research, development, information services, engineering, pre-sale and post-sale services, physical services related to primary production activity, rent of any production and facilities."[48]

Finally, industrial services may also be defined in contrast to outsourcing, which exhibits a longer customer-service provider relationship, and a total transfer of the business process to third-party service providers.[49] Though this distinction is legitimate, however, the nature of services provided in both cases is the same.

---

45 See Povorina, 11–12.
46 Research Study Monitor Group, 10.
47 Ibid., 10–11.
48 A. I. Mamishev, "The Development of the Sphere of Industrial Services in the Conditions of Modernization of the Economy" (PhD diss., St. Petersburg, 2013): 3. http://dlib.rsl.ru/viewer/01005555145#?page=33. (in Russ.)
49 See M. V. Kudymov, "Criteria for Identifying Outsourcing in Instrument-Making and Machine-Building Enterprises," *Russian Entrepreneurship* 10, no. 2 (2009): 43–47. (in Russ.)

The role of industrial services in the process of labor reproduction is one of its fundamental characteristics. "From the point of view of economic relations, an industrial service is a production process that allows for the standard length of the product's consumer value. It allows for the partial reproduction and value transfer to products or labor produced with their help."[50] This definition, however, loses the specificity of industrial services, which here may be interpreted as any material service, like catering.

As services continue to become an integral part of the industrial process, the boundary between services and material production grows blurrier. On the other hand, industrial services are also emerging as a continuation of the production process following the output of the finished product, because after-sales services also involve material production processes: installation of equipment, its adjustment, repair, technical upgrade, etc. Kowalowski refers to a number of such arguments.[51] As far back as 1977, Peter Hill suggested that a job can be considered both as service and as industrial production, depending on whether the work is done by an industrial enterprise or by a service company.[52]

Production (industrial) services can be considered both broadly and narrowly. In the latter sense, we would include only services for industrial equipment and industrial technological processes. But even within this verry narrow definition, there is a wide range of possible services. Services in the broad sense includes any services that are necessary for the operation of industrial companies. On top of services like technical and technological services, personnel training, internal transportation, etc., this would also include insurance services, industrial R&D, information services, etc., and other services all the way up to catering, i.e., everything that falls within the scope of B2B relations.

Industrial services are a growing and profitable segment of the market. To remain competitive and technologically ahead of the curve, a task important to the Russian economy, the development of industrial services is a must.

* * *

50 I. N. Zadorina, "Management of Organizational-Economic Development of Enterprises of Industrial Services in Transport," (Thesis, Kostroma State University N. A. Nekrasova, 2010). (in Russ.)

51 See for example St. Fölster and J. Gr. Göran, "Industri Och Tjänster – Båda Behövs För Tillväxt, Svenskt Näringsliv (the Confederation of Swedish Enterprise)," *The Economist*, 377, no. 8446 (2005): 69–70.

52 See Peter T. Hill, "On Goods and Services," *Review of Income and Wealth* 23, no. 4 (1977): 315–338.

Having analyzed the main components of the production process in contemporary industrial production, as well as the relationship between various services and material production, we are led to the following conclusion: that technological development (the technological application of scientific knowledge) determines the technological structures of production, which unite all the components of production at a certain level of development. Technology becomes the basis of the whole production process: from the selection (or creation) of raw materials, to the quality of human labor and tools necessary to the organization of the production process and the receipt of the final product. The nature of the technologies that are used depends on their interaction at the macro level, at the scale of social production, and on the integral technological structure, which defines the industrial mode of production at a given stage of its development.

The nature of the technological mode largely determines the impact of the industrial mode of production on other levels of the social structure, determining the shape of society itself. This influence is, of course, complex, mediated, and multistage, interacting with patterns of development throughout the different spheres and strata of society. But what is decisive is the thrust of technological progress.

Much depends on the way technology is developed. Historically, we see a natural transition away from a reliance on experience and skill based on empirical observations and patterns, and toward the development of technology based on scientific knowledge. As the technological application of scientific knowledge grows more common, the characteristics of an industrial begin to change: such a society *begins* its transition to a new stage of social production. This stage differs significantly from the "traditional" industrial state (and even from Galbraith's "new" one) yet *remains industrial in its mode of production*. For this reason, we must delineate the preconditions for the emergence of this new generation of the industrial state, which I term the second generation of the new industrial state (NIS.2).

This society will be built on the terms of the latest technological paradigms (the fifth and sixth), their new institutional and organizational structures, a new conception of the worker, and indeed, a renewed sense of life . . .

It is a mistake to think that the new industrial state will only recreate the mid-twentieth-century late-industrial system of Galbraith. We will only see this result when and where shortsighted economists and policymakers fails to envision a way out of the dead ends of post-industrialism, dooming their country to new (or, rather, quite old) ways of playing catch-up. Eventually, their attempts at catch-up will fail, leaving those leading economies behind for good.

Part Two

THE RUSSIAN ECONOMIC SYSTEM AND (DE) INDUSTRIALIZATION

Chapter 3

Industrialization of the Economy as a Factor of Social Development; The Phenomenon of Modern Deindustrialization

---

3.1. Industrialization

Economic *industrialization* is traditionally understood as the process of the development of industrial production. In the sphere of the organization of production, this includes the complication of production structures and the introduction of innovative managerial methods. In the sphere of technological development, it includes the complication and expansion of the base of production, an increase in the technological level of equipment, based on the spread and improvement of machine technologies. In the field of human resources, it includes a continuous increase in the worker's necessary qualifications and his technological specialization, and the growth of labor productivity. Finally, industrialization also means a higher product complexity, number of process stages, knowledge-intensity, etc. All these processes lead to structural changes in the economy, resulting in a sharp increase in the share of industrial products and services in the GDP. Accordingly, the role of this industrial component in the national economy grows, becoming the economy's basic element.

In the course of *industrial production* various processes and material objects (industrial technology, technological equipment) are used, as well as human *labor.* As a result, there also emerge goods designed to meet the material needs of people: *industrial products.*

The transition to the industrial mode of production—the industrial revolution—marks a profound shift in the technological basis of material production, and no less significant changes in the entire system of social relations. The Dutch experience is instructive here. One of the most important extractive industries in the United Provinces was fishing, [1] which employed a large part of the population. The industry relied primarily on catching and harvesting herring, and the herring trade. There was even a Dutch proverb: Amsterdam grew up on herring bones. Whaling also played an important role. The seventeenth-century expeditions to Spitsbergen "involved 200–250 ships annually, 1,300–1,400 whales were caught, and the net income in some years exceeded 10 million guilders."[2] Whaling expeditions to Iceland were also organized.

The Dutch manufacturing industry had two main sectors: textile production and shipbuilding. Their textile manufactories and craft workshops were famous throughout Europe for their production of dyed cloth, cotton, linen and silk fabrics, ribbons, thread, and lace. Dyeing, whitewashing, and other ancillary industries also developed.

Leiden became the largest center of cloth production not only in Holland but in all of Europe. Hundreds of smaller workshops clustered around dozens of large textile factories, which provided tens of thousands of workers with a living. The peak of cloth production in Leiden was in 1664, when the city produced a total of one-hundred-forty-four thousand pieces of various fabrics.[3] Amsterdam and Rotterdam also produced large quantities of fabric. Haarlem, then an independent city, developed the production of silk and linen fabrics, and whitewashing workshops also popped up and concentrated in the city.

The Dutch shipbuilding industry became internationally important and an example to follow. It was not without reason that Peter the Great went to the Netherlands in search of technical knowledge and specialists to establish his own shipyards. The late seventeenth and early eighteenth centuries saw the flowering of the industry. Hundreds of ships were built in dozens of shipyards. Production costs were significantly lower than in other European countries, which ensured

---

1   The Republic of the United Provinces was formed in the sixteenth century as a result of the Dutch Bourgeois Revolution; it existed until 1795.

2   "The Netherlands in the second half of the seventeenth century and in the eighteenth century," in *New History* (Tiumen: Tiumen State Academy of Culture, Arts, and Social Technologies, 2015). http://www.studfiles.ru/preview/3493421/./

3   Ibid.

a flow of foreign orders. Even the British, their main competitors, often placed orders for the construction of their ships in the Netherlands.

Shipbuilding led to the development of related manufacturing: rope- and sail-making, sawmills, and woodworking. Dutch navigational instruments became renowned for their quality. This flourishing of major industries facilitated the demand for a wide variety of industrial products among the Dutch populace. Book publishing led to more paper manufacturing; house construction led to more brick and glass manufacturing. The food industry also developed: breweries, cheese factories, butter mills, sugar, and tobacco production. Population growth accompanied this industrial boom, and the number of affluent townspeople and their demand for luxury goods increased accordingly. The country was producing artistic tiling, porcelain, watches, and jewelry.

But, as is now widely known, the Netherlands was plagued by an economic disease: usury. Industrial growth and the trade that accompanied it led to the accumulation of large amounts of capital, which were increasingly concentrated in trading and money lending, where they made the biggest profits. The Netherlands dominated the European financial market, and the Amsterdam Stock Exchange and banks attracted capital from all over Europe. The country became Europe's main moneylender.

It seemed as if the Netherlands was at the height of its prosperity and power. But the dominance of merchant and moneylending capital over industrial capital led to its demise. "The Dutch bourgeoisie flooded its domestic market with cheaper foreign products, thus strangling domestic industry. As a result of this trend, by the end of the seventeenth century the Netherlands had already lost its industrial dominance, and then lost its standing in trade to England, a state of rapidly developing industrial capitalism."[4] The industrial bourgeoisie's attempts to enact protective policies like in England, France, Prussia, etc. were thwarted by the usurious merchant oligarchy.

The Dutch experience teaches us that industrial development must be accompanied by economic and institutional policies that allow for continued technological development in production. Though the Netherlands at first built its economic power of an already advanced industry, the Dutch bourgeoisie changed its priorities after they gained a significant share of European and intercontinental trade and finance markets. The Dutch ruling classes exploited their monopoly on trade and finance while ignoring material production. As a result, the Netherlands dropped from a first- to second-rate power in a historically short amount of time.

---

4 Ibid.

England, on the other hand, chose a different part of industrial development. The agrarian revolution and the spread of manufacturing served as a solid basis for the industrial revolution in England. In the struggle for economic supremacy, the English ruling classes relied on protectionist measures for their industries (the transition to free trade policies only occurred after England had already seized its industrial monopoly). These policies encouraged entrepreneurs to introduce technological innovations that strengthened their competitive position in domestic and foreign markets.

The transition toward an industrial mode of production in England was not smooth. Inventions that disrupted the old craftwork-style manufacturing process came slowly. Decrepit workshops did not help the matter. And workers were initially unenthusiastic about new methods and technologies, especially when they were not immediately effective. In 1733, John Kay invented the flying shuttle, though it was at first not widely used in the production of cotton fabrics. It was only in the 1760s that use of the flying shuttle became widespread. A bigger demand for yarn followed, and with it, the emergence of technical improvements in spinning.

In 1738, John Wyatt invented the mechanical spinning machine, though its inadequate construction meant it was little used (detailed information about its construction has not survived). Then in 1764 James Hargreaves invented the simple but effective spinning jenny. The next logical step in the industrial revolution was to attach a mechanical engine to the spinning wheel, an accomplishment accredited to Richard Arkwright, a barber. He applied previous innovation to his spinning mill, first powered by a waterwheel, then by a steam engine. "By 1780 there were twenty spinning mills in England, and then years later, 150 spinning mills modeled after Arkwright's."[5] During the first half of the nineteenth century, a wave of inventions swept over the textile industry. Its technologies saw constant improvement, as did its quality of goods and labor productivity.

James Watt's steam engine innovations made it possible and economical to use it on a large scale. Widespread use of the steam engine had revolutionary consequences: factory production became virtually independent of natural energy sources like wind and water.

More machines in use meant more demand for metal and more need for improvements in metallurgical production technology. England outpaced Russia in iron production thanks to the use of coal-fired iron smelting. Further

---

5 *World History: Encyclopedia*, Vol. 5 (Moscow: Socio-Economic Literature Publishing, 1958). (in Russ.)

improvements, including the invention of puddling, led to an increase in steel production.

Important changes in other industries were also taking place. The railway steam locomotive, and Stephenson's later, more efficient model, made long-distance transportation easy, which dramatically increased the volume of people and industrial goods in transport (especially coal and iron ore). It became more common for certain parts of the country to specialize in certain industries thanks to the ability to move large quantities of freight quickly. The first steam-powered railroad linked the industrial centers of Liverpool and Manchester. The first steamship made its maiden journey on the Clyde River in 1812.[6]

The industrial revolution, which saw the transition of most material production to machine technology, gave Britain an industrial monopoly, and with it, enormous political influence. Britain became the "world's workshop." Big changes were taking place in the whole structure of society. The first visible consequence of the industrial revolution was the growth of the urban population. "Rapid industrial growth gave rise to new industrial cities and centers of economic activity. Birmingham, for example, had only 4,000 inhabitants in 1696; this number grew to seventy thousand a century later. Manchester's population grew fivefold between 1717 and 1773. The new industrial cities and districts that sprang up in the north of the country, closer to coal and iron deposits, attracted people from the southern and southwestern parts of the country."[7] Profound changes in the structure of British society continued to take place throughout the industrial revolution. The industrial bourgeoisie became increasingly more powerful, displacing the landed gentry. The number of small, independent manufacturers declined, while the number of the factory proletariat grew. Compulsory schooling was introduced to feed the need for skilled industrial labor.

People's living quarters changed as new products were introduced. Indoor plumbing, gas, electric lighting spread widely. People began to look different, as clothing and footwear became standardized. New methods of communication altered the nature of everyday social contact. Railway mail dramatically accelerated the circulation of personal and business correspondence.

At the same time, new economic and political institutions developed, reflecting the needs of economic development and the changing balance of

---

6 For more, see "The Industrial Revolution in England," http://www.istmira.com/drugoe-novoe-vremya/7394-promyshlennaya-revolyuciya-v-anglii.html. (in Russ.)

7 *World History: Encyclopedia*, Vol. 5 (Moscow: Socio-Economic Literature Publishing, 1958). (in Russ.)

social forces. "The transition from protectionism to free trade was becoming inevitable. In the 1820s, duties on industrial goods were reduced from 50 percent to 20 percent. The 1830s and 1840s saw further reduction or even abolition of duties, and finally, in 1853 all duties on raw materials and semi-finished goods were abolished and duties on finished goods were greatly reduced. In 1846 the "bread laws" were repealed, partly as result of a bad harvest in 1845. In 1849, the Cromwell Navigation Act was repealed, and in 1851 restrictions on cabotage trade ceased to exist."[8]

Sharp social and political contradictions accompanied these dramatic changes. Profound social changes marginalized large segments of the population and led to mass impoverishment. Large-scale social movements, like the Luddite movement, the struggle for universal suffrage, the Chartist movement, mass strikes, etc., were often met with violent resistance. Nevertheless, they forced the ruling classes to legislate on working hours and other labor conditions.

The history of industrialization in most countries is replete with many dramatic and even tragic turns. As we remember the human toll that we paid to enter this new stage of development, we should also be careful to avoid moving backwards, toward industrial degradation or deindustrialization, and losing ground for naught.

3.2. Diagnosis: Deindustrialization

The phenomenon of deindustrialization is well known. It has taken different form in different countries, as per historical and national peculiarities. Here are some examples.

I have already discussed the Dutch case, its role as a leading industrial power in the mid-seventeenth century, and its subsequent deindustrialization of sorts, which affected its entire real economic sector. Cloth production in Leiden, the largest center of the wool industry, dropped fourfold; the number of ships under construction dropped ten to fifteen times; and commercial fishing dropped seven to ten times. The country was importing more than it was exporting. The flight of industrial capital accompanied the collapse of local industry, mostly to England, the Dutch's most dangerous rival.

---

8 F. Y. Polyansky and V. A. Zhamin, eds., "Industrial Revolution in England," in *Economic History of Capitalist Countries: Textbook*, (Moscow: MGU, 1986), http://www.gumer.info/bibliotek_Buks/Econom/bubl/18.php (in Russ.)

Industrial capital was not the only thing leaving the country. By the end of the eighteenth century, nonresidents (mainly the Dutch) owned 2 percent of the shares of the largest English companies—the Bank of England, the East India Company, the South Sea Company—which were often direct Dutch competitors. Those same foreigners (again, mostly the Dutch) also owned 14 percent of the national English debt, which was largely due to wars with the Dutch. Deindustrialization led to an economic stagnation that lasted throughout the eighteenth century, accompanied by a fall in incomes, the impoverishment of many workers, and permanent political instability. As a result, the population welcomed the French army when it came to liberate them from its own government.

Deindustrialization began in the US in the mid-1960s. For example, during the Reagan and Bush Sr. presidencies, total employment increased by an average of 1.4 percent, but the opposite was true of industry. Each year the steel industry lost 6.1 percent of workers, metalworking 4.5 percent, automotive and equipment manufacturing 1.5 percent, clothing and textiles 2 percent. As a result, by the beginning of the Clinton administration, almost two million manufacturing jobs and half a million mining jobs had been eliminated. In 1997, some 17.5 million people were employed in American industry.

There were two precipitous drops in employment between 2000–2003 and 2007–2009, and as a result American industry now employs twelve million people out of a total one hundred forty-three million workers. At the same time, between 1990 and 2008 the number of people employed in the US increased from one hundred twenty two to one hundred forty three million, and twenty seven million new jobs were created, 40 percent of which were in the public sector and healthcare, and the rest in retail, construction, hotels, and restaurants. On the whole, 98 percent of these jobs were in "non-traded" [netorguemyi] sectors, producing goods and providing services for the domestic market only. In other words, by 2008 the US health care industry employed more people than did industry, yet the government employed nearly one and a half times as many people as the health care industry (twenty-two million versus sixteen million). Industry lagged behind the services also in the export sector.

By 2010 the US had become a leader in deindustrialization, second only to Hong Kong, whose economy is actually an appendage of China's colossal industry. At the same time, industry was not (and could not be!) replaced by services in the American export sector. Consider the consequences of this process:

1. US *exports were growing rapidly, but they were falling further and further behind imports.* American industry was losing out on the domestic market but could not compensate for this loss on the external market. The balance of trade in industrial goods fell from -2 percent in 1992 to -8 percent in in 2008. US trade balance was deteriorating rapidly (it had been in a deficit since 1976). While in 1997 the deficit was around one hundred billion dollars (insignificant considering the scale of the US economy), by 2000 it was close to four hundred billion, and in 2007–2008 it was around seven hundred billion dollars.

    The negative trade balance generated a negative balance of payments, which were covered by foreign loans and debt issuance. From 2.7 trillion dollars in 1989, US foreign debt rose to 5.7 trillion dollars in 2001, thirteen trillion in 2009, and 15 trillion in 2011. In 2023 it exceeded 31.4 trillion dollars, with government debt accounting for less than a quarter.

2. Deindustrialization has led to a *"mutation" of domestic demand*, which was long considered a strength of the American economy given its independence from the ups and downs of foreign markets. Since the Reagan administration, domestic demand has been growing at the expense of specific "tools" [instrumentariia]. Real wages reached their peak in the 1970s, declined by the mid-1990s, and after a brief rise in the second half of the 1990s and the beginning of the 2000s, they fell back to their previous level. Moreover, according to the well-known economist Phillips, the real rate of inflation in the United States after 1983 was higher than the official rate (especially since 1996). If this is true, that wage growth is fictitious, and the picture in the 2000s is even more depressing.

    More and more affordable credit allowed for the growth of domestic demand and general prosperity. But the result was a population in extreme debt, and banks left with "bad" debts. These factors led to the fragility of domestic demand and the instability of the banking system. And because personal income tax is the primary source of revenue for the US federal budget, stagnating incomes meant there was no active growth in the taxable base. In such a situation, a growing budget deficit and national debt were only a matter of time. Deindustrialization preceded all these events. Wages in the service sector are on average one and a half times lower than in manufacturing. Skilled workers are harder to replace than waiters. Temporary and part-time work is common in the service sector, which has grown enormously in the last two decades. Today the trade union movement is for obvious reasons weaker. The contraction of industry has been accompanied by the stagnation or decline of real wages. But even the latter has not increased the competitiveness of the American economy— cheap labor has concentrated mainly in the nontradable sector.

3. Since 1980, deindustrialization has led to the *growth of social inequality* in the US. Back then, 0.1 percent of the population received slightly more than 1 percent of the national income, and now it receives 5 percent. This is more than the elite earned in the 1870s–1880s. The present level of income inequality is comparable to that in the 1920s. The reasons for this are the specifics of labor in the private sector that I have enumerated above, but also the absence of a large, united, and active "proletariat." This high level of social inequality also leads to a further decline in domestic demand.

4. Stock market and mortgage bubbles, as well as distortions in the banking system, are all the consequences of deindustrialization. Industry is more capital-intensive than the service sector and the average economy. As a result of deindustrialization, sooner or later a situation arises where there is "lots of free money—few good deals." The actions of the financial authorities may help or hinder the situation, but in the end this result is generally inevitable. As I mentioned, the first consequence of this situation was increasingly more affordable credit, including mortgages. The second was the influx of speculative capital in financial markets. The results of this are well known: the financial crisis of 2008–2009.

The US seems to understand the reasons for the crisis and the dangers of a Dutch-style scenario. Money flows into the economy, but economic growth is slow to recover, mostly because the money actually finances foreign industries and fossil fuel suppliers.

The US still has its strengths. Firstly, it has a technological advantage; even Germany and Japan are still lagging behind. Secondly, the US has unique opportunities to promote its economic interests in foreign markets. Thirdly, and as a consequence of the first two points, the US has a competitive and rapidly growing exports market. Fourthly, it has an impressive reserve of natural resources and much lower domestic energy and electricity prices than in Europe and Japan. Finally, the US has a much younger population than the EU and Japan, which places less of a burden on the pension system and the budget, and which can provide manpower for industry.

As we can see from the American case, deindustrialization is a major problem even for a country with such powerful industrial potential and world-leading technologies. Deindustrialization is even more dangerous for Russia, which had to make considerable sacrifices to approach the level of industrial development of other, more advanced countries.

Thirty years ago, the British economist Alexander Cairncross, an expert on deindustrialization,[9] pointed to a general decline in industrial production, a decrease in the share of industrial production in the GDP, and even a decline in the export of industrial products as the main symptoms of deindustrialization. At the same time, he also noted that these are not all the symptoms of this economic disease—deindustrialization—and listed some others: a transition from the predominant production of goods to that of services; a reduction in the export of industrial products, with a sufficiently long decline that then creates a trade deficit (though this is not always true), etc. On the basis of this argument, Cairncross builds a chain of consequences that lead to the economy's dependence on imports and its general degradation. Our approach at the Institute for New Industrial Development differs from his and shows that deindustrialization can also take place in the absence of the factors that Cairncross enumerates.

It seems more productive to study deindustrialization by analyzing negative trends in the four basic components that characterize industrialization itself: the organization of production, its technological provision, the nature of labor in production, and its product. Deindustrialization is accompanied by a simplification of labor and technologies, a decrease in scientific and "knowledge-intensive" production, the destruction of productive capacity, etc. In other words, under deindustrialization there occurs the simplification, or primitivization, of industrial production and the economy as a whole. Instead of scientific, technological, and economic progress, there is regression.

Under deindustrialization, technology becomes less complex, raw materials are processed more simply, production equipment, tools, and other devices are rendered simpler. We see a reduction in personnel qualifications, loss of skills and abilities, loss of specialties and competencies, and so on.

At INID, we call this effect the "4D effect" (analogous to the well-known "4I effect").

---

9 A. Cairncross, "What is Deindustrialization?," in *Deindustrialization*, ed. F. Blackaby (London: Pergamon, 1982), 5–17.

The main features of the 4D effect are:

- the **dis**organization of the production process (reduction in the level of organization and management of production);
- the **de**gradation of technologies (drop in the technological level of production);
- the **de**qualification of labor in production;
- the **de**complication (simplification) of the product of production.

The inevitable consequences of these trends are:

- the **de**stabilization of the economic condition of industrial companies;
- the **dis**integration of industrial structures and relations;
- and many other such "de-"s.

The economic result of deindustrialization is a general decline in and loss of entire productive activities and sectors, often without the ability to rebuild them.

As a result of deindustrialization, national production is replaced by *importing*, which begins to saturate the national market. Due to a shortage of domestic goods, imports meet the needs of the people, and their income goes to foreign markets. This chain of events *destabilizes the national economy*, leads to its degradation and eventual collapse, with the concurrent social instability and so on.

The current state of the Russian economy is fundamentally the consequence of its deep deindustrialization, which has led not only to a decline in gross industrial product, but also to negative structural changes in the economy: a bigger share of extractive industries and a smaller share of manufacturing industries in the economy. This decline was especially sharp in mechanical engineering, whose products are the technological basis of many economic and social activities.

Chapter 4

Industrial Development in Russia: Lessons from the Past

4.1. Russia's difficult path to industrialization

Industrialization came late to Russia, at least in comparison with most developed countries. The steps toward industrialization in the eighteenth and first half of the nineteenth century were limited due to the overall backwardness of the economic system. Though this process sped up in the last third of the nineteenth century, industrialization was hindered by the peasant reforms of 1861 and other economic reforms that followed. By the beginning of the twentieth century, the Russian Empire was still primarily an agrarian economy, though it had developed a sizable industrial sector, too.

The country went through an accelerated process of industrialization when the Bolsheviks took power, who attempted to restore the country's industrial potential that was destroyed during the First World War and the Russian Civil War. New, large-scale industrial production facilities popped up. The Soviets adopted the GOELRO plan, the first Soviet state program for the comprehensive development of industry. The goal of further industrialization was built into every five-year plan that followed the first Five-Year Plan of 1928. The Soviets introduced industrialization by force, and there were significant human and economic losses as a result. Their methods brought the industrial revolution to completion in Russia and created a complex of modern industrial sectors, providing the country with the necessary military and economic might to defeat Hitler's Germany, the most powerful war machine of its time.

Industrialization continued after the Second World War. Up until the 1980s, industry was regarded as the leading sector of the Russian economy, a fact that was reflected in state economic policy. The Soviets created and maintained the potential for impressive industry, and it exists to this day.

The Russian economy has seen big successes and equally big crises. It has been an outsider on the world economic stage, but it has also delivered on its flagship economic projects. It has undergone many reforms and revolutions. Its economic development has been contradictory, and some important lessons can be gleaned from this history.

The first lesson: all fundamental changes in the Russian economy were caused by major advances in material production technologies.

In the Russian Empire industrialization began in the eighteenth century. Technologically, Russia kept pace with the most advanced countries in the world: new technologies for melting metal and the first steam locomotive were invented simultaneously in Russia and England. During the second wave of industrialization at the beginning of the twentieth century, Russian scientists and engineers created the radio and the airplane at the same time as their Western counterparts. Russia was the first country to venture into space during the techno-scientific revolution of the mid-twentieth century, and the creator of the world's first nuclear power station.

Historical experience demonstrates that economic progress comes with technological development. Classical political economy argues that the material-technical basis of social production is the fundamental basis for economic and social progress. It seems that this once-obvious conclusion has been forgotten by some domestic reformers, and we are still paying the price for our technological backwardness and deindustrialization.

The history of the Russian state, however, also leads us to other conclusions.

The second lesson: it is necessary to form a system of economic relations and institutions that not only ensures technological progress, but also generates strong and constant material momentum for its continual innovation.

There are both positive and negative examples of this principle in Russian history. Among the first are the successes of the Russian economy's modernization, when an energetic state, combined with private entrepreneurship, provided the potential for strong technological development. On this basis, productivity grew, as did the quality of products, and with it, the overall quality of life, all leading to Russia's greater geopolitical power.

Examples of modernization are well known. They include the reforms of Peter the Great, the reforms of Sergey Yulyevich Witte (whose name the INID proudly bears), and the reforms of Pyotr Arkadyevich Stolypin, whose half-heartedness led to revolution. All these reforms were controversial and costly, as was the experience of Soviet modernization. The foundations of Russia's industrial and military power in the 1930s were watered with the blood of millions of prisoners, and the 1950s and 1960s were remembered not only for their scientific and technological revolutions, but also for Khrushchev's "corn craze" [kukuruzomaniya].

Russia's history also shows numerous examples of conservative economic and social institutions hindering modernization. The institution of serfdom persisted in Russia for centuries after it was abolished in Europe. The overly centralized, bureaucratic system of state administration in the USSR also hindered progress. Finally, in post-Soviet Russia, we see the negative impact of another extreme: market fundamentalism.

To avoid the same traps, economic reforms should refrain from absolutizing theoretical dogmas about the power of centralized planning and state ownership, or about the progressive potential of the free market and private entrepreneurship. As the economists Mikhail Tugan-Baranovskiy and Sergey Glazyev suggest, these moments of great economic transformation in Russia teach us that Russian economic institutions should provide as much space as possible for technological development, the progress of material production, and the human element in production.

The *third lesson is still being formulated* based on the experiences of recent history.

The twenty-first century presents challenges full of contradictions to both the domestic and global economies. As our technologies and institutions develop and take on various and complex new forms, life becomes more unpredictable, more chaotic, indeed, more destructive. Neither the self-regulating mechanisms of the free market nor the old forms of state bureaucracy can cope with these changes. This precarity is reflected in the economy in the EU's uncontrolled financialization and centrifugal tendencies, in the "revolt of the peripheries," in global economic crises, and so on.

In the sociopolitical sphere, the contradictions of the contemporary age have led to extremes, like, on the one hand, the fetishization of democratic procedures, resulting in a decline in social morale and the interruption of human biological norms, and on the other hand, the rise of conservative fundamentalism, plunging us into a medieval darkness.

Russia's economic and social policies are also struggling to meet the challenges of the recent past. Growing geo-economic and geopolitical conflict and new technological challenges are met with an "ostrich" policy of burying our heads in the sand. There is a sharp contradiction between our liberal market-oriented economic policy and our conservative geo-political ideology.

There is no doubt that Russia must be reborn as a major world power, for the benefit of its citizens, the Russian state, and the global community. But Russia cannot and should not be a colossus on clay feet.

The twenty-first century Russian economy necessitates technologically advanced material production coupled with progressive scientific, educational, and cultural policies. Such is the preliminary formulation for the third lesson of Russian history.

4.2. Russia's industrial potential: Lessons from Sergey Witte

There are some spaces in Russia that fill you with a sense of history. In St. Petersburg, almost every building seems to contain a world of history within. But for me, an economist who has dedicated his life to this practice, the house of Sergey Witte is special. Both because it is near our Institute for New Industrial Development, and because during his time at the turn of twentieth century, and during ours at the turn of the twenty-first, economists are faced with similar problems: how to modernize the economy and society at large in order to multiply Russia's industrial and intellectual wealth.

Unfortunately, these problems only reached partial conclusions during the era of Witte's reforms at the end of the nineteenth century. And at the end of the twentieth century, the Russian Federation took an entirely different path: that of total deindustrialization. More than one-hundred years have passed since the time of Witte, but we are faced with the same problems. Standing in front of his house, I ask myself once again: what was right and what was wrong in the approach of our former reformer, whose name decorates our institute?

What can we take from Witte's legacy to solve the twenty-first-century problem now in front of us: the reindustrialization of the Russian economy. The most fundamental answer to this question is that we must create in our domestic economy the conditions for technological and human potential to flourish. This is the first lesson to glean from the success of Witte's reforms. But it is as correct as it is abstract, and life demands concrete suggestions. To arrive at concrete examples of future recommendations, we must look critically at achievements of the past.

It is well known that Russia saw the significant growth of industry based on machine production in the last third of the nineteenth century. Many of the successes of this development are associated with Witte, who was Minister of Finance of the Russian Empire for eleven years.

Witte began his economic career after graduating from the Imperial Novorossiysk University in Odessa. On May 1, 1870, Witte began to work in the management of the Odessa railroad, and quickly grew close to the director of the Russian Society of Shipping and Trade, Nikolai Matveevich Chikhachev, who was in charge of the railway. In February of 1880, Witte was appointed head of operations of the Southwestern Railway Company and moved to Kyiv. His career quickly took off. In 1886, he became the manager of the same company, and in February of 1892 he became Minister of Railways. Within a few months of his tenure, Witte succeeded in eliminating large accumulations of nontransported cargo, which had become commonplace, reforming railroad tariffs, and more.

His successes did not go unnoticed, and at the end of 1892, Witte was appointed Minister of Finance, a post he held until 1903. After retirement, Witte was given a minor post as chairman of the Committee of Ministers. Then, during the turbulent times of the First Russian Revolution, Witte was brought back into government, and in October of 1905, he headed the Russian government as chairman of the Council of Ministers. His name is associated with the Manifesto of October 17, 1905, which some celebrate as the first step to democracy in Russia, while others criticize it for its inconsistency and narrowness.

Witte began his career as statesman at a time when Russia was already experiencing lively industrial growth. But this growth was largely based on timid, half-hearted steps toward developing domestic industry, which for the most part relied on small artisanal or semi-artisanal establishments. The share of industry in the national economy was very low, and the discrepancy between Russia and the advanced industrial powers of England, Germany, and the US was huge. The peasant reform of 1861 revived agricultural production to some extent, but did not lead to a real agrarian revolution, one which could create a reliable basis for industrial growth in the production of food and raw materials, freeing up workers for industrial labor.

To intensify industrial growth, Witte proposed intensifying railway construction. He had his personal reasons for this suggestion, given his extensive experience in railroad management and railroad tariffs. In 1883, he published his book on *The Principles of Railway Tariffs for Cargo Transportation* (the second edition came out in 1884, and the third came out in 1910 with considerable additions). The book is primarily an *appeal to market principles of price-setting*. According to Witte, when determining railroad charges, one should not rely on the expenses of transport companies, but on the potential prices of the transported goods at their points of departure and destination, which are formed according to supply and demand.

Witte also argued that the effective functioning of the domestic economy was impossible without a sufficient network of railroads. The Russian railway system connected different economic regions of the country, promoted the efficient distribution of industries, and ensured the flow of new resources into the economy. Moreover, railway construction stimulated the production of locomotives, wagons, rails, sleepers, metal structures for bridges, and the construction of station buildings and facilities, bringing together many branches of Russian industry.

As Minister of Railways, Witte pursued a policy of buying up private Russian railroads. He understood that *Russia's railways would be much more effective as part of a unified state complex*. Some of his innovations while in this office are still in place today. For example, it was in 1889 that Russian passenger trains were fitted with modern metal cup holders.

Through Witte's efforts construction on the Trans-Siberian Railway was accelerated. Rail communication with remote areas of Siberia and the Far East was not only of strategic military and political importance but was also a necessary condition for the economic development of new territories with rich reserves of natural resources. Without railroads, it was impossible to ensure the timely and necessary flow of people to the developed territories. Witte understood that *big investments in infrastructure would ensure progressive structural shifts in the entire economy*. The table below demonstrates the sharp rise in the rate of railway construction under Witte, both as Minister of Railways and then Minister of Finance (table 3).

Russia still suffers from the underdevelopment of its transport infrastructure. Operational speeds in freight and passenger rail traffic are lags far behind world standards. The development of air transport, which now plays the same role as did rail transport one century ago, is also lagging. Because the country's many regions are poorly connected, they have developed unequally, only fortifying the trends of economic disintegration and deindustrialization in the country. Investment in transportation will not only lead to the more efficient transport of goods and people, but it will also create centers of domestic demand for high-tech production. Witte realized as much at the turn of the twentieth century, but more than a hundred years later, this fact seems underappreciated and ununderstood by politicians and economists.

TABLE 3. Lines operated by state and private companies in the European and Asian parts of Russia, excluding Finnish railroads and CER (1889–1912)

Three-year periods	Length of lines put into operation during the period (versts)	Length of lines in service at the end of the period (versts)
1889–1891	1 202	28 389
1892–1894	4 013	32 402
1895–1897	5 520	37 922
1898–1900	10 643	48 565
1901–1903	4 526	53 091
1904–1906	4 850	57 941
1907–1909	2 539	60 480
1910–1912	2 296	62 776

Source: Edmond Teri, *Russia's Economic Transformation*, trans. A.A. Peshkov (Moscow: Russian Political Encyclopedia (ROSSPEN), 2008), 100.

Witte paid considerable attention to Russia's foreign economic ties. He believed in the German economic theory, developed by Friedrich List and others, that argued that *domestic markets must be protected by customs tariffs in order for the national economy to develop*. This was at odds with free trade, which argues for the reduction or downright abolition of customs tariffs. History demonstrates that almost all countries in the first stages of their industrial development used protectionist tariffs to protect domestic producers from economically more powerful countries. It is those economically powerful countries that benefit from free trade with weaker competitors.

By hindering the import of manufactured goods, protective tariffs encourage manufacturers to move production into the country in order to gain access to the domestic market. In this way, they encourage the flow of foreign investment into the country. They have also been an importance source of revenue for the Russian state.

Witte put these ideas into practice. In 1891, Russia adopted a new customs tariff, which Witte developed with Dmitriy I. Mendeleev and others. The tariff became an important part of Russia's foreign trade policy, a bulwark for its developing industry. Revenue from customs increased from 130.5 million rubles in 1892 to 212.17 million rubles in 1901 as more imports flowed into the country (403.9 million in 1892 and 593.4 million in 1901) with higher duties on some goods.[1]

---

1 W. Brandt "Sergey Y. Witte (addition to article)," in *Encyclopedic Dictionary of F. A. Brockhaus and I. A. Efron*, Vol. 1, edited by K. K. Arsenyev and F. F. Petrushevsky (St. Petersburg: Brockhaus-Efron, 1890–1907). (in Russ.)

It is worth noting the parallels between this situation and Russia's recent, hasty accession to the WTO, which significantly curtailed its ability to protect its domestic market. But even in the current situation, it is possible to implement *resilient but flexible policies aimed at the protection of domestic production, though we must rely mainly on methods other than tariffs due to different historical circumstances.*

Another significant source of state revenue for the Russian Empire was the state alcohol monopoly introduced by Witte in 1895. The private production and trade of raw alcohol was allowed, but the production of purified alcohol as well as the production and trade of spirits were placed in the hands of the state. One of Witte's main goals was to improve the quality of spirits. Together with the Central Chemical Laboratory, a group of scientists composed of Dmitriy Mendeleev, Vasiliy D. Mendeleev, Nikolai I. Tavildarov, Mikhail G. Kucherov, Aleksandr A. Verigo, Gleb M. Krzhizhanovsky, and others, Witte tackled the problem of introducing a vodka monopoly in the country. The goals of the reform were to place vodka production solely in the hands of the state, to establish a high standard of quality for vodka production, and to remove artificial impurities from ethyl alcohol produced exclusively from grains.

From that point on, the state alcohol monopoly became a major source of revenue for the Russian and later Soviet governments, producing as much as a quarter of all state revenue. After the state alcohol monopoly was abolished in the 1990s, vodka production rose steadily against a backdrop of overall industrial decline, and *underground* vodka distribution swelled. Vodka was likely the only industrial product that did not decline in production. And yet, it did neither the state budget nor Russian citizens any good. For this reason, it is worth seriously considering another *state alcohol monopoly* in Russia, especially in view of current budgetary constraints.

Another of Witte's reforms that had considerable impact on the Russian economy was his currency reform, placing the Russian ruble on the gold standard in 1897. This *stabilized the ruble, ensured its wider circulation, simplified foreign economic operations, and facilitated the influx of foreign investments.* At the same time, *the switch to the gold standard made it easier to transfer capital to foreign lands and, in the event of economic difficulties, created the risk of capital flight.*

Moreover, the switch required large gold reserves, which increased the cost of maintaining money in circulation. In 1899 the quantity of gold in circulation amounted to 451.4 million rubles (three times more than in 1898 and 12.5 times more than in 1897), while the amount of paper money in circulation dropped to 661.8 million rubles. During 1900 the amount of gold in circulation increased by 1.42 times. Though this growth then stabilized, the amount of gold in circulation increased almost eighteen-fold in four years. At the same time, the amount of paper money in circulation declined by 2.175 times, which led to an acute paper money shortage among the population. In 1899, the amount of paper currency in the Russian Empire amounted to ten rubles (twenty-five francs) per citizen, while in Austria it was fifty francs, 112 in Germany, 115 in the United States, 136 in England, and 218 francs in France. For the sake of comparison, note that in 1857, when Russia had not yet transitioned from a subsistence economy to a monetary economy, the exchange rate was twenty-five rubles to 62.5 francs.[2] Economists and politicians had ambivalent feelings about the switch to the gold standard.

By modern standards, the gold standard may look anachronistic. But making the ruble more convertible to foreign currencies is not an unrealistic goal, nor is increasing the scale of foreign trade operations using the ruble. But the Russian experience, as well as that of other countries, shows that *the best way to guarantee the stability of the convertible ruble is via available, reliable, and diversified export commodities.*

Witte's policies aimed at *attracting foreign capital in the form of direct investments and loans* also had *contradictory results.* On the one hand, while foreign investments expanded opportunities for industrial growth, the Russian economy suffered from its narrow base of domestic industrial capital. Witte had this to say on the topic: "to bring Russia to a strong economic position that would consolidate its independence from foreign powers and enable it to satisfy its needs in proportion to its natural wealth: that is our greatest task."[3] To solve this task the influx of foreign capital was necessary. "Therefore, it is my deep conviction that the influx of foreign capitalists into the country should not be hindered, but on the contrary, we should open our doors wide for them, for they inject the necessary energy into the country's economic organism." Moreover, foreign capital provided Russia with modern industrial equipment, especially in the chemical and electrical industries. On the other hand, foreign capital occupied key positions in almost all of Russia's modern industrial sectors and held back the spread of the most advanced technologies of the time, not wanting to contribute to Russia's competitive edge.

Debt dependence on foreign financial capital (mostly French) did not cause serious threat of a payment crisis under Witte. But under his successors,

---

2 Nechvolodov, A, *From Ruin to Prosperity* (St. Petersburg: Printing house of the Headquarters of the Guard Troops and the St. Petersburg Military District, 1906). (in Russ.)

3 *Minutes of the Speeches of the Minister of Finance S. Witte and Foreign Minister M. N. Murav'ev at the Ministerial Meeting Chaired by Nicholas II on the Foundations of Russia's Trade and Industrial Policy* (n.p., March 17, 1899). (in Russ.)

the accumulation of foreign debt continued, which made the Russian Empire dependent on French foreign policy and affected Russia's position before and during World War I, and contributed to Russia's involvement in the war as part of the Triple Entente.

The contemporary Russian economy also requires foreign investment for the same reasons that guided Witte's policy. But we should not ignore the downside here: *the possibility of losing control over critical sectors of the national economy and the risk of mounting foreign debt.* There is not as great a shortage of domestic sources of capital today as there was at the turn of the last century, and much depends on *national banks providing cheap and accessible credit to industry.*

In 1898, Witte began to reform trade and industrial taxation. While he was head of the treasury, the national budget more than doubled: from approximately one billion rubles in 1892 to more than two billion in 1903. The annual budget grew by 10.5 percent, while in the previous decade it grew by 2.5 percent, and in the following by 5 percent. This budget growth was ensured primarily by increases in revenue from state property, in indirect taxes (in the 1890s they grew by 42.7 percent), and a progressive tax on corporate profits, which replaced the former system of industrial taxation. Increases in direct taxes were insignificant and limited mainly to increases in housing and city real estate taxes. In fact, some direct taxes were reduced, including the land tax, which was halved.[4]

Witte's tax policies should hardly be seen as an example to follow in the modern day. Over the past century plus, the circumstances surrounding revenue generation and tax administration have changed dramatically many times. Instead, what we should take from Witte is his capacity to *adapt the tax system to the conditions of the economy at a certain stage of its development.*

Witte understood the close relationship between the agrarian and industrial sectors, and how the backwardness of Russian agriculture hindered its industrial development. With this in mind, he wanted to take measures to promote agricultural production. He believed it necessary to reform the peasant *obshchina* and advocated moving away from this economic structure. He suggested that communal land management in its current form, "its ambiguity on the right to property acquired by a member of the peasant household, and its uncertainty on the householder's duties, sapped the energy and productivity out of labor. The peasant population, due to the lack of a firm and clear legal order in personal, family, and property relations, suffers from numerous and severe difficulties." For these reasons, Witte advocated transforming the system into one based on

---

4 "Introduction. S. Y. Witte and financial policy in Russia." http://www.xserver.ru/user/vitmr/1.shtml. (in Russ).

common private law. "Now that the main provisions of the emancipation reform have been implemented, it is absolutely necessary to definitively organize the peasants [okonchatelnoe ustroystvo krestian], to lift up the peasant and grant him the rights that all of the Emperor's subjects enjoy."[5]

The ruling elite did not understand Witte's approach at first. Witte also allocated additional funds to the resettlement of peasants and eased administrative barriers to their resettlement in eastern parts of the country. With a law passed on February 12, 1903, he also abolished the corporal punishment of peasants by the volost courts and eased stringent passport requirements for peasants. Witte participated in the expansion of the Peasants' Land Bank. New laws and regulations on small-scale credit for peasants were also instituted with his participation.

On the whole, however, Witte failed to effect significant change in agricultural production. In his later reforms, Pyotr A. Stolypin further developed a number of Witte's proposed solutions.

The economy's growth and stability today depend on the development of agricultural production. Improving the situation in the agricultural sector is a prerequisite for the reindustrialization of Russia.

We can still apply much of what Witte taught us to our modern-day problems, like the "specification [spetsifikatsii] and protection of property rights." As in Witte's day, this problem is related to the vestiges of the past: then it was the feudal land tenure system, now it is the command economy system.

Witte did not reduce the country's industrial and overall economic growth merely to fiscal, monetary, and credit policies. He also tackled social problems and recognized the importance of the human element in economic growth, which meant hiring specialists and training the masses. With his participation, *labor laws came to pass, most importantly the 1897 law limiting working hours.*

Under the Ministry of Finance, Russia's first state-owned press agency opened in 1902, the Merchant-Telegraph Agency (later called the Petrograd Telegraph Agency). It was Witte who invited Mendeleev to head the Chamber of Weights and Measures, and the noted scientist quickly put the agency in order.

Witte's Ministry of Finance invested heavily in technical and commercial education. The act of May 19, 1894 put the Ministry of Finance in charge of commercial schools. On April 10, 1896, a regulation on commercial schools ensured that communities, cities, estates, and *zemstvos* participated in the dissemination of commercial knowledge. Trade schools and courses on commerce were set up. Before 1894 there existed only eight commercial

---

5   S. Witte, *Abstract of Lectures on the National and State Economy, Delivered to His Imperial Highness the Grand Duke Mikhail Alekseevich in 1900–1902* (St. Petersburg: n.p., 1912), 112.

schools; from 1896 to 1902, 147 commercial schools existed, with more than twenty thousand students in attendance. Among the 147, there were fifty-one business colleges [uchilishche], forty-three trade schools, thirty classes and twenty-three courses on commerce. With the March 10, 1897 act on rural artisanal workshops, technical knowledge began to spread among the rural population. The act of March 19, 1902 encouraged the development of practical technical education in the working class. The Ministry promoted artistic and industrial education and women's vocational training. The Kyiv, Warsaw, and Petersburg Polytechnic Institutes opened their doors for the first time. In 1902, the total number of students enrolled in the various educational institutions under the Ministry of Finance exceeded thirty thousand.[6]

A hundred and some years later, Russia "suddenly" finds itself lacking in qualified workers. But the past hundred plus years have taught us *that economic development depends largely on state support of education, especially vocational education.* Following Witte's lead, we should consider education a worthwhile expense. In fact, the success of Witte's network of commercial schools was not even based on big government spending, but on business investments, taking some of the financial burden of training the masses off the state.

There is no doubt that Witte's policies had a significant impact on Russia's industrial growth. But his plans were hindered by the limited economic and social structure of the Russian Empire. As a result, periods of crisis followed periods of remarkable recovery. Although Russia's overall rate of economic growth exceeded that of Great Britain and France, it was not sufficient to compete with the most dynamic industrial powers, the US and Germany (table 4).

TABLE 4. Production of major industrial products in the Russian Empire (1887–1913) in poods

Types of products	1887	1900	1913
Cast iron	36.1	176.8	283
Charcoal	276.2	986.4	2215
Steel and iron	35.5	163	246.5
Oil	155	631.1	561.3
Cotton (processing)	11.5	16	25.9
Sugar	25.9	48.5	75.4

Source: R. Portal, "The Industrialization of Russia," in *Cambridge Economic History of Europe*, Vol. 6 (Cambridge: Cambridge University Press, 1965), 837, 844.

6   W. Brandt, "Sergey Y. Witte (addition to article)." (in Russ.)

Witte seemed to understand the precarity of the situation and made a concerted effort (especially in 1905–1906) to balance the stability of the monarchy, which he considered a prerequisite for economic development, and the implementation of urgent socioeconomic reforms. The perfect balance was, however, never achieved, and the situation ultimately ended in revolution. We should not forget this lesson either.

Chapter 5

The Deindustrialization of Russia and the Challenges of Reindustrialization[1]

Russia has long pursued an economic policy that had, in principle, the correct *goal*: to create a modern social market economy with modernized development. But the *means* toward this end have been less than successful: an ideology of market fundamentalism coupled with the practice of a shadow market and manual state management. This combination has led to economic stagnation and all its negative consequences.

As I detailed above, Russia's road to industrialization was not an easy one. Its economic development was not without several periods of deindustrialization.

Before World War I, Russia's industry was growing and so was its economic potential. Sergey Y. Glazyev writes that during this period, "the second techno-economic paradigm [vtoroy tekhnologicheskiy uklad] began to dominate as it entered its maturity, and the individual technological chains of the third techno-economic paradigm had already formed in its technological base and were rapidly spreading."

However, the First World War, followed by the Civil War and its attendant devastation, ruptured established economic ties and led to economic

---

1 This chapter is based on a report from the meeting commemorating the 250th anniversary of the Free Economic Society of Russia.

deterioration. Russia stepped off the path of scientific, technological, and industrial process. The country entered an era of prolong deindustrialization.

The first significant step toward economic recovery was the GOELRO plan, a long-term state program for the restoration and development of domestic industry, using the advanced technologies of the third techno-economic paradigm. But the economic devastation and deindustrialization of the previous five years forced the Bolshevik government to put the industrial elements of the GOELRO plan on hold, and instead institute the New Economic Policy, which restored small-scale entrepreneurship and manufacturing. As a result, by the 1930s the Soviet state was left with an inefficient industry, primarily nationalized, with outdated technology. A decisive breakthrough in the economy was impossible under these conditions. It was necessary to industrialize the national economy, a process that began in earnest at the beginning of the 1930s.

There were two possible paths to industrialization: by accelerating the development of light industry, or the development of heavy industry. The Soviets decided on the second option, in essence a reincarnation of GOELRO but accelerated.

I will not dwell on the specifics of this period of industrialization here, but I will mention that elements of the third techno-economic paradigm took hold in various industries.

Yet again, however, the process of domestic industrialization was interrupted by war. Widespread industrial destruction forced another period of deindustrialization. Postwar reconstruction restored the elements of the third techno-economic paradigm in Russian industry, which still lagged behind as the fourth techno-economic paradigm developed in better-off countries. This trend has continued to the present day, as Russia *continues to lag behind by one techno-economic paradigm*, and the gap has only grown in recent decades.

Russia's attempts to make up for lost time and catch up with more developed countries has often come at a heavy price. Although in the latter half of the twentieth century, the USSR grew into a successful industrial power with flourishing industrial and technological potential, various problems plagued this development. In the 1980s, Russia continued to lag behind the world's economic leaders. Its critics blamed this lag on the flaws of the Soviet planned economy. But from the start of the market reforms, the new Russian government had radically changed its position on industry. The very term "industrial policy" virtually disappeared from the official vocabulary, and a liberal take on economic development prevailed, mixed an ideology of post-industrialism. The so-called "economically developed" countries believed that humanity had entered a new phase: "postindustrial society," in which the importance of industry and industrial workers was constantly on the decline while the importance of the service sector grew.

This new state position on industry resulted in the largest industrial decline in the Russian economy since WWII. In line with its new position, the Russian government adopted new economic policies and reimagined the role of private industry. Cooperation among different industrial sectors also took a nosedive during the political turmoil of the late 1980s and early 1990s: the "fall" of the USSR, which caused the breakdown of traditional economic ties. The industrial production index in Russia (as percentage of the previous year) was 84.0 percent in 1992, 86.3 percent in 1993, 78.4 percent in 1994, 95.4 percent in 1995, 92.4 percent in 1996, 101.0 percent in 1997 and 95.2 percent in 1998.[2] If we take 1991 as the baseline, then the cumulative index of industrial production according to the Rosstat data for 1998 was 48.2 percent, i.e., the total industrial production in the country decreased by more than twofold from 1991 to 1998. Russia's economy underwent large-scale *deindustrialization* as a result of the so-called shock therapy of the 1990s. Those responsible for these policies did not take into account the most important characteristic of industry: the time lag between when a policy is introduced and when it shows its positive effects. Sometimes the positive effects of industrial investment are not apparent until long after the reforms that made them possible. Industrial enterprise was not given sufficient time to flourish during this period and could not adapt in time to the new economic reality, which saw the breakdown of economic ties between the former Soviet republics and the hasty introduction of market economics.

I want to stress again that national industry was ignored on the basis of liberal economic theory that pushed for less government interference in the economy and argued that a "postindustrial" age had come. Though the fallacy of this position is now obvious, it is this brand of liberal economic thought that set the tone for economic policy in the Russia of the 1990s. The government adopted this viewpoint in its policymaking, and unfortunately continues to do so, to a very large extent, to this day.

The *planned* deindustrialization of Russia is well underway. Due to a significant reduction in domestic production, the share of imports, for example, in machine tools and light industry today exceeds 90 percent. In heavy engineering, radio-electronics, and medical equipment, this share exceeds 80 percent. The situation is similar, if not worse, in other basic sectors of the economy (food, mining, energy, communications, etc.). For example, if in 2000 Russia imported ten

---

2   Here and below, unless otherwise noted, data is from Rosstat, the Ministry of Economic Development of Russia, the Ministry of Finance of Russia, and the Bank of Russia.

billion dollars' worth of machinery, equipment, and transport vehicles, fourteen years later it was one hundred fifty billion dollars (fifteen times more). Today Russia is critically dependent on imports.

This situation makes the role of industrial policy pivotal in tackling the problem of economic, and indeed, social development.[3] The geopolitical and geo-economic challenges that face the Russian economy and society have greatly exacerbated the existing problems, which have been festering for decades. I believe that these problems have reached such a pitch that they now pose a threat to Russia's national security. The challenge is to find a new model of economic growth that is based on a fuller use of our own capabilities and resources.

The approaches and principles of economic regulation that are currently in use are in desperate need of reconsideration. Russia has long pursued an economic policy that had the correct intention: to create a modern social market economy and ensure the modernization of development. One cannot but agree with the goals, tasks, and priorities set forth in various government documents on its strategy. The means, however, toward those goals—above all, the state's insistence on market fundamentalism coupled with a shadow market and manual state management—have caused the economy to stagnate. More than twenty years of liberal economic policy has led to the collapse of industrial production, economic instability, and a dramatic rise in dependence on imports, which is especially evident in the high-tech industries. According to the World Bank's website, the share of high-tech products in Russia's industrial exports more than halved between 2003 and 2013, from 18.3 percent to 8.4 percent, the most serious decline of any developed or developing country cited in the study. Russia's export model is still focused on exports of low value-added products (raw materials and energy). For example, the top eight oil and gas producers accounted for more than 60 percent of the value of all Russian exports in early 2014, according to Rosstat, while the share of the nonresource export sector has shrunk to a quarter.

Russia is one of the richest countries in the world in terms of resource potential. Only 2.4 percent of the world's population lives in the country, while its territory occupies 10 percent of the Earth's area. Russia has 45 percent of the world's natural gas reserves, 13 percent of oil, and 23 percent of coal. Arable

---

3   See S. D. Bodrunov, R. S. Grinberg, and D. E. Sorokin, "Reindustrialization of the Russian economy: imperatives, potential, risks," *Economic revival of Russia* 1, no. 35 (2013): 19–49; A. I. Popov, "Creating a New Model of Development: Modernization and Conditions for Transition to an Innovative Economy," *Proceedings of the St. Petersburg State Economic University* 4 (2012): 18–26. (in Russ.)

land per capita in Russia is 0.9 hectares, 80 percent more than in Finland and 30 percent more than in the US. Expert studies show that the degree of resource efficiency in the Russian economy is as follows: 25 percent efficiency of natural resources, 15 percent of human resources, 10 percent of financial resources, and 3.3 percent of intellectual resources.[4] The developmental level of the country's resource potential is estimated at 18 percent. In comparison, in the US it is 76 percent, in the EU 78 percent, and in Japan it is 88 percent. The current economic system relies primarily on the export of natural resources, which does not allow for their most effective use, nor for the use of export revenues for technological modernization and structural economic renewal.

I would argue that the current recession is, in principle, the consequence of the *profound deindustrialization* of the Russian economy.

In the absence of modern technologies that are available and ready to be put to use, a qualitative leap in development, especially innovative development, is impossible, as is economic growth in general. With this in mind, I will note the following:

1. The processes of deindustrialization, including of high-tech industries, are closely related to the specificities of the Russian market transformation. Privatization and other macroeconomic policies created relatively more favorable for the fuel and raw materials sectors, the financial market, trade and intermediary services, and some other service sectors. The manufacturing industry, already behind global market standards, was starved for investment and had no resources to modernize and become more competitive. This problem was not a policy priority and went unattended. But the problem was not only the lack of investment from abroad; internal sources of technological renewal also went unused and were thereby degraded. The state sharply cut its spending on research and development, and the emerging business sector failed to supply R&D with the necessary funding. Not only that—it eliminated more than 80 percent of internal R&D organizations. The policy to blame for this is, again, that of market fundamentalism.

2. When discussing the host of problems related to industrialization, mention is often made of the necessity of a "competitive economic environment." The dominant interpretation of this term is no more

---

4   A. O. Blinov, "Innovative and Technological Modernization of Russian Industry—the Basis of State Security," *Economics of Sustainable Development* 13 (2013): 44–50. (in Russ.)

sophisticated than you would find in an economics textbook, which explains that the ideal competitive environment is one with many small firms. This was also the guideline for those Russian "privatizers" who broke up various large enterprises. There is no doubt that competition is necessary for a functioning market economy, but the structure and organization of those former Soviet enterprises differed greatly from those of Western companies. Big Soviet enterprises were broken up during an unstable transition period that saw many economic ties break across multiple former Soviet republics. As a result, increased competition led to the downfall of the emerging enterprises, which were unprepared to exist in such an environment. Note that due to structural reforms, industry science was separated from industrial enterprises. Without ties to production, research, design, and technological divisions went bankrupt and were redeveloped [pereprofilirovalis]. As a result, the technological level of production declined significantly. None of these factors led to a competitive environment, but only to a disorganized industry and to further deindustrialization.

3. I argue that one of the main causes of deindustrialization is the "Dutch disease" I detailed above. In the 2000s, the flow of financial resources into Russia, thanks to its growing profile on the world oil market, did little to correct the chaotic situation. Surplus liquidity was not channeled into the modernization of production and renewal of fixed assets, but was either sterilized in various funds, or boosted domestic demand, which was satisfied mainly through imports and therefore poorly stimulated the development of domestic production.

4. Russian industrial enterprises lag far behind in their management and organization of production. The low profitability of the manufacturing industry (lower than in the financial sector, services, etc.) hinders investments in industrial innovation, both in technologies and management. State credit and tax policy are mainly to blame for its low profitability. The problem of access to "long" and "cheap" money in Russia remains unsolved. Real interest rates significantly exceed the profitability of almost all manufacturing industries, which suffocates them financially and further contributes to deindustrialization.

5. The role of state-owned enterprises in the economy is worth reconsidering. In the traditional liberal economic framework, it is

considered a negative for the state to expand its reach in the economy. But there is simply no convincing evidence that state-owned enterprises are always less efficient than private enterprises. It is merely an axiom of economic liberalism that should not be taken at face value. Increased state ownership is not a problem in itself. The main problem is that the state support of large enterprises, though it affects high-tech sectors, especially in the defense industry, has not led to technological renewal in manufacturing. This problem is primarily due to the ambiguity of state strategy when it comes to industrial policy, which is mired in vague goals and means for achieving them.

We must radically change course and transition from *de*industrialization to *re*industrialization. The task is clear. First, I will delineate our starting position. Russia has yet to recover its pre-Perestroika scientific and industrial potential, more than half of which was destroyed during the systemic crisis of the 1990s. This is the first feature of today's Russian economy that we must consider on the road to reindustrialization (table 5).

TABLE 5. Recovery of industrial production (1991 = 100 percent)

	1998	2008	2009	2012	2015 (forecast) [5]
GDP	60.5	117.8	108.6	122.1	138.2
Industry as a whole, including:	48.2	85.4	77.5	90.0	101.3
Mineral extraction	167.2	105.6	104.9	112.0	113.6
Manufacturing industries	40.7	82.9	70.3	87.1	101.4

Let us take machinery as an example. According to output in 2012, the volume of machinery production was a little more than half of its 1991 level, and there was unprecedented decline in certain types of products (table 6).

---

5   It is now clear that this forecast was overly optimistic.

TABLE 6. Output of individual types of products in machinery

	1990	2011
Turbines, million kW	12.5	6.8
Wheeled tractors, thousand pcs.	77.8	12.7
Crawler tractors, thousand pcs.	63.8	1.72
Grain harvesters, thousand pcs.	65.7	6.2
Forage harvesters, thousand pcs.	10.1	0.286
Milking machines, thousand pcs.	30.7	2.6
Spinning machines, pcs.	1509	27
Looms, pcs.	18300	9
Trucks, thousand pcs.	665	207

The Russian economy lags far behind its main competitors by share of machinery production in the structure of its manufacturing industries (table 7).

TABLE 7. Share of machinery and equipment production in the structure of manufacturing industries

Country	Year	Share of machinery and equipment, %
Russia	2011	21.5
USA	2007	32.5
Germany	2008	42.8
UK	2007	29.8
France	2008	27.9
Japan	2007	44.4
Brazil	2007	26.9
China	2009	33.6

The decline in the domestic machinery industry occurred primarily due to the rapid decline of production in the machine tool industry (table 8). By 2012, the volume of machinery and equipment production barely exceeded 50 percent of the 1991 volume. That number did not even reach the volume level of 2008, when the machine tool industry shrunk to the same extent as it did in 1991. Meanwhile, these same figures are increasing in developed countries, as Russia lags far behind (table 9).

TABLE 8. Production by types of economic activity in industry (1991 = 100 percent)

	1998	2008	2009	2012	2015	2020 (forecast)
Production of machinery and equipment, incl.	38.1*	63.3	43.4	53.5	66.8	
Machine tools	11.2	7.2	2.8	5.1	7.7	9.6**
Forging presses	5.4	11.5	5.3	8.3	8.2**	11.3**

* 1995

** RF state program, "Industrial development and increasing its competitiveness up to 2020," Russian Ministry of Industry and Trade, 2013.

TABLE 9. Production of metal-cutting machines, pcs.

Machine type	Drilling and milling machines		Lathes	
Country	2007	2008	2007	2008
Russia	2 826	2 408	1 360	1 412
Germany	15 721	45 370	6 574	23 342
USA	9 246	8 139	6 210	7 416
Japan	16 544	14 311	27 761	26 998
Brazil	9 127	11 799	13 344	5 429

When the machine tool industry falls behind, so does the entire technological base of production. Such is the *technological challenge* facing us in the current economic situation. On to the *second* relevant feature of today's Russian economy as we consider the path to reindustrialization. Since 2012, the pace of economic development has been in steady decline. By 2014 the economy came close to rock bottom, or "near-zero" [okolonolia], as Russia is likely entering a full-fledged recession. The situation in the manufacturing industry is particularly worrisome. The nonzero average of growth in mineral production in 2013, added to the average of growth in manufacturing in that same year, gives us the "near-zero" industrial average for 2013. And industry, the backbone of the economy, had little impact on these figures. The obvious conclusion to be drawn from the fact of industrial stagnation is that of economic stagnation, which also leads to the state's political instability.

I argue that the solution to this problem must be based on reindustrialization via advanced technology. I want to stress that I am not advocating that Russia restores Soviet industry as it was, but that Russia upgrades its technological base of production. As an economic policy, *the main goals of reindustrialization* ("new industrialization" or "neoindustrialization") are to *restore industry as a basic component* of economic development, to *prioritize material production* and the real economy, and to *modernize Russia with new and advanced technology.*

I also want to stress that the current task, to create a new techno-industrial base, does not contradict the theses of established economists who argue that we must establish a new material base for production by utilizing technologies of the fifth and sixth paradigms (S. Glazyev), or informatization, miniaturization, customization, and network-organized production (M. Kastells), or the creative potential of workers (A. Buzgalin, A. Kolganov, T. Sakaiya), and so on. These priorities do, however, contradict the priorities of the reigning liberal economic ideology, with its stress on services, financial transactions, brokering, etc.

It is impossible to tackle the current challenges without *integrating* material production with science and education. Practically, the reindustrialization of the Russian economy necessitates as an *organizational principle* the *integration of science, production, and education.*

Moreover, material production itself must meet the challenges of technological and human development. Changes in material production must be made systemically and holistically. Allow me to highlight the key features of this transformation:

- updating the content of technological processes;
- changing the structure of industrial enterprises (micro-level);
- changing the structure of industrial sectors (macro-level);
- changing the approach to the organization/localization of production;
- forming of new types of industrial cooperation;
- increasing integration of production with science and education;
- transitioning to an ideology of "continuous innovation in production processes";
- forming economic relations and institutes aimed at industrial/techno-scientific progress.

Firstly, it is necessary that we do not copy and recreate the sectoral and technological structure of industrial production as it existed before the latest phase of deindustrialization in Russia. The challenge is to create a *new industrial system that corresponds to the latest, twenty-first-century frontiers in science and technology.* Such a system implies: knowledge-intensive production; flexibility and adaptability to constantly changing needs; customization (one method thereof is 3D printing, for example); "just-in-time" [tochno vovremia] and "lean" [berezhlivo] production organization. *Secondly,* we must change the *structure* of industrial sectors and *location* of industrial production, their internal *structure* and *types of cooperation* between them, as well as models of their integration with science and education. Thirdly (and perhaps most importantly), it is necessary to form economic *relations* and *institutions* that ensure the progress of a fundamentally new material production. This can only happen with an active industrial policy aimed at supporting those entrepreneurs who implement the above-mentioned imperatives of creating qualitatively new material production; creating favorable credit and financial conditions for them; increasing the prestige of conscientious material labor and reducing social inequality; prioritizing on the state level the development of science and education; protecting domestic production and promoting it in global markets.

Chapter 6

Techno-Economic Paradigms and the Renewal of the Russian Economy: The Political-Economic Aspect[1]

1. Techno-economic paradigms

Technological development in the context of economic industrialization leads to significant improvements not only in production, but in the entire life of a society. After enough technological upgrades, society advances to a new level of development where needs are better met and there is greater opportunity for its expansion.

But the situation calls for more than abstract theorization about the influence of progressive production on socioeconomic relations. There must be criteria to distinguish between different periods of technological development and the differences in a society's needs and how to satisfy them during those different periods. Sergey Glazyev and Dmitriy Lvov's theory of techno-economic paradigms allows us to make these qualitative judgements, which can then lead to quantitative criteria. According to Glazyev and Lvov, a techno-economic paradigm is a system of interconnected productions [proizvodstva] (including interdependent technological chains) of the same technical level, essentially a subsystem of a more general economic system.

---

1 Based on a report from the All-Russian Economic Forum: "Political Economy: Shaping the Subject of Research," Moscow, Free Economic Society of Russia, June 10, 2015.

Different interrelated sets of technologies correspond to different stages of technological development, as scholars have long noted. As early as the early twentieth century, Joseph Schumpeter noted that technological innovations develop discretely in time. Schumpeter considers innovative entrepreneurial activity, which drives the improvement of production technologies, to be an advantage in economic competition and the main driver of economic development.[2] Schumpeter termed those periods of extreme innovation "clusters" [klastery] or "bundles" [puchki] of innovation,[3] though the term *waves* of innovation is now more common.[4]

In 1975, the West German scientist Gerhard Mensch coined the term "technical mode of production" (from the German *Techniksysteme*). In the 1970s and 1980s, the English economist Christopher Freeman, who believed in the "diffusion of innovations," formulated the concept of technical-economic paradigms, which was further developed by his student Carlota Perez.[5] The Russian economic term "techno-economic paradigm" [tekhnologicheskii uklad] is an analogue of these other concepts: *waves of innovation, technical-economic paradigm*, and *technological mode of production*. Lvov and Glazyev coined the term in 1986.[6]

According to Glazyev's definition, a techno-economic paradigm is an integral, stable formation, within which develops a closed cycle: it begins with the extraction and production of primary resources, and ends with the final product, which corresponds to the given type of public consumption. The *core* of the techno-economic paradigm is a certain set of basic technologies used for an extended period of time or characteristic of the various sectors of an economy. The technological innovations that determine the formation of the core are called *key factors*. The sectors that use the key factors and play a leading role in the spread of the new paradigm are called *carriers*.[7]

2   I. A. Schumpeter, *Theory of Economic Development*. (in Russ.)
3   S. M. Menshikov and L. A. Klimenko, *Long Waves in Economics: When Society Changes its Skin*, 2nd ed. (Moscow: LENAND, 2014), 192. (in Russ.)
4   M. Blaug M. "I. A. Schumpeter," in *Great Economists before Keynes: An Introduction to the Lives & Works of One Hundred Great Economists of the Past* (St. Petersburg: Economikus, 2008), 333. (in Russ.)
5   See K. Peres, *Technological Revolutions and Financial Capital: The Dynamics of Bubbles and Golden Ages* (Moscow: Delo, 2011). (in Russ.)
6   See See D. S. Lvov and S. Y. Glazyev, "Theoretical and Applied Aspects of STP Management," *Economics and Mathematical Methods* 22, no. 5 (1986): 793–804. (in Russ.)
7   S. Y. Glazyev and V. V. Kharitonov, eds., *Nanotechnology as a Key Factor of the New Techno-Economic Mode in the Economy* (Moscow: Trovant, 2009), 11.

The material conditions for the formation of each new techno-economic paradigm are formed in the course of the previous paradigm's development. Economic development proceeds by the successive and gradual change of paradigms, and at their initial stage, each paradigm uses old energy-carriers [energonositeli] and infrastructure, like transportation (according to Glazyev) and info-communications infrastructure (according to the majority of economists on the topic). After the new paradigm takes hold in the economy and replaces the old one, the appropriate infrastructure also forms and asserts itself. Besides the core, the defining characteristic of a techno-economic paradigm according to Glazyev is its organizational-economic mechanism of regulation.[8]

Each new paradigm significantly extends the limits of a society's production possibilities curve. As the organization of production simultaneously and significantly improves, labor and capital, the two main factors of production, can be put to much more efficient use. Since the fourth techno-economic paradigm, technology has been included as the third factor of production. According to the estimations of foreign economists, its contribution to economic growth has varied in different periods of time from 20 percent to almost 80 percent (taking into account the peculiarities of different research methods). In developed countries, the development and implementation of technological innovations is a decisive factor of socioeconomic development and a guarantee of economic security. In the US, for example, the increase in per capita national income due to technological innovation is up to 90%.[9]

This theoretical approach has much in common with the approach of Western sociologists and futurists like Daniel Bell, Alvin Toffler, Manuel Castells, T. Sakaiya, and others, who study the mutual influence of technological evolution and economic development. The rise of concepts like "postindustrial society," "information society," the "third wave," etc. points to a growing interest in studying the influence of technology on socioeconomic change. But the work of the aforementioned authors was primarily descriptive. They did not sufficiently develop theories that could explain the nature and patterns of the interaction between technology and the economy. Moreover, they greatly exaggerated the importance of postindustrial trends and ignored the processes of deindustrialization and financialization that are currently taking place and undermining the productive potential of developed countries.

---

8   See L. K. Gurieva, "The Concept of Techno-Economic Paradigms," *Innovational Economics* 10 (2004): 70–75.
9   Ibid.

Daniel Bell's suggestion that a "service society" based on a "knowledge economy" is the future economic standard appears unconvincing in light of all the facts that I have offered above, though many Russian economists have also subscribed to this view.[10] If we utilize their studies critically, however, we can still come to some useful conclusions on economic systems undergoing change by technological progress. Studies have quite convincingly shown that *changes in technology, which effect the transition from one dominant production factor to another, or from one dominant industry to another,* lead to changes in the economy and in social life as a whole: in institutions, social structures (from the global to the family level), ideological attitudes, methods of political action, etc.

Such historical transitions were based on shifts between five techno-economic paradigms, corresponding with Nikolai D. Kondratyev's concept of the "long waves of economic conjuncture" [dlinnye volny ekonomicheskoi kon'iunktury"]. Note that if the emergence and spread of a new technoeconomic paradigm coincides with the upward phase of a Kondratyev cycle, this paradigm lives on even when the wave that gave rise to it has already passed and been replaced by another. Economic scholarship has identified six techno-economic paradigms.

The *first* techno-economic paradigm (1770–1830) developed as a result of the spread of machine technology in the textile industry, which is the primary industry of this paradigm.

The *second* techno-economic paradigm (1830–1880) is associated with the advent of the steam engine, the development of the railroad, and transcontinental steamship service. The mechanization of many industries was underway. The main industries of this paradigm are railroad machinery, steam engines, and steel.

The *third* techno-economic paradigm (1880–1930) is characterized by the development of electric power and internal combustion engines; the development of heavy mechanical engineering and electrical engineering, and growth of aviation and the automobile industry; and the use of radio, telephone, and telegraph as means of communication.

The *fourth* techno-economic paradigm (1930–1980) is based on the widespread use of internal combustion engines that run on oil, petroleum, and

---

10 "Post-industrial society is a society whose economy has shifted from predominantly producing goods to producing services." Daniel Bell, *The Coming of Post-Industrial Society: A Venture of Social Forecasting* (New York: Basic Books, 1973), 120; see also Daniel Bell, "The Social Framework of the Information Society," *The New Technocratic Wave in the West* (Moscow: Progress, 1986). In Russia, V. L. Inozemtsev has carried on Bell's research. See V. L. Inozemtsev, *Beyond the Economic Society* (Moscow: Academia, 1998). (in Russ.)

gas; the development of petrochemical technologies; and the emergence and distribution of synthetic materials. Computers and computer software emerged, and space exploration began.

The *fifth* techno-economic paradigm (early 1980s to the present) is characterized by the wide spread of info-communication technologies based on developments in microelectronics and informatics. Biotechnology (including genetic engineering), robotics, fiber-optic and space communication systems have begun to develop.

In the first decade of the 2000s, the *sixth techno-economic paradigm* began, which will likely be characterized by the wide spread of biotechnology, other nonmachine and hybrid machine technologies, and nanotechnology.

Different studies may disagree on the key technologies and industries that make up the core of any given paradigm, as well as their chronological frameworks. But the main point is that these paradigms are a coherent technological system, in which the core of a paradigm connects all its parts by technological chains. The degree of technological and economic connectivity of the various parts determines the efficiency of the techno-economic paradigm, and the speed at which new technologies move to other sectors and regions.

Each paradigm becomes the basis for a new stage of society's development. At the same time, we should not deduce new stages of social development directly from changes in technology and reduce all changes in society to the impact of technological innovations. The structure of society, even when considering only its socioeconomic system, is much more complex, and the changes taking place in it can be understood only by relying on a well-developed methodology based on political economy.

6.2. Principles of political economy on the study of socioeconomic systems

Theoretical economic research should lead to practical solutions for society's everyday economic problems. Though we can all more or less agree on this statement, a conclusion drawn directly from it may be more controversial. It is now more than ever necessary to revive a *political and economic* vision for the problems of Russia's economic system.[11]

At first glance, political economists seem far removed from the rhythms of everyday economic life. This, however, is not the case. Our work seamlessly

---

11 See *Journal of Economic Theory* 2 (2013). (in Russ.)

combines theoretical and practical issues, confirming the expression that *nothing is more practical than good theory.*

It is *political economy* that can provide answers to today's main challenges, determine a strategy for the socioeconomic development of the country, and illuminate the *far horizons* of our destination. The key problem of the modern Russian economy is its *industrial revival,* the creation of high-tech material production that is integrated with science and education. It is not just a question of determining the most effective structure of industrial production,[12] but of forming a *new economic system* capable of internal momentum toward technological *modernization* and industrial *growth.*

Allow me to highlight some of the political economic aspects of the problem before us, so as to clarify the methods and specifics of this approach. I will outline the contours of the political-economic method using the works of A. V. Buzgalin[13] and A. A. Porokhovsky.[14]

Firstly: the subject of political economy is mainly the *objective* relations of people in the process of *material production* in the broad sense, both production proper and exchange, distribution, and consumption. Note the emphasis on the word *objective* and the word *production.* This is the fundamental difference between political economy and the current economic discourse that is summed up by the word "economics," where the focus is on choice of the *individual, primarily* in the context of *exchange* rather than production.

To consider a challenge like *reindustrialization,* we must approach it specifically from the perspective of political economy, which allows us to pinpoint our focus on production itself, and to formulate the objective laws of its development and which methods are best for the revival of material production. Supporters of market fundamentalism have long attempted to distract from the fact that our economic priority can and should be material production itself, which has led to a deeply entrenched deindustrialization throughout the economy. Reindustrialization demonstrates the correctness of those political economists who criticized the intense development of intermediary (secondary) sectors to the detriment of material production.

---

12 S. D. Bodrunov, "What Kind of Industrialization Does Russia Need?," *Russia's Economic Revival* 44, no. 2 (2015): 6–17; V. T. Riazanov, "New Industrialization of Russia as a Real Goal and Post-Industrial Ideal," *Economic Revival of Russia* 40, no. 2 (2014): 17–25. (in Russ.)

13 See A. V. Buzgalin, "Economics and 'Economic Imperialism': There Are Alternatives," *Questions of Political Economy* 1, no. 2 (2012): 19–35. (in Russ.)

14 See A. A. Porokhovsky, "Political Economy at the Turn of the Century," *Questions of Political Economy* 2, no. 1. (2012): 3–18. (in Russ.)

Secondly: political economy has always emphasized the need for development where there is an *equal dialectical interrelation* [dialekticheskaia vzaimoadekvatnost'] *between the material-technological base of production* (in Marxist terms, the productive forces) and *socioeconomic production relations*. To study the *interaction between the economy and the technosphere*, however, we must have an understanding of the technosphere's evolutionary patterns.

Using Glazyev's theory of techno-economic paradigms, I will analyze the Russian economic system. Many of his conclusions are applicable here. I will consider the conditionality of economic dynamics in the timely transition to a new economic stage, and the interconnection between techno-economic paradigm formation and changes in a society's economic structure and overall way of life.

As I have noted, scholars of so-called "postindustrial" problematics have voiced similar views on the role of technology. The above-mentioned authors, including Alvin Toffler,[15] typically emphasize the development of new technologies in material production, the structure of employment, etc. This aspect of their argument is important, and I will return to it when analyzing the specifics of the Russian economic system.

Note that these arguments are drawn from analyzing the economies of primarily developed countries. It is important to determine *to what extent the arguments of Western sociologists and futurologists apply to the Russian case.* Are the same shifts and trends taking place or not? To what extent can we rely on the prognostics of Western studies? The answers to these questions largely determine how we approach the socioeconomic level of our research. It is at this level that the specifics of the socioeconomic structure of Russian economic relations and institutions may be defined.

If my conclusion about preserving the primary role of material production and its basic sectors is correct, at least for countries like Russia, then we must study the system of economic relations and institutions primarily as a system of relations taking shape in material production. The future system of economic relations and institutions depends on the well-being and direction of material production's development. As a result, the following conclusion about the reindustrialization of Russia is inevitable: free-market relations and classical

---

15 According to Alvin Toffler, 1955 was the new economy's turning point, when the number of white-collar workers and service sector workers in the United States for the first time began to exceed the number of blue-collar workers. Over this decade began the wide-scale implementation of computers and the proliferation of new technologies available for the general population. See Alvin Toffler, *The Third Wave* (Moscow: AST, 1999), 40–53, 68. (in Russ.)

forms of private property are insufficient for the progress of high-tech material production. For example, the development of complex clusters [klastery] that integrate modern material production, science, and education requires not only adequate market conditions (guarantees of property rights, contracts, etc.), but also, at the least, public-private partnerships and long-term state-sponsored programs in support of those clusters (cheap loans, tax breaks, state investments coupled with private investments, etc.).

Thirdly: again, I emphasize the importance of our political economy, a historical and systemic method for investigating *economic reality*. Political economy, though widely known as a methodology, is rarely applied when the economy is discussed according to ideological lines, whether liberal or conservative, and this is particularly so when it comes to the Russian economy.[16]

This historical-systemic approach requires that we study the internal systemic relations of different elements of the economy. It is even more important to understand the economic system, in relation to factors external to the economy, as a contiguous piece of a greater whole. In my viewpoint, the economy is not merely one realm where more or less rational entities operate, but a diversity of economic systems developing in time, one of which is the Russian system. It has its own *developmental patterns* that refract the general laws of economic development into something *unique* to our land and civilization. This is not to say that our political economists have developed an Ohm's law particular to Russia. Rather, they have demonstrated that objective economic relations inherent in the market and other economic phenomena have their own characteristics in different social spaces at different stages of their development. It is for this reason that, when discussing the pros and cons of, for example, market and state

---

16 G.B. Kleiner, Corresponding Member of the Russian Academy of Sciences, emphasizes: "a system is not a multitude of elements connected in a certain way (endogenous definition), but a relatively spatially and temporally stable integral part of an environment; an observer can distinguish the system from its environment by spatial or functional characteristics (exogenous definition). The systemic paradigm, which represent the economy as a unity of interacting, transforming, and evolving systems, is on the one hand an alternative to the neoclassical paradigm with its division of the economy into macro- and microeconomics, and on the one hand, a concept that integrates neoclassical, institutional, and evolutionary approaches. G. B. Kleiner, "Strategic Planning: The Basis of the Systemic-Approach," *Modernization of Economy and Socio-Economic Development*, Vol. 2 (Moscow: GU-HSE Publishing House, 2008). http://www.kleiner.ru/skrepk/strategplan-2008.pdf. (in Russ.); A similar approach can be found in the works of Ia. Kornai, who also believes that the object of an economist's research "is an integral system, which interacts with other systems, including larger ones that contain it. Every economic system in this case is represented as the sphere of interaction of the economy, politics, ideology, psychology, culture, and other fields; for this reason, an analysis from the perspective of only one of the relevant disciplines would be incomplete and superficial." J. Kornai, "The Systemic Paradigm," *Questions of Economics* 4 (2002): 10–12. (in Russ.)

regulation, or private or state ownership, we should take into account which national system we are talking about: that of the biggest state in Eurasia, or that of a smaller one such as, say, Belgium. It is important to remember that the Russia of the 1990s and the Russia of today, with its policy of reindustrialization and import substitution, are "two big differences" (as they say in Odessa, *dve bol'shie raznitsy*), two systems with different geo-politico-economic orientations. For this reason, we must approach each case individually and solve each problem differently.

Thus, to understand an economic system, it is necessary to study the material and technological prerequisites of its existence and operation, as well as the sociocultural environment in which it was or is being formed. The latter includes ideological, sociopsychological, political, ethno-cultural and other components—a country's civilizational specificity. It is important to understand the influence of these factors on the economic relations and institutions, on the laws that create them and make them function. This task implies the analysis of the forward and backward linkages of the economic system at the following levels:

1. techno-economic paradigms;
2. socioeconomic relations and economic-legal institutions;
3. civilizational and sociocultural invariants and trends.

Fourthly: without political economy, we cannot understand the "human dimension" of economic development, like the increasingly more important role of knowledge in the modern economy. Political economy demonstrates the critical role of science and education in the transition to a new model of economic development, one based in high-tech reindustrialization and continuous economic modernization.[17]

Fifthly: political economy considers social and political determinants, dominants, and trends. Noneconomic factors play an important role in the Russian economic model. Anatoly A. Porokhovsky has emphasized the importance of this fact in the Russian case.[18] And the state's influence on the trajectory of the

---

17 O. N. Smolin, "Development of Human Potential as the Basis for XXI Century Modernization," *Economic Revival of Russia* 44, no. 2 (2015): 34–37. (in Russ.)

18 "To implement the Russian market model, there is no alternative to democratic institutions in the structure of economic and non-economic factors toward this goal. It is historically and practically evidenced that only the full domination of democratic institutions can destroy both the official's monopoly, the dictate of big business, and the population's distrust of the authorities. The loss of any link in this chain maintains the Russian people's recent prejudice

economic system is only increasing, particularly during transitional phases. As a result, the quality of sociopolitical institutions largely determines the quality of economic institutions and the conditions in which they are formed,[19] a fact that economic strategists are well aware of, yet often ignore.

The more theoretical work being done in political economy at Moscow State University (MGU) is complemented by the work at the Institute of Economics of the Russian Academy of Sciences. The MGU school of political economy aims to consider an economic system in the context of its interaction with political, social, cultural, and other such factors, thereby developing a complex historical context for economic processes. Leonid I. Abalkin's output shows this approach at work. He stresses that the logic of modern progress can be described in terms of historical synthesis. To approach this logic, we must consider socioeconomic changes in their broad historical context, the result of the combination and entanglement of global development trends, individual rights and freedoms, the socialization of social and political life, and the peculiarities of the social structures of different societies.[20] Dmitriy E. Sorokin and other economists of the same school further developed Abalkin's arguments.[21]

It is no accident that political economy combines those two concepts, politics, and economics. Its focus on the sociopolitical component of economic processes is its distinct advantage. Political economy pays particular attention to public interests, the social structure of society, the activities of the state, and economic policies. The works of Ruslan S. Grinberg make this fact especially clear.[22]

---

against the market and democracy." A. A. Porokhovsky, "The Russian Market Model: The Path toward Its Realization," *Questions of Economy* 10, no. 35 (2007): 35–49.

19 "Non-economic factors continue to dominate the objective laws of market development, as a result of which the mechanisms of competition are suppressed, owners and companies often find themselves defenseless, and the economy as a whole is still unable to realize a structure adequate for the information-technological stage." A. A. Pokhorovsky, "Modern Development and Economic Interests," *Questions of Political Economy* 2, no. 1 (2013): 25. (in Russ.)

20 L. I. Abalkin, *Russia: The Search for Self-Determination: Essays.* 2nd ed. (Moscow: n.p., 2005), 51. (in Russ.)

21 "The integration of the totality of institutions that secure social integrity is what determines the movements of economic agents in a society." This includes the nonmarket institutions of civil society and market and state mechanisms of economic regulation. The organic integrity and complementariness of "these three components of the modern mechanism of economic regulation produces a synergistic effect, expressed in the sustainable pursuit of implementing society's values, which just one of these institutions cannot guarantee by itself." D. E. Sorokin, "Political and Economic Guidelines for Institutional Transformation," in *China and Russia* (Moscow: Nauka, 2003), 72, 75, 76. (in Russ.)

22 See R. S. Grinberg, *Freedom and Justice: Russian Temptations of False Choice* (Moscow: Magister: INFRA-M, 2012). (in Russ.)

6.3. The dynamics of economic systems

A society's economic subsystem is dynamic and rapidly developing. Such systems are characterized by internal contradictions, which grow and intensify in the course of development: tension between a system's different elements, which may also change and be upgraded, or the connections between them may change, or the basic principles of the very structure may change. Such contradictions lead to changes in the system, and they are resolved when the system transitions to a different mode—a qualitative transformation of the system.

Economic systems throughout history and those that are still in place today evince a process of constant change, which from time to time leads to the replacement of a society's socioeconomic system by another. Changes in the technological basis of society, the main catalyst of these changes, lead to new needs in a society; to new social "players" (new social classes, strata, socio-professional groups, etc.); to different social content and different constellations of social interests. As a result, tensions grow between the elements of an economic system and in their links, and the struggle intensifies between different social groups as they attempt the satisfaction of their interests, a process that is inevitably connected to the distribution of economic resources and the competition over their access.

Such transitions are rarely made in an evolutionary way. Much more often they take the form of a nonevolutionary breakdown or of a revolutionary transformation. Periodic revolutionary changes take place regularly in economic development, but their forms can vary. By introducing scientific methods of planning and forecasting of economic and social processes into economic management practices, we can soften the dramatic social upheavals and the negative side effects of such radical transformations. The use of such methods in China plays an important role in the fact that the Chinese economy and society are highly manageable and predictable in their development. Over the past thirty-five years, China has evaded serious social and economic turmoil. At the same time, the ruling class must not use scientific methods for social management merely as an ideological façade for its decisions.

A political-economic approach allows us to explore the internal social dynamics of society, to understand the essence of potential social tensions and contradictions, and sources of economic and technical progress. Toward this end, a political economist must know which social strata are produced by a particular economic system and in what ratio to one another they exist. Which social group will become the driver of progress? Which social forces will be brought to the forefront by the objective laws of economic development, and how will the activity of these social forces relate to the task at hand, that of reviving material production? To answer such questions is the task of political economy. The work of scholars at the RAS Institute of Economics and their colleagues at Moscow State University investigates the historical dynamics of a given economic system and clarifies the nature of its systemic shifts. From this point of view, *it is insufficient to operate under the simple assumption that Russia is a market economy without digging deeper, and to list a textbook set of guidelines as a recipe for solving Russia's problems.*[23]

Political economy makes it possible not only to show the *functional connections* between various economic phenomena, but also to distinguish between what happens *naturally* and *accidentally* in an economy, to consider it *in development, systemically* and *historically*. Most importantly, political economy is a science based in the processes of material production, *not only of exchange.* For this reason, it pays close attention to *relations between people* and between social communities, or in other words, to the interactions of *different socioeconomic interests.*

All this allows us to consider political economy, in the words of Lomonosov, *not only a luminous science, but also a fruitful one* [naukoi ne tol'ko svetonosnoi, no i plodonosnoi], a science that provides important theoretical foundations for practical recommendations, both fundamentally and topically.

As I have many times mentioned, one of the most urgent problems of today is that of the *renewal and development of the Russian economic system.*

We may consider Russia's *economic system proper* using the methodology of the MGU school of political economy. This methodology is based on both classical political economy[24] and a modern systemic approach.

From this viewpoint, the following assessment seems correct: "The specifics of the economy in Russia are determined, on the one hand, by its external and historical conditions, and on the other hand, by the internal features of the socio-economic system."[25] This excerpt comes from a university book on Russia's economic transition in the 1990s, written as it was still taking underway. Its approach singles out some of the peculiarities of the modern capitalist model's formation in Russia that distinguish it from other countries. These features are determined by the starting point of the process in Russia (the planned economic

---

23 This is also necessary because the institutions of market economy in the modern era have evolved: "The modern mechanism of economic self-regulation only by inactivity continues to be called a market mechanism, though essentially different from the classical notions of the latter. These differences are so great that one wonders whether a fundamentally new mechanism of self-regulation is in place." D. E. Sorokin, "Political and Economic Guidelines for Institutional Transformation," in *China and Russia* (Moscow: Nauka, 2003), 73. (in Russ.)

24 See N. A. Tsagolov, ed., *A Course on Political Economy* (Moscow: Ekonomika, 1973). (in Russ.)

25 V. V. Radaev and A. V. Buzgalin, *Economy of the Transition Period* (Moscow: n.p., 1995), 48.

system) and a special, as if restorative [vosstanovitelnaya] attitude toward the existing capitalism in the country.[26]

Some fruitful developments in Russia's economic revival are based in this political-economic approach. Of particular note are a few events that took place in the last years: "The Economic System of Modern Russia: Paths and Goals of Development," an international scholarly conference held at Moscow State University on November 19, 2014; and "The Return of Political Economy," the second international Political Economy Congress, held in Moscow City Hall in May 2015. The S. Y. Witte Institute of New Industrial Development was one of the congress's organizers, and I participated as co-moderator of the main plenary session. International forums such as these have demonstrated the enthusiasm that exists for approaching Russia's economic system from the perspective of political economy and analyzing its current condition, problems, possible paths of development, and models for economic growth through this lens.

A collective monograph also came out of the second International Political Economy Congress, titled *The Russian Economic System: Anatomy of the Present, Alternatives for the Future.*[27] The book includes profiles of some famous political economists from Russia and other countries. The book's authors include Aleksandr V. Buzgalin, Ruslan S. Grinberg, Soltan S. Dzarasov, Andrey I. Kolganov, Viktor M. Kulkov, Dmitriy E. Sorokin, Kaisyn A. Khubiev, Georgiy N. Tsagolov, David B. Epstein, and other prominent Russian scholars, as well as professors from Cambridge and the Sorbonne.

The book provides a *systematic analysis* of contemporary Russia's *industrial relations and institutions*, and outlines some of the laws of its economic processes and historical dynamics. From the *perspective of political economy*, it proposes *alternative policies for economic renewal*, with the goal of overcoming the negative effects of *deindustrialization* and *import dependence* in the Russian economy.

It is important to develop evidence-based practical recommendations in this way. Let's take one example. An economic policy aimed at reindustrialization and import substitution has been repeatedly discussed in the Duma and the Federation Council, in speeches by state leaders, and at various academic forums. These problems were discussed at Free Economic Society events, at

26 "Firstly, there is the historically unprecedented transition to a market economy not from a traditional economy, but from a special, planned economy that existed in a relatively small number of countries. Secondly, today's Russian society, which on the path of reform-evolutionary development, should make some kind of return [vozvratnoe dvizhenie]." Radaev and Buzgalin, 49.
27 S. D. Bodrunov and A. A. Porokhovsky, eds., *The Economic System of Modern Russia: Anatomy of the Present and Alternatives of the Future*, 2nd edition (Moscow: LENAND, 2015).

Russian Academy of Sciences conferences, at the Moscow Economic Forum, the St. Petersburg Economic Congress, etc.

But the question remains: on what theoretical and methodological basis are these or other practical recommendations based? The proposals of the INID are based on a systemic political-economic approach.[28] The systemic approach, as I have discussed,[29] involves the study of *systemic elements*, their *internal relations*, *systemic qualities*, etc. It is especially important that the economic system be approached not as an isolated and self-sufficient system, but as an *integral part of a bigger whole*; it must not be approached endogenously but exogenously, in interconnection with external factors. To understand the essence of the *economic system*, it is necessary to study, on the one hand, the material and technical preconditions that determine its existence and functioning, and, on the other hand, the sociocultural environment in which the system is formed. The latter includes ideological, sociopsychological, political, ethno-cultural, and other components, often defined as the *civilizational specificity* of the country.

It is important to understand the influence of all these factors on economic relations and institutions, on their internal patterns of formation and functioning, and on the dynamics of their development.

At the same time, given that an economic system is always under dynamic development, this dynamism is also "dynamic": there are different rates of development developing in different directions, continuously changing an economic system's essence and its elements, interrelations, etc. This makes it imperative that we use political economy as our main tool of economic analysis toward practical recommendations and decisions.

The above is, of course, a very schematic picture of the Russian economic system. I have not touched on several issues, like the systemic quality of the Russian economy, its internal contradictions, integrity, its qualifications [kvalifitsirovaniia] according to various attributes, etc. I have outlined only the necessity of using political economy in its analysis. Nevertheless, even such a broad-stroke analysis based on *political economy* allows me and other INID scholars to propose *theoretically* substantiated *practical* measures to improve *economic policy*.

---

28 See, for example, S. D. Bodrunov, "The Russian Economic System: The Future of High-Tech Material Production," *Russia's Economic Revival* 2 (2014): 5–16; S. D. Bodrunov, "Reindustrialization of the Russian Economy and Import Substitution Based on the Integration of Production, Science, and Education," in *Integration of Production, Science, and Education as a Basis for the Reindustrialization of Russian Economy: Proceedings of the Scientific Seminar "Modern Problems of Development"* (St. Petersburg: Institute for New Industrial Development (INID), 2015), 25–51. (in Russ.)

29 G. B. Kleiner, "What Kind of Economy Does Russia Need and Why? (The Experience of Systemic Research)," *Questions of Economics* 10 (2013): 4–27. (in Russ.)

Chapter 7

The Russian Economic System: The Future of High-Tech Industrial Production[1]

Complex systems like Russia's economic system cannot be studied without a well-defined methodology. The last chapter laid out the methodology in use here: political economy. I will now turn to its application.

7.1. A transnational Russian economic system: A positive synthesis of current debates

It is given that any economic system eventually withers and decays and that a new one takes its place. The transition from one system to another is always fraught with significant problems. Grinberg and Rubinstein rightly suggest that such stages of development in social evolution "are characterized by incompleteness, lack of integrity, and the coexistence of elements from the new and the old economies. Therefore, the period between two mature states is both

---

1 Based on a report from the Council on Economic Theory of Lomonosov Moscow State University, prepared by the INID team under the guidance of Dr. S. D. Bodrunov.

the formation of the new economic system and at the same time the downward development of the old one."[2]

During the 1990s, the forced disintegration of the old planned economy system coupled with the simultaneous slowdown in debugging [otladki] the economic relations and institutions of the new market system led to the fact that, "during the reform years the country lost half of its potential. Worse still, it did not succeed in stopping the primitivization of production, deintellectualization of labor, and degradation of the social sphere. To this list we must also add the advent of mass poverty, which increased quickly during those years of radical change."[3] Relying on the market being automatically self-regulating in moments of transitions such as this one delayed the formation of market institutions.

Even worse, economic policy oriented new economic relations in a direction that did not correspond to their material, economic, and sociocultural prerequisites. The economy consequently reacted to this distortion with shrinking demand and, as a result, production; with the shortening the horizon of economic decisions; and with the rejection long-term investments and high-risk projects. While this was going on, a bigger and bigger social stratum was developing that could not support itself financially via typical economic activity.

An economy with growing social problems like income inequality and wealth disparity creates a trap for itself: it undermines the main source of economic development. As notes Grinberg, a corresponding member of the Russian Academy of Sciences, the sharp downturn in scientific, technical, and human potential was one of Russia's most severe losses during its years of reform, from both an economic and social perspective. In his opinion, "the main tragedy of life nowadays is the monstrous stratification where 10 percent live normally and 70 percent merely survive."[4]

How can the modern Russian economy solve the inefficiency of its economic and social institutions? Scholars of the classical and new institutionalist schools, who study the patterns of the evolution, adoption, and formation of institutions, raise the question of the historical conditionality of Russia's institutional problems. Aleksandr A. Auzan writes: "Russia is as if suspended in a space where traditional society cannot be restored, and no one seems to want to restore it, while a modernized society with its corresponding institutions cannot be built.

---

2 R. S. Grinberg and A. Y. Rubinstein, eds., *Economic Socio-Dynamics* (Moscow: ISE press, 2000), 85. (in Russ.)

3 R. S. Grinberg, "Russia: Economic Success without Development and Democracy?" *Russia's Economic Revival* 2 (2005): 11. (in Russ.)

4 R. S. Grinberg, *Freedom and Justice: Russian Temptations of a False Choice* (Moscow, Magister: INFRA-M, 2012), 61.

This interrupted modernization has been going on for three centuries since the time of Peter the Great."[5] Further research in this direction pushes the date of Russia's "wrong" institutional turn even further back: "We can observe not only that Russia is stuck in a rut, but even the point when the initial [decisive] institutional choice was made: in the fourteenth and fifteenth centuries, when thee institutions of autocracy and serfdom began to emerge."[6]

This formulation of the problem orients the study of Russian economics toward an institutional critique, questioning the extent to which institutional choices are arbitrary (i.e., can be interpreted in terms of right and wrong decisions), and the extent to which decisions made in the historical past can determine the trajectory of institutional development in the present.

Other scholars are focusing on the study of *civilizational* peculiarities (ethnocultural, ideological, social, etc.), and their influence on technological, economic, and institutional development. But the most far-reaching conclusions are drawn by scholars working on the *philosophy of economics*. From their point of view, economic reality cannot be grasped without an understanding of the higher meaning of human existence. "The focus of attention—not as research, but as revelation—is not a human being seeking consumer satisfaction like any animal, but a human being seeking meaning, but not only in personal, but also in collective, public, universal existence,"[7] notes Yuri M. Osipov, the leader of this school of thought. This methodological approach complements an approach that looks for nationally specific, sustainable determinants for economic development, which differentiate a given economy from other national economic models. "Russia has a number of sustainable factors (many of them unique) that have a significant impact on the country's economic system. Their stable, constant, long-term character allows us to characterize them as an objective basis for the specifics of the Russian economy."[8]

This national specificity and does not exclude, however, the influence of global development trends on the Russian economic system. On the contrary,

5   A. A. Auzan, "We Are Approaching the Moment of Truth of Our Civilization," *Free World* (2011). http://www.liberty.ru/Themes/Aleksandr-Auzan-My-priblizhaemsya-k-momentu-istiny-nashej-civilizacii. (in Russ.)

6   A. A. Auzan, *The Economics of Everything: How Institutions Determine Our Lives* (Moscow: Mann, Ivanov, and Ferber, 2014). http://read.bizlib.org/aleksandr-auzan-ekonomika-vsego. Html. (in Russ.)

7   Y. M. Osipov, "Centenary of S. N. Bulgakov's Philosophy of Economy—One Hundred Years of Economic Philosophy," *Sophia. One hundred years of Russian Sophian philosophy*, ed. Y. M. Osipov, A.I. Ageev, and E.S. Zotova. (Moscow: Teis, 2012), 9–22. (in Russ.)

8   V. M. Kulkov, "Dominants of Russia's Economic System," *Russia Today* (Moscow; Volgograd, 2000), 31. (in Russ.)

it is by synthesizing specifically national features with global trends that we can see the progressive movement of the Russian economy. "The Russian economic system should be a type of modern mixed economy that is inherently regulated, socially oriented, labor-oriented, spiritually oriented, postindustrial-oriented. In this way it will organically combine Russian originality with the progressive tendencies of global development."[9]

Though such concepts may be highly abstract, these scholars have still come to some specific practical conclusions that are very much in line with those from other scholars mentioned above. Their recommendations include a more active state role and more attention paid to reviving material production and to social justice.

There are also those visions of Russia's economic future that I have already mentioned, based on ideas like *reindustrialization* and *neoindustrialization*; a *postindustrial society* born of liberal thought; and economic development that prioritizes *education, science,* and *culture.*

I have presented my ideas on a new industrialization in a series of INID reports, in a joint project by INID and the RAS Institute of Economics (this report was presented to the Expert Council under the Chairman of the Federation Council of the Federal Assembly of the Russian Federation in March 2013), in a number of monographs and reports at the Abalkin lecture series at the Russian Economic Society, at the plenary session of the Moscow Economic Forum (2014), and in a number of articles.[10] Other programs to improve Russia's economic system and lift the country out of stagnation were considered at the Moscow Forum.[11] These proposals are based on the gap between Russia's human, resource, and economic potential and its consequential results: "We know that our country has great potential for dynamic and long-lasting development: resources, people who want to work, vast land for agriculture, all the conditions for expansion into foreign markets.

---

9 Ibid., 35.

10 See, for example, S. D. Bodrunov, "The Question of Reindustrialization of the Russian Economy," *Russia's Economic Revival* 38, no. 4 (2013): 5–27; S. D. Bodrunov and V. N. Lopatin, *Institutional Modernization of Russian Industry in the WTO* (St. Petersburg: Institute for New Industrial Development (INID), 2012); S. D. Bodrunov, R. S. Grinberg, and D. E. Sorokin, "Reindustrialization of the Russian economy: imperatives, potential, risks," *Economic Revival of Russia* 1, no. 35 (2013): 19–49; S. D. Bodrunov, *Strategy and Politics of Reindustrialization for Russia's Innovative Development,* ed. S. D. Bodrunov and V. N. Lopatin (St. Petersburg: Institute for New Industrial Development INID, 2014). (in Russ.)

11 See, for example, K. A. Babkin, *Reasonable industrial policy, or How we get out of the crisis* (Moscow: n.p., 2008). (in Russ.)

What is missing is a sound economic policy to get the country on the right track again."[12]

A realistic perspective on Russia's economic evolution demonstrates that "post-industrialism" has not taken hold throughout the global economy and it is especially premature to attempt it in Russia. Even those who tout the benefits of the postindustrial approach have admitted as much. For example, Vladislav L. Inozemtsev, a prominent Russian scholar of postindustrial society, notes: "The modern world is still an industrial one. Raw materials accounted for 16.1 percent of world trade in 2009, services accounted for 18.9 percent, and manufactured goods for 65 percent. Among the twenty largest U.S. exporters, fifteen are industrial giants, and only five are technology giants. Technology is nothing unless it can be applied to industry and conquer global markets in the form of a finished product. Today technology does not in itself change the nature of a country's exports, but as a means of the effective and mass production of industrial goods."[13] From this point of view, Russia is not in the ghostly postindustrial world of the future, or even in the industrial world of the present. Rather, Russia has lost its footing in mass industrial production. "The country must become familiar to the average consumer, who is confronted daily, even hourly with many countries' 'business cards' in the form of industrial product labels. The frequency of these references to different nations on such essential media [as product labels] leads people around the world to make judgments on a country's importance on the global economy, as well as the abilities and talents of is people. Spreading the *Made in Russia* label must become the national strategy for modernizing Russia. This is the only significant indicator of the success of domestic modernization."[14] This approach corresponds to international practice, as evidenced in both historical examples and the current situation in the global economy. It is important to remember that the transition to machine industrial production led the countries of Western Europe, the US, and Japan to the forefront of the world economy, a position previously occupied by China and India. First, the UK ensured its economic and political dominance on the world stage via its industrial monopoly, and then, the whole of the West followed, and now they stand to benefit from this fortunate position for a long time to come.

---

12 K. A. Babkin, Speech at the Moscow Economic Forum, Moscow, 2014. http://www.umpro.ru/index.php? page_id=17&art_id_1= 489 &group_id_4= 54&m_id_4=27. (in Russ.)

13 V. L. Inozemtsev, "Modernizatsia.ru: Made in Russia," *Vedomosti*, December 7, 2010. (in Russ.)

14 Ibid.

Despite changes in the structure of GDP, the countries that are today's leaders in the world economy are in that position thanks to their technological leadership, not their service sectors (they were also the countries to first set forth on the path of industrialization). Those states that have successfully overcome economic backwardness—South Korea, Taiwan, China, Brazil, Malaysia, Vietnam, etc.—have chosen to do so by industrial development as a strategy for economic revival. Industrialization allowed these countries to rapidly increase their economic potential, creating the prerequisites for the development of high-tech industries. Now they face the difficult task of challenging the scientific and technological monopoly of the most advanced countries. In any case, without industrialization, the prospect of forming an independent and national scientific and technological core for a national economy is a pipe dream. It is industrial production that provides the material base for industrial innovation and creates real demand for research and development.

To prioritize the development of science, education, and culture in this process is merely common sense, though this prospect seems premature for Russia as things stand. Scholars have long emphasized the fact that the main productive force of the economy is the human being at the center of it. In the modern day, the human aspect is more important than ever. It is also true that a modern economy based on high-tech production requires a worker with a high level of education, and this education should be and universally accessible and take place throughout life. Human development is an essential part of the social production process. Scientific progress, including fundamental science, is a prerequisite for technological renewal. Public and private support for these spheres should be substantially expanded in Russia. Kolganov and Buzgalin have written on the topic.[15] Boris S. Kashin, an Academician at the Russian Academy of Sciences, and Oleg N. Smolin, a Corresponding Member at the Russian Academy of Education, have also frequently addressed the question.[16]

---

15 A. I. Kolganov and A. V. Buzgalin, "Reindustrialization as Nostalgia? Theoretical Discourse," *Sotsis* 1 (2014): 80–94; A. I. Kolganov and A. V. Buzgalin, "Reindustrialization as Nostalgia? Polemical notes on targets of an alternative socio-economic strategy," *Sotsis* 3 (2014): 120–130.

16 "First of all, it is necessary to develop a roadmap for Russian economics, so that the latter can address well-defined tasks and their solution. On the other hand, it is necessary to raise the status of the Russian economist. And to not be guided by fictitious indicators, developed by incomprehensible Western experts, on the quality of his scientific work," writes B. S. Kashin. He continues: "The impression is that the authorities are not interested in the opinion of professional economists. Apparently, they only need an entourage of 'expert' representatives to legitimize decisions that they have already been made. It turns out that economics is separate from the sphere of managerial decision-making. Moreover, these two groups are sometimes hostile to each other. We can say that there is an anti-scientific approach to decision-making

7.2. The current status of the Russian economic system and prospects for its development

A critical synthesis of these various, often quite different approaches and perspectives will reveal some common constructive ideas. And in the process, we can abandon some of the peculiarities that limit each argument according to the author's specific enthusiasm for one solution or another (whether their emphasis is on techno-economic paradigms, civilizational specificity, reindustrialization, the priority of education, and so on).

The general terms of this synthesis should include:

- advanced development of modern material production based on technologies of at least the fourth and fifth paradigms, and the provision of these industries with R&D and highly qualified personnel;
- new industrialization with the fullest consideration of Russia's civilizational specifics;
- economic policy based on thorough analysis of the real structure and contradictions of the existing economic system.

Recommendations for the future should take into account the significant influence of politics and ideology on implementing economic policies toward economic change.

The specifics of the post-Soviet Russian economic system deserve further attention. The systemic approach is particularly useful here. To analyze the structure of the Russian economic system, I will select key subsystems that reflect different historical stages of its formation and the levels of its development, per international criteria for technological and economic stages of development.

I will analyze the structure of the economy at three levels: 1—techno-economic paradigms; 2—socioeconomic relations and economic and legal institutions; 3—civilizational and sociocultural invariants and trends. With this approach, we can clearly distinguish the *three subsystems of Russia's economic system*.

---

in the sociopolitical and economic spheres." B. S. Kashin, "The Philosophy of Innovation Parasitism," *The Free Press*, December 13, 2011. http://commpart.livejournal. com/15221. html. (in Russ.); Smolin emphasizes: "Until the education system is restored, Russia will remain a third-world country. Either we change our economic course, or the national security of our country, its integrity, its future will be threatened." O. N. Smolin, Speech at the Moscow Economic Forum, 2014. http://me-forum.ru/media/events/plenary_discuss_I/. (in Russ.)

The first subsystem is the *traditional-conservative subsystem*, which is characterized by:

1. Traditionally important, but often conservative industries (agricultural production and other "old" material production industries growing out of the nineteenth and early twentieth centuries); technological systems based on manual and little-industrialized labor; machine production of unprocessed products, which includes the raw materials sector;
2. market relations burdened by the vestiges of a subsistence economy, patriarchal attitudes, and state and bureaucratic protectionism and paternalism;
3. "traditional Russian civilizational invariants," gravitating toward conservative ideology.

The second subsystem is the *liberal-market subsystem*, which is characterized by:

1. predominantly assembly production as part of transnational corporations; service, trade, finance, and other intermediary spheres;
2. market-based capitalist economic relations and institutions close to the "classical" kind though considerably modified by Russian specifics;
3. a predominantly liberal-western ideology.

The third subsystem—*the buds of a future mixed economy*—prioritizes high-tech production on the basis of socially oriented, regulated economic development. To overcome the systemic defects of the past, like shortages, bureaucratism, and unjustified egalitarianism [uravnilovku], this future system should take a critical look at the best features of the Soviet system, including its impressive military-industrial complex, and those of other countries like China, Vietnam, etc.

This nascent subsystem will (should) include:

- high-tech industries of the fifth and sixth techno-economic paradigms, as well as clusters that combine production, science, and education;
- the programming and selective regulation of the market economy, state-private sector partnerships, and other mixed forms of economy, combining the advantages of both the market and state regulation;
- an ideology of accelerated development based on the critical integration of Western achievements and traditional Russian values.

Formulating the problem in this way reflects the Russian economy's current situation as illustrated by statistical data. In the structure of the gross domestic product (table 10), even during the economically favorable 2000s, the share of manufacturing industries was declining, as was Russia's food security, based on domestic agricultural production. At the same time, the share of mining, financial activities, and real estate transactions was growing. Only a slight decrease in the share of trade can be regarded as a positive structural change. At the same time, sectors that depend on human development have been slow to recover since the economic failure of the 1990s. For example, the share of education has remained at the same low level, and the share of health care has increased by only a fraction of a percent.

TABLE 10. Structure of Russia's GDP in Percentage

	2002	2011	2012	2012–2011 (% points)	2012–2002 (% points)
GDP in market prices	100	100	100		
Agriculture and other	5.3	3.5	3.1	−0.4	−2.2
Fishing, fish farming	0.3	0.2	0.2	0	−0.1
Mining	5.9	9.2	9.3	0.1	3.4
Manufacturing industries	15.2	13.2	13	−0.2	−2.2
Including refining and coke fuel	1.8	3	3	0	1.2
Electrical power and other	3.2	3.3	3	−0.3	−0.3
Construction	4.7	5.6	5.5	0	0.8
Trade and other	20.2	16.7	16.9	0.1	−3.4
Hotels and restaurants	0.8	0.8	0.8	0	0
Transportation and communications	9	7.1	7	−0.1	−2.1
Financial activities	2.6	3.5	3.7	0.2	1.1

(continued)

	2002	2011	2012	2012–2011 (% points)	2012–2002 (% points)
Real estate, rentals	9.4	10.1	10.1	0	0.7
Public administration and defense	4.5	4.8	5.6	0.8	1.1
Education	2.6	2.5	2.6	0.1	0
Healthcare	3	3.1	3.3	0.2	0.4
Other social services	1.7	1.4	1.4	0	−0.3
Net taxes on products	11.5	14.9	14.5	−0.3	3

Similar trends in the distribution of investment in fixed assets (table 11) only reinforce the current inefficient economic structure rather than improve it.

TABLE 11. Structure of investment in fixed assets (by types of economic activity, excluding the informal economy, as percentage of the total) in 2008–2012

Indicator	2008	2009	2010	2011	2012
Volume of investment in fixed capital by large and medium-sized organizations, total (%)	100.0	100.0	100.0	100.0	100.0
Agriculture, hunting, and forestry	11.2	10.1	9.6	12.92	11.6
Mining	0.2	0.4	0.2	0.58	0.5
Manufacturing industries	27.7	21.5	13.4	23.23	28.8
Production and distribution of electricity, gas, and water	10.3	8.4	11.0	12.09	17.1
Construction	1.5	0.7	1.0	1.09	0.6
Wholesale and retail trade; repair of motor vehicles, motorcycles, household goods, and personal items	1.4	5.5	1.8	3.47	1.8
Hotels and restaurants	0.4	0.3	0.3	0.69	0.6

(continued)

Indicator	2008	2009	2010	2011	2012
Transport and communications	14.8	13.7	24.2	18.14	14.1
Financial activities	1.5	1.5	1.9	1.53	1.8
Real estate operations, leasing, and services	8.6	9.9	19.9	10.01	9.4
Public administration and military security; social insurance	5.4	4.2	4.7	2.51	1.9
Education	2.7	3.8	2.0	2.64	4.1
Healthcare and social services	5.4	10.6	6.5	5.57	3.8
Provision of other utilities, social, and personal services	8.9	9.5	3.6	5.52	3.9

The dynamics of industrial production during the entirety of the reforms (table 12) and during only its last years (table 13) reflects the general decline of industrial production and the oversimplification of its structure. In this context only the growth of the weight of electrical and electro-optical equipment looks like a positive. Innovation slows down when production and the country's intellectual base fall to such lows. Inadequate levels of innovation characterize the Russian economy across practically all sectors, including high tech (fig. 5), and the total share of innovation-active enterprises remains at an unacceptably low level (fig. 6).

TABLE 12. Dynamics of industrial production 1991–2010

Indicator	2010 to 1991, %
General economic indicators	
Index of industrial production, as % of the previous year	83.8
Indices of production by types of economic activity in sections C, D, E of OKVED (in % to the previous year, adjusted for informal activities):	
• Mineral extraction	108.8
• Manufacturing industries	78.6
• Production and distribution of electricity, gas, and water	89.1

(continued)

Indicator	2010 to 1991, %
Mining	
• Coal, million tons	91.2
• Oil, including gas condensate, million tons	109.5
• Natural and associated gas, bcm	101.2
Manufacturing industries	
Metallurgical production and production of finished metal products	
• Production of finished rolled ferrous metals, million tons	104.7
• Steel pipes, million tons	87.6
Production of certain types of machinery and equipment	
• Household refrigerators and freezers, thousand pcs.	95.9
• Metal-cutting machines, thousand pcs.	4.1
Production of vehicles and equipment	
• Passenger cars, thousand pcs.	117.5
• Truck cranes, thousand pcs.	22.5
• Mainline freight cars, thousand pcs.	225.4
Electricity production and distribution	
• production, billion kWh	97.2
• consumption, billion kWh	96.6

TABLE 13. Shipped products, work, and services by types of economic activity, percentage of total volume of industrial production

	2008	2009	2010	2011	2012
Total by section	**100**	**100**	**100**	**100**	**100**
Mining	**0.4**	**0.5**	**0.5**	**0.4**	**0.5**
Extraction of fuel and energy minerals	0.2	0.2	0.2	0.1	0.2
Extraction of minerals, other than fuel and energy	0.2	0.3	0.3	0.3	0.4
Manufacturing industries	**82.0**	**78.3**	**79.5**	**81.4**	**81.9**

(*continued*)

	2008	2009	2010	2011	2012
Production of food, including beverages and tobacco	12.1	15.8	14.3	12.5	14.0
Textile and apparel production	0.8	0.8	0.7	0.6	0.7
Manufacture of leather, leather goods, and footwear	1.1	1.3	1.3	1.2	1.5
Wood processing and production of wood products	4.9	5.1	6.5	6.5	6.2
Pulp and paper production, publishing and printing activities	2.2	2.0	2.0	1.7	1.9
Chemical production	20.9	17.2	17.6	20.4	20.4
Production of rubber and plastic products	6.2	6.0	6.7	7.6	3.8
Production of other non-metallic mineral products	2.6	2.0	1.5	1.6	1.8
Metallurgical production	11.0	8.2	10.0	9.9	9.8
Machinery and equipment manufacture (excluding production of weapons and ammunition)	3.5	3.8	4.3	3.5	3.4
Production of electrical, electronic, and optical equipment	4.5	4.4	5.0	5.8	7.1
Vehicle and equipment production	4.0	4.3	3.3	3.8	4.8
Other production	6.3	5.8	5.1	4.8	5.1
Production and distribution of electricity, gas, and water	**17.6**	**21.2**	**20.0**	**18.2**	17.6

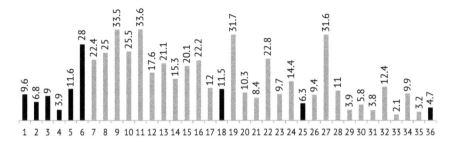

FIGURE 5. Share of organizations that implemented technological innovations in the total number of organizations of industrial production, by types of economic activity (2011):
1 - total; 2 - mining (3 - fuel and energy; 4 - other than fuel and energy); 5 - manufacturing industries; 6 - high-tech; 7 – pharmaceutical manufacturing; 8 - office equipment and computer technology; 9 - equipment for radio and tele-comms; 10 - medical devices, measuring instruments, optical instruments and devices, watches; 11 - aircraft, including spacecraft; 12 - high-level medium-tech (13 - chemical production; 14 - manufacture of machinery and equipment; 15 - electrical machinery and electrical equipment; 16 - vehicles, trailers, semitrailers; 17 - other vehicles); 18 - low-level medium-tech (19 - production of coke and oil products; 20 - rubber and plastic products; 21 - other non-metallic mineral products; 22 - metallurgical; 23 - finished metal products; 24 - shipbuilding and repair; 25 - low-tech; 26 – food manufacture, including beverages; 27 - tobacco products; 28 - textiles; 29 - clothing, dress making, dressing; 30 - leather, leather products, and footwear; 31 - production of wood and cork products, except furniture; 32 - manufacture of pulp, wood pulp, paper, cardboard, and their products; 33 - publishing and printing, reproduction of recorded media; 34 - manufacture of furniture and other goods not included in other groups; 35 - processing of secondary raw materials); 36 - production and distribution of electricity, gas, water

Debate Night, "Will Russia become one of the leaders in high-tech production," October 1, 2013, http://www.hse.ru/data/2013/10/28/1282559304/Skolkovo%20Booklet.pdf.

There have been some positive trends in recent years, but they testify only to the first and rather timid steps toward the development of new industrialization. This direction, as I have already noted, has considerable support among economists (both theorists and practitioners). Grinberg, who is the director and a corresponding member of the RAS Institute of Economics, as well as the scientific director of INID, has repeatedly emphasized that Russia needs to move to a new economic policy that ensures the development of the real production sector based on a mixed, socially oriented and state-regulated market economy.[17] Glazyev, who is advisor to the president of the Russian Federation, also shares this position: "Today we see the collapse of liberal theory, a liberal utopia—a

---

17 See R. S. Grinberg, K. A. Babkin, and A. V. Buzgalin, eds., "Myths about the Free Market We Should Leave in the Past: 'Economy for the People,'" in *Socially-Oriented Development Based on the Progress of the Real Sector: Materials of the Moscow Economic Forum*, 32–43. Moscow: Cultural Revolution, 2014. (in Russ.)

completely false view of how the world works and what needs to be done."[18] He stresses the decisive role of the state in supporting the basic industries of a new techno-economic paradigm at any stage of development.

Drawing on these suggestions does not mean that the prospects of the Russian economy lie only in the development of the third subsystem outlined above. Significant adjustments are necessary throughout the Russian economy.

I will lay out the key objectives of each of the three above-mentioned subsystems:

1. *The traditional-conservative subsystem*: it is imperative to reduce production costs in the agrarian and raw materials sectors and significantly increase innovation in order to provide the necessary basis for the other two subsystems. Factors of economic security play an important role here (food independence; long-term importance of revenue from fuel and raw materials export). It is best to combine the developmental impulses and the stabilizing role of patriarchal and conservative traditions.

2. *The liberal-market subsystem*: The in-demand subsectors of the market necessitate: the restoration of mass flow production; the general growth of small and medium business; ensuring the availability of credit, financial, insurance, and other services for business; the improvement of competitive institutions and institutions for the protection of property rights; the effective use of personal initiative.

3. *The buds of a future mixed economy*, which assumes the priority of high-tech production on the basis of socially oriented, regulated economic development: As already noted, this third subsystem is in its nascent stages. This subsystem should provide the foundation for the formation of an innovative economic environment. Without this, the implementation of the positive functions of the first two subsystems is for naught, and an effective policy of reindustrialization is impossible. The development of the third subsystem will require a significant change in the system of economic relations, institutions, policy, and cultural and ideological attitudes.

---

18 S. Y. Glazyev, "The Transition to a New, Humanitarian Techno-Economic Paradigm," in *Modernization of the Russian Economy: Lessons of the Past, Opportunities, Risks* (Moscow: IKF, 2012), 23. (in Russ.)

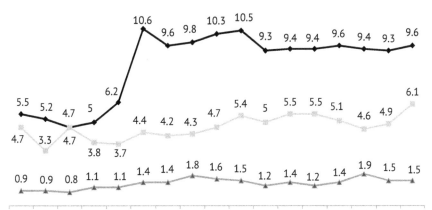

FIGURE 6. Level of innovation of industrial enterprises in Russia[19]
http://www.hse.ru/data/2013/10/28/1282559304/Skolkovo%20Booklet.pdf. Сайт ГУ-ВШЭ

By studying the specifics of the Russian economy, we can better understand its *prospects of developing a high-tech sector of material production, and the requirements toward this goal and toward reforming the economic system as a whole.*

Russia has historically prioritized the development of the basic sectors of material production, which use raw materials and other natural resources for the development of machinery, aircrafts, nuclear power, the space industry, and related industries, and for the economic foundations of Russia's national defense capabilities and related high-tech industries. I consider this trend a positive one, and one that should be preserved. Its revival is evident in recent years, and there is much room for growth if Russia continues on this path. For example, state investment in the development of the military-industrial complex has grown. This trend is in line with Russia's "civilizational codes" [tsivilizatsionnym kodam], which assume the priority of *the state* [derzhavy] over private interests but still trust entrepreneurial initiative to meet the challenges of the country's revival.

19 Website of the Higher School of Economics, http://www.hse.ru/data/2013/10/28/1282559304/Skolkovo%20Booklet.pdf.

Russia's economic system must ensure the development of this kind of material production, which will in turn ensure total economic, military, and other forms of security for the country.

It is essential that the development of high-tech material production (like the above-mentioned industries) integrates production with science and education, a system that was destroyed during the reform years. This integration must be implemented at a new level and in fundamentally new economic forms that make use of state, market, and private property potential. These new economic forms should have some independence. They should focus not only on solving problems of production development, but also the fundamental problems of technological development, social and environmental problems, and more broadly problems of the human condition.

To solve social and environmental problems, there must be a state system for financing the sciences and university education. There should be both public and private, medium- and long-term demand for both.

Systemic changes must take place if we are to implement these various possibilities of development in the Russian economy. Such changes include development and implementation of long-term programs, medium-term indicative plans, and an active industrial policy. To stimulate market initiative, there must be state support of modern domestic production, and an active fight against parasitic intermediation and the expansion of MNCs in the Russian economy. Public-private partnerships with stable, systemic institutional support that guarantees long-term investments by private business into R&D and the technological modernization of production could play a big role in this process. The tax and credit systems of the real sector (especially high tech) should stimulate the development of these industries and their innovation potential.

Finally, the whole system must ensure a moderate level of social differentiation, in which income differences would depend mainly on the workers' real contribution to the economy.

Part Three

THE NEW INDUSTRIAL STATE V.2

Chapter 8

The New Industrial State of the Twentieth Century

The publication of Galbraith's *New Industrial State* was a major event in global economics and for a large part of the ruling economic and political class. [1] The book was testament to Galbraith's rethinking of the modern production-economic system, especially that of the US, one of the world's two dominant powers. The work of this titan of twentieth-century economics was seemingly overshadowed by the developments of the following decades. Recent years have, however, cast doubt on those arguments for post-industrialism that overshadowed Galbraith's in the 1990s.

8.1. The concept of "postindustrial society"

Scholars of the "postindustrial wave" have, with varying degrees of detail, laid out the fundamental characteristics of this new society and economy. Their arguments usually begin with reference to a shift in *technology* and *structure of the economy*. Starting with Daniel Bell's work on postindustrial society[2]

---

1   John Kenneth Galbraith, *The New Industrial State* (London: Hamish Hamilton, 1967).
2   Daniel Bell, *The Coming of Post-Industrial Society: A Venture of Social Forecasting* (New York: Basic Books, 1973).

and Alvin Toffler's work on the "third wave,"[3] an economic paradigm that denied the primacy of material production began to take hold. Theories of the "Information society" and "information economy" began to appear, followed by the concept of the "society (or economy) of knowledge," followed by that of the digital economy. The work of Taichi Sakaiya, Manuel Castells, and many others became very popular.[4] In Russia, the work of Vladislav Inozemtsev was a kind of encyclopedia of Western post-industrialism.[5]

The proliferation of computer technology, and later of the Internet, has in recent decades become a distinctive feature of a new economic and social life. One of the defining features of the postindustrial trend were the growth of the service sector and simultaneous decline of the share of material production.[6] Indeed, over the course of the twentieth century there were significant changes in the share ratio of services to material production in almost all developed countries. By the 1970s and 1980s, the role of material production decreased sharply; the service sector became the dominant one. It still generates more than 70 percent of the GDP in developed countries and employs more than 75 percent of workers.[7]

Most scholars have devoted attention to obvious issues like the structure of the service sector and the labor content of its workers. Though the post-industrialists have emphasized the significant differences between the various service sectors and their activities,[8] they have been nothing but optimistic about the growth of information, telecommunications, and professional services. Meanwhile, the questionable "post-industrialism" of job growth in such sectors as trade, loading and unloading, the restaurant and hotel business, cleaning, etc., has been overshadowed.

---

3 Alvin Toffler, *The Third Wave* (London: Pan Books Ltd.; William Collins Sons & Co. Ltd, 1980).

4 See, for example, T. Sakaiya, "Cost created by knowledge, or the History of the Future," in *The New Post-Industrial Wave in the West: An Anthology*, ed. V. L. Inozemtsev, 337–371 (Moscow: Academia, 1999). (in Russ.)

5 See V. L. Inozemtsev, *Modern Postindustrial Society: Nature, Contradictions, Prospects* (Moscow: Logos, 2000); V. L. Inozemtsev, *At the Turn of Era: Economic Trends and Their Non-Economic Consequence* (Moscow: Economika, 2003). (in Russ.)

6 Daniel Bell, *The Coming of Post-Industrial Society: A Venture of Social Forecasting* (New York: Basic Books, 1973); Daniel Bell, "Post-Industrial Society," in *"The American Model": In Conflict with the Future*, ed. G. K. Shakhnazarova, 16–24 (Moscow: Progress, 1984).

7 International Labour Organization. *World employment and social outlook 2015: The changing nature of jobs* (Geneva: ILO, 2015), 25.

8 For example, Daniel Bell, the grandfather of post-industrialism, writes about the separation of different sectors in the service sector: Daniel Bell, *The Coming of Post-Industrial Society: A Venture of Social Forecasting* (New York: Basic Books, 1973).

The second most important characteristic of a postindustrial system is a fundamentally new *type of resources*. The main resource and product of the postindustrial economy is information, according to Castells, Sakaiya, and many others.[9] This shift is essential. Indeed, information has various characteristics that distinguish it from material products. It does not disappear when consumed, the cost of its production is disproportionately higher than the cost of duplication, its creation requires a highly educated worker, and even its consumption in many cases requires a certain level of skill.[10]

Accordingly, the *dominant type of worker* in a postindustrial information economy is, according to postindustrial scholars, the professional, usually one with higher education, who owns a certain labor force and "human capital." This is a special resource that is not only industrial, but also an investment [investitsionnogo]. For this reason, many scholars of the postindustrial wave have suggested the birth of a "society of professionals."[11]

In this world where information is produced by a highly qualified professional (the owner of "human capital"), there is a radical change in the *primary link of the economy*: large production factories are now replaced by individual "electronic cottages" linked together by the World Wide Web. This fact, coupled with new computer and Internet technologies, led to a predominantly *network-based economic* and societal *structure*.

As far as economic relations are concerned, no fundamental changes were intended. Moreover, the new structure of the economy, new computer and Internet technologies, the individualization of production, and the increasing role of the individual worker were supposed to reduce (and partly did reduce) the state's role as an economic regulator and social protector. These changes were seen as a kind of renaissance of market relations and private property. The post-industrialists also believed that the rise of small-scale individual private

9   See, for example, M. Castells, "The Formation of Network Society," in *The New Post-Industrial Wave in the West: An Anthology*, edited by V. L. Inozemets, 496–510 (Moscow: Academia, 1999); M. Castells, "Network Society," *The first of September*, no. 12 (2001). https://ps.1sept.ru/article.php?ID=200101210; T. Sakaiya, *The Knowledge-Value Revolution, or a History of the Future* (Tokyo: Kodansha USA Inc., 1991); Y. Masuda, *The Information Society as Post-Industrial Society* (Washington: World Future Society, 1983).
10 G. J. Mulgan, *Communication and Control: Networks and the New Economics of Communication* (Oxford: Polity, 1991), 174; R. Crawford, *In the Era of Human Capital* (New York: Harper Business, 1991), 11.
11 I. Sergeeva and V. Bykov, "Material and Non-Material Factors of Labor Motivation," *Man and Labor* 9 (2010): 43. V. L. Inozemtsev, "The Post-Industrial Economy and 'Post-Industrial" Society (on the Problem of Social Trends of the XXI Century)," *Social Sciences and Modernity* 3 (2001): 145. (in Russ.)

enterprises would soon become a reality, as would the spread of private property to sectors previously less impacted by it, like intellectual products.

All these changes were to result in a new social structure, with knowledge as the dominant factor in the formation of social strata.[12] But to what extent has this theory proved realistic?

8.2. The mirage of post-industrialism

The growing importance of the production, dissemination, and application of knowledge plays an enormous role in the development of modern society. If we consider the situation more broadly, it is not just about knowledge, but about the socioeconomic importance of each part of human culture. The "cultured person" is one of the most important pillars of societal development. Moreover, without an authentic culture, there can be no effective industrial development, which is based on, but not limited to, essential knowledge. The norms and rules enshrined in human behavior are not a mere projection of human knowledge. Such rules are largely determined solely by the culture of a society: the rules of conduct (individual, collective, corporate); the rules of doing business (you give your word and fulfill it, you do not go behind someone's back, you are responsible for your own actions, etc.). These rules, coupled with other important factors, determine the atmosphere of doing business, including the comfortable (or uncomfortable) conditions of industrial activity.

In the early twentieth century, Ivan Kh. Ozerov, a well-known Russian economist and professor at the Imperial Moscow and Imperial St. Petersburg Universities, wrote on this topic: "We have too little culture. [...] All our failures are due to this ... No matter the issue at hand, we will always run into the dead end of our low culture ... Routine, worship of the "maybe" [avos']—all this is rooted in low culture. Our industry—again, low productivity due to low culture, low worker development ... And our ruling classes and our government are also affected by our low level of culture. Otherwise, our politics, whether domestic or economic, would have changed. But because of this culture, we do not understand that organic treatment, changing the basic conditions of the body, has

---

12 The spread of information technology, processes of miniaturization, flexible production systems, etc. in the late twentieth century stimulated the development of non-corporate ways of organizing labor. Most Western and domestic economists who study this phenomenon note the development of forms of capital-free intellectual labor. For a critical analysis of these processes, see J. Rifkin, *The End of Work: The Decline of the Global Labor Force and the Dawn of the Post-Market Era* (New York: G. P. Putnam's Sons, 1995).

to come first, while in our culture we rely more on quack methods [znakharskie metody]." To remedy the situation, the professor offered a piece of advice still relevant today: "Yes, we have to create a business-like atmosphere around us, reorganize the school, reorganize our behavior, destroy the brakes that hamper the initiative and scope of energetic individuals, create strong guarantors for the development of the human personality and of self-determination . . ."[13]

The post-industrialists are willfully blind to the connection between the cultural sphere and the sphere of material production and its proper functioning. Rather, they look at the direct impact of technological and structural shifts on the social system, in what is a simplistic interpretation. Moreover, they tend to extrapolate the profound changes in the lives of a relatively small subset of workers—those working with modern information, telecommunications, and media technologies—to the lives of a majority of society. The post-industrialists tend to ignore the fact that their enthusiasm does not carry over to the entire service sector, and more generally, they also tend to ignore the growing social contradictions of this trend in their conclusions in favor of post-industrialism.

They paint an attractive image of the near future, or even the present, one in which most people own personal computers, and can thus be considered potential private owners capable of running their own business—the "self-employed" class. Meanwhile, they ignore the very real ruins of industrial Detroit. In their eyes, this postindustrial wasteland is the relic of a bygone past. They would much rather imagine that in that wasteland there exist "electronic cottages" connected by the World Wide Web, populated by the modern "creative class." This class produces electronic toys for "advanced" users, designs clothes meant for catwalks, invents gadgets with useless but fascinating functions—and for a considerable amount of money at that. And other equally "creative" managers, marketing experts, and financiers think about how to make the consumer buy all those products, or at least get them to believe in the prospect of endlessly rising stock prices, produced by the "creative" corporations that direct the work of the "self-employed."

In this world there is no class struggle, no contradictions of socioeconomic interests. Yes, there is competition, but it rewards the worthy: the most knowledgeable, the most creative, who do not shrink from transforming their abilities and their human relationships into "human" and "social" capital. Somewhere at the edge of this brave new world are dishwashers, maids, salespeople, chauffeurs, and dockworkers, and somewhere far away, across the

---

13 E. Zhirnov, "Time of Despair, Panic of Thought," *Kommersant Vlast* 49 (December 14, 2015): 35. http://www.kommersant.ru/doc/2861286. (in Russ.)

ocean, there are Mexicans, Koreans, Filipinos stitching fancy dresses for twelve hours a day, making sneakers, assembling computers, and overheating in steel mills. What can we do, those of us who have not demonstrated the skills to succeed in postindustrial society, they are left behind.

How sweet it is to leave behind the dangers of the "technogenic future," the gloom of industrial reality, create your own virtual reality—and make big money doing so, while at the same time falling deeper and deeper into that virtual world. But after all, who cares? As long as the mirage of the virtual world does not crumble when it collides with our somber reality.

Post-industrialism effectively rejects the industrial basis of societal development. This is its fundamental mistake. As a rule, the post-industrialists look at the structure of the economy, the GDP, exports, the number of people employed in various sectors of social production, and other quantitative indicators that characterize the state of the economy. And when industrial figures decrease, they draw the mistaken conclusion that the industrial path of development is at its end.

The post-industrialists fetishize knowledge and information and the role of creators, transformers, and distributors of this knowledge and information. They see in them a self-sufficient significance. The mirage of information, or "white noise," becomes a symbol of postindustrial progress. To some extent, their attitude makes sense, especially on the financial market, where modern alchemists turn virtual "white noise" into considerable profits by taking them out of the real economy. For such dealers, the content of the information itself or what purpose it serves is irrelevant. The main thing is to turn the *virtual* into money.

From the point of view of the neoliberal market economy, the only adequate system for a postindustrial, information-network technological base is one in which the main sphere of business is services, the main means of capital accumulation is financial transactions, and the free market, which extends to the whole of society, is the dominant mechanism for ensuring balance and growth. This myth of a "new economy" promised crisis-free growth and development for the developed countries. The dominance of this economic position, known as "market fundamentalism,"[14] is directly linked to a number of processes that have developed in the global economy.

Firstly, the financialization of the economy took hold, leading to the expansion of financial institutions and forming a new mode of economic

---

14 R. S. Grinberg, "The Big Crisis: It's Time to Get Away from Radical Liberalism," in *The Main Book on the Crisis*, ed. A. V. Buzgalin (Moscow: Iauza; Eksmo, 2009), 59–72.

regulation, property relations, etc.[15] Investment priorities changed. They were increasingly directed from the sphere of production to the sphere of financial transactions, and production investments became dependent on the illusory financial market. Control over property and basic property rights shifted to financial institutions. The rapid development of the financial sector as one of the main (and in some cases the main) sources of GDP growth began. All this led to bloated "financial bubbles" and, through a series of intermediaries, to the global financial and economic crisis.

Secondly, the postindustrial wave resulted in the massive drift of industrial production to the Global South and accelerated the industrialization of semi-peripheral and eventually peripheral countries, making up almost half of the world population (table 14). The growth of the geopolitical and economic influence and power of China, India and the BRICS as a whole has led to new challenges for the Global North.

TABLE 14. Distribution of employed persons by economic sector, world, and regions (%)

	1998	2003	2004	2005	2006	2007	2008
Industrial sector							
Whole world	21.1	20.7	21.1	21.5	22.1	22.7	23.2
Developed countries and EU states	27.9	25.6	25.3	25.0	25.0	25.0	25.1
Central and South-eastern Europe (not including EU members) and CIS	27.7	25.6	25.3	25.5	25.5	25.4	25.3
South Asia	15.4	18.7	19.4	20.1	21.0	21.8	22.6
Latin America and the Caribbean	21.8	21.6	21.8	22.2	22.4	22.6	22.9
North Africa	20.0	19.2	19.7	20.8	21.7	22.7	23.6
Sub-Saharan Africa	9.5	9.5	9.7	9.7	9.9	10.1	10.3
Service sector							
Whole world	38.1	40.7	41.5	41.9	42.4	42.9	43.3

(continued)

---

15 C. Lapavitsas and I. Levina, "Financial Profit: Profit from Production and Profit upon Alienation," *Research on Money and Finance* 24 (2010).

	1998	2003	2004	2005	2006	2007	2008
Developed countries and EU states	66.3	69.8	70.4	70.8	70.9	71.1	71.2
Central and South-eastern Europe (not including EU members) and CIS	45.5	51.7	52.6	53.2	54.2	55.1	56.0
South Asia	25.1	27.9	28.5	29.0	29.5	30.0	30.4
Latin America and the Caribbean	56.8	59.0	58.9	58.9	59.6	60.3	60.9
North Africa	44.1	46.1	45.1	44.8	44.5	44.2	43.9
Sub-Saharan Africa	22.9	25.1	25.9	26.3	26.7	27.4	28.0
Agrarian sector							
Whole world	40.8	38.7	37.5	36.5	35.5	34.4	33.5
Developed countries and EU states	5.8	4.6	4.3	4.2	4.0	3.9	3.7
Central and South-eastern Europe (not including EU members) and CIS	26.8	22.7	22.1	21.2	20.4	19.5	18.7
South Asia	59.5	53.4	52.1	50.8	49.5	48.2	46.9
Latin America and the Caribbean	21.4	19.4	19.3	18.9	18.0	17.1	16.2
North Africa	35.9	34.7	35.3	34.5	33.8	33.1	32.4
Sub-Saharan Africa	67.6	65.4	64.4	64.0	63.4	62.5	61.7

Source: International Labor Organization, *Global Employment Trends* (Geneva: ILO, 2009), 36.

Thirdly, many economies in the Global North, especially that of the United States, underwent deindustrialization, leading to a new reality in the global economy: the Global North's production dependence on the Global South. With the rapid rise of contemporary high-tech production in China, the Global South finds itself less and less technologically dependent on the North, threatening the technological dominance of the US and the EU. This new challenge has forced the economists of developed economies to consider how to restore material production and develop a new industrial economy.

The postindustrial "virtualization" of production and human needs has led, among other things, to a slowdown in the pace of scientific and technological progress, while innovation has seemingly exploded. But the *illusion of innovation* is widespread: to distinguish your product or service on the market, it is enough simply to make it look novel, or at best, to improve its consumer characteristics only slightly. It is no coincidence that actually new technologies capable of changing the face of modern material production occupy very small niches, and the technological revolutionization of material production is still far off. This problem is also extremely relevant for many post-Soviet countries, especially for the Russian Federation, where the deindustrialization has taken strong hold of the economy.

8.3. Is Galbraith making a comeback?

Note that, for all the changes in material production over the last century, it is still the basis of the economy, and remains predominantly industrial. Industrial production ensures the continuous growth of productivity in material production on the basis of scientific and technological progress. It also creates the possibility of employment growth in the service sectors.

I will recall some of Galbraith's arguments, now largely forgotten, and select those that reflect most adequately the interrelation of the material-technical and economic aspects that determine this or that type of economy.[16]

I will begin my analysis with the changes in the material and technological basis of the economy. Galbraith states that the most visible change "is the application of increasingly intricate and sophisticated technology to the production of things. Machines have replaced crude manpower. And increasingly, as they are used to instruct other machines, they replace the cruder forms of human intelligence."[17] These changes lead to the expansion of production, which requires a greater investment of capital and more and more highly skilled workers. The result (and remember that we are discussing mid-twentieth-century economics) is the development of large corporations as the main type of economic organization, which dominate the economy and attract the necessary capital for production.

---

16 These parameters are based on the main provisions of works by Glazyev, Buzgalin, and Kolganov. See S. Y. Glazyev and V. V. Kharitonov, eds., *Nanotechnology as a Key Factor of the New Techno-Economic Mode in the Economy* (Moscow: Trovant, 2009); A. I. Kolganov and A. V. Buzgalin,eds., *Comparative Economics: Comparative Analysis of Economic Systems: Textbook for University Students Majoring in Economics* (Moscow: INFRA-M, 2005). (in Russ.)
17 Galbraith, *The New Industrial State*, 1.

According to Galbraith, in the mid-twentieth century, it was those large corporations that could provide the labor force with the required qualifications and ensure scientific and technological progress.

As large corporations rose in power, Galbraith noted, *unions declined in power*. "Union membership in the United States reached a peak in 1956. Since then, employment has continued to grow; union membership in the main has gone down."[18] Even more significant was the *structural change in the professional composition of the labor force*. The number of people pursuing higher education increased substantially, while the increase in actual educational opportunities was more moderate.

"Seventy years ago," writes Galbraith, "the corporation was still confined to those industries—railroading, steamboating, steelmaking, petroleum recovery and refining, some mining—where, it seemed, production had to be on a large scale. Now it also sells groceries, mills grain, publishes newspapers and provides public entertainment, all activities that were once the province of the individual proprietor or the insignificant firm."[19] The distinction between the *entrepreneur-owner, the organizer of production, and the income recipient* was becoming quite evident, though it had begun long before. Picking up on the work of economists from the first third of the twentieth century, like Thorstein Veblen,[20] Adolf Berle and Gardiner Means,[21] Stuart Chase,[22] and others, Galbraith's thinking overlaps somewhat with that of Marx when it comes to the division of capital in joint-stock companies into capital-ownership and capital-function [kapital-sobstvennost' i kapital-funktsiiu]. He notes that, at the beginning of the twentieth century, "the corporation was the instrument of its owners and a projection of their personalities. The names of these principals—Carnegie, Rockefeller, Harriman, Mellon, Guggenheim, Ford—were known across the land. They are still known, but for the art galleries and philanthropic foundations they established and their descendants who are in politics. The men who now head the great corporations are unknown. Not for a generation have people outside Detroit and the automobile industry known the name of the current head of General Motors."[23]

---

18 Ibid., 3

19 Ibid., 1.

20 T. Veblen, *The Engineers and the Price System* (Kitchener: Batoche Books, 2001), 1921. http://socserv2.mcmaster.ca/~econ/ugcm/3ll3/veblen/Engineers.pdf.

21 Adolf A Berle and C. Gardiner, *Means: The Modern Corporation and Private Property* (New York: The Macmillan Company, 1932). http://www.unz.org/Pub/BerleAdolf-1932.

22 Stuart Chase, *A New Deal* (New York: The Macmillan Company, 1932). The title of this book, *A New Deal*, was later used by Roosevelt for his election program, "The New Deal."

23 Galbraith, 2.

This trend, which Galbraith absolutizes to some degree here, stimulates efficiency by distributing functional duties among specialists and widely involving professionals in management. But the ascent of technocracy also conceals another development: the increasing concentration of capital in the hands of the very few, because top managers, despite their massive incomes, remain mostly a "function" of the real masters' activities, those at the very top of the corporations.

The growth of corporate capital inevitably led to a change in the economic role of the state. Under these new conditions, which Galbraith beheld at the middle of the twentieth century, "the state undertakes to regulate the total income available for the purchase of goods and services in the economy. It seeks to insure sufficient purchasing power to buy whatever the current labor force can produce."[24] Firstly, *the role of planning consequently increased* considerably. "The large commitment of capital and organization well in advance of result requires that there be foresight and also that all feasible steps be taken to insure that what is foreseen will transpire."[25] This is an important conclusion of Galbraith's. Secondly, *consumer demand became an object of management.* Galbraith correctly points out that the nature of technology and of the capital it requires, as well as the time needed to develop and produce a product, dictate the need for government regulation of demand.

A corporation that is considering producing a new car must be able to convince people to buy one. And it is just as important that people have the means to do so. This becomes crucial when production requires very large and long-term capital investments, and products are as likely to reach the market during a depression as during an upswing. Thus, there is a need to stabilize aggregate demand. The state and, even more importantly, corporations are tasked with *creating demand*, not only taking it into account. Galbraith emphasizes: "The decisions on what will be saved are made in the main by a few hundred large corporations. The decisions as to what will be invested are made by a similar number of large firms to which are added those of a much larger number of individuals who are buying dwellings, automobiles, and household appliances. No mechanism of the market relates the decisions to save to the decisions to invest."[26] Galbraith admitted that this last statement something of an exaggeration in an era that has returned to the neoliberal model of market economy. But I believe his words here are becoming relevant again in a number of countries.

---

24 Ibid.
25 Ibid., 4.
26 Ibid., 42.

Galbraith concludes that there is a profound difference between a small enterprise, which is entirely under the control of an individual and owes all its success to that fact, and a corporation. This distinction, which can be seen as the boundary that separates millions of small firms from thousands of giants, underlies the broad *division of the economy into a "market" and a "planning" system.*

The dominance of the industrial mode of production results in the widescale technological application of scientific knowledge and in constant changes in the technological basis of production. This then leads to better opportunities to meet the needs of the people (and not only the material ones), and to fundamentally new needs. The result is a change in the characteristics of human life: production activities, qualifications, education, culture, everyday life, the entire social environment, and in the end, the social fabric.

The development of services in R&D, education, health care, information, and telecommunications, and professional (business) services, which the post-industrialists regard as a symbol of the rapid growth of the "service economy," is in fact closely dependent on their application to material production. It is no coincidence that the so-called industrial services sector, based on material production processes and oriented toward their service, has recently become so important.

Above all, knowledge is needed to move to new stages of technological progress. Where are the technologies of material production currently headed?

Chapter 9

The New Industrial State v.2: The Paramaters of its Genesis

———

9.1. Modern technological development: Revolutionary prospects

The new industrial society and economy of the twenty-first century must become a "negation of a negation," a dialectical sublation of both Galbraith's late industrial system and the postindustrial system of Bell and others. How is this "negation of a negation" conceived? To answer this question, I will analyze real trends in the revival of modern material production rather than paint an unrealistic picture of a future economic utopia.

Using the methodology outlined above, I will first look at *technological* changes, primarily those that have become (or are becoming) a reality in the sphere of material production. The most important of these changes is the increasing importance of information technology, as the post-industrialists have correctly suggested. But unlike the post-industrialists, I do not see this change as evidence of the decreasing importance of material production. Indeed, this change leads me to conclude that the *knowledge-intensity of material production* is constantly growing.

Unlike those who theorize on the rise of the information society, I do not want to focus on the increased role of information itself,[27] nor on the *production of information*, but on a *new form of material production* growing out of these other facts.[28]

The difference is significant. As developments in the global economy demonstrate, creating information often leads to informational noise. Economic resources now go toward creating signs[29] and simulacra[30] of useful goods [blaga] instead of contributing to labor productivity, human progress, and social and ecological solutions. This kind of "informatization" ultimately leads to the virtualization of social existence, which destroys the human personality, its spiritual world, social ties, and the unity of peoples and states.

The knowledge-intensive technology used in material production synthesizes the achievements of both the industrial and information technologies. This critical synthesis is reflected in the fact that, in high-tech production, operations and processes where the worker acts not as an appendage of a machine (like at a conveyor belt), but as a source of knowledge that is transformed into technology, begin to play a defining role. "The man stands beside the production process" and "relates himself to that process as its overseer and regulator."[31] In this context, then, it is appropriate to talk about the "knowledge-intensity" of material production and its product.

On this basis, a fundamentally *new type of material production* is born: *knowledge-intensive production*. Its main features are:

- the continuous increase of information and reduction of the material component; miniaturization, i.e., a tendency toward the reduction of energy, material and, capital that goes into production;

---

27 The "information society" and "knowledge-based society" have been a longstanding subject of interest for post-industrialists. See P. Drucker, *The Age of Discontinuity; Guidelines to Our Changing Society* (New York: Harper and Row, 1969); Fritz Machlup, *The Production and Distribution of Knowledge in the United States* (Princeton: Princeton University Press, 1962); Y. Masuda, *The Information Society as Post-industrial Society* (Washington: World Future Society, 1983) and others.

28 The question of knowledge-intensive industry has been debated for a long time. But there is a lack of certainty about what we mean by "knowledge-based economy" and "knowledge-intensive industry." See K. Smith, *What is the 'Knowledge Economy'? Knowledge Intensive Industries and Distributed Knowledge Bases* (Oslo: United Nations University, 2000), 2, 7–9.

29 J. Baudrillard, *For a Critique of the Political Economy of the Sign*, trans. D. Krachkin (Moscow: Academic Project, 2007).

30 A. V. Buzgalin and A. I. Kolganov, "The Simulacrum Market: A View Through the Prism of Classical Political Economy," *Philosophy of Economy* 2, no. 3 (2012). (in Russ.)

31 Karl Marx. Economic Manuscripts of 1857-58. In: Karl Marx and Friedrich Engels, *Collected Works*. Vol. 29 (New York: International Publishers, 1975): 91. (It is also necessary to add this book to Bibliography list at p. 272).

- the peculiarities of the *production process* and trends in *technological* development (flexibility, modularity, standardization, etc.);
- *network-model structuring*, replacing vertically integrated structuring;
- the use of modern methods of production and management (just-in-time, lean-production, etc.);[32]
- environmental friendliness and new sources of energy;
- the development of new technologies in material production, transport, and logistics (nanotechnologies, 3D-printing, etc.);
- the spread of additive technologies, leading to the reduced role of traditional manufacturing;
- emphasis on quality and efficiency.

The application of new knowledge in production is a continuously accelerating process; beneficial effects tend to compound and multiply, a process that is inherent in knowledge itself. As a result, knowledge-intensive production makes it possible to meet growing needs more quickly. As new technologies develop and ascend to new levels, there is a consequential decrease in the capital, material, and energy needed for production. In the long term, this allows us to reduce the number of resources necessary to satisfy human needs. Demand for resources will then fall, consequently changing the position of resource-producing countries in the global economy. This will, on the one hand, reduce pressure on their natural reserves, and on the other, allow for environmentally conscious development that preserves (and even restores) the environment.

Biotechnology, genetic engineering, alternative energy, nanotechnology, additive, cognitive, and social technologies are actively developing, building on the world of traditional machine technology. The transition to hybrid technologies may open the door to a new technological revolution, where machine technology, together with information technology, is used to regulate and direct natural processes toward human aims. To estimate the parameters of this technological breakthrough, I will use an approach based on Glazyev's theory of techno-economic paradigms (see ch. 6).

A new, integral [tselostny] way of life is emerging and becoming dominant, in response to the emergence and wide spread of the next wave of technologies. As

---

32 For more, see T. Ohno, *Just-in-Time for Today and Tomorrow* (New York: Productivity Press, 1988); W. Wadell and N. Bodek, *The Rebirth of American Industry* (Vancouver: PCS Press, 2005); B. Malakooti, *Operations and Production Systems with Multiple Objectives* (New York: John Wiley & Sons, 2013); S. Tillema and M. Steen, "Co-Existing Concepts of Management Control: The Containment of Tensions Due to the Implementation of Lean Production," *Management Accounting Research* 27 (2015): 67–83.

these technologies find more and more new applications, and as they become more refined in their many uses, they gradually penetrate not only the sphere of direct production, but all spheres of social life. This leads to technological shifts, and to changes in the social system as a whole.

Of course, not every new technological mode entails revolutionary changes in the social structure. The first two techno-economic paradigms that led to the industrial revolution in Western Europe did indeed reorganize the social structure of the European world. The role of small independent producers in both agriculture and handicraft production was drastically diminished, and society became divided between wage-earners (proletarians) and capitalists. From the late eighteenth century to the mid-twentieth century, history is punctuated by episodes of intense, sometimes violent struggle between these classes, from the Luddite movement to the guerrilla movements in Latin America.

At the same time, the transition to the third and fourth techno-economic paradigms, although accompanied by significant evolutionary shifts (including the emergence of monopolies, the development of state regulation, the transition to a social state, etc.), did not cause a revolution in the entire social system. Though it has changed markedly, it remains fundamentally the same.

Today we are witnessing the transition to the sixth techno-economic paradigm: the world of biotech, nanotech, robotics, VR technology, new medicine that will increase the length and quality of human life, and so on. The contours of the technologies that will become the basis for tomorrow's economy are beginning to appear.

We cannot yet predict what specific social shifts this technological revolution will lead to, because even the structure of its basic technologies is not yet sufficiently clear. One thing is certain: the sixth techno-economic paradigm will be based, even more than the fifth, on the generation [generirovanii] of scientific knowledge and its application in production toward knowledge-intensive products.

The *knowledge-intensive material product* is the new primary resource and result of the new industrial economy of the twenty-first century. It has the features of both the informational and "typical" material product. From the former, the knowledge-intensive product inherits its information content and many of its properties and problems; from the latter, it inherits its real utility for the reproduction of both material production itself and the human qualities necessary for it.

Using the concept of the level (complexity) of a product (see ch. 1), we can determine the specifics of a knowledge-intensive product. The general trend in the development of industrial production is a significant reduction in the use of "natural" energy and natural forces for the production of products. At the same time, as a rule, the specific consumption of raw materials and materials used in production decreases, but at the same time, the share of knowledge in the product structure sharply increases. Ultimately, it is the knowledge implemented in a product that determines its level, consumer properties and characteristics, or its ability to meet the growing needs of a person.

9.2. Features of modern technological development: The sixth techno-economic paradigm

When determining strategies of industrial development, it is important to remember that changes in material production are always *systemic* and, thus, *integrally interconnected*. I will highlight some of the key changes, corresponding to *cutting-edge twenty-first-century science and technology*, that will contribute to the *creation of a new industrial system*.

Some features of twenty-first-century industrial development include:

- updated content of technological processes;
- changes in structure of industrial enterprises (micro-level);
- changes in structure oof industrial sectors (macro-level);
- changes in organization and localization of industries;
- new types of industrial cooperation;
- stronger integration of production with science and education;
- an ideology of continuity when it comes to innovation in production;
- economic relations and institutions aimed at industrial/scientific-technological progress.

We must update: the *content of technological processes*; the *structure* of industrial sectors and the *location* of productions; the internal *structure* and *types of cooperation* between industries and their integration with science and education; economic *relations* and *institutions* that ensure the progress of fundamentally new material production.

We must not limit ourselves only to mastering modern technologies of manufacturing. We must also update our standards in product quality management, logistics, and personnel. And we must *extend these updates to the entire production process*: its *organization, technological base, product*, and, of course, the *nature* and *quality* of industrial *labor*. As the *nature* and *organization* of industrial production continue to develop, we must take note of the growing trend toward the *individualization of production*. A given job is increasingly organized around an *individual consumer*.

We must take up the following challenges of twenty-first-century industry:

- higher rates of new technological innovation, increasing labor productivity, and making production cheaper;
- increasing the "individualization" of production, of technologies, and products;
- introducing the principle of product modularity [modul'nost'];
- accelerating the intellectualization, computerization, robotization of production;
- developing network technologies and introducing the network principle into production;
- the miniaturization/compactization of production;
- supporting the trend of creating low-cost and zero-waste production facilities;
- continuously increasing the rate of technological transfer;
- the convergence of developer and manufacturer;
- reducing the time it takes to introduce new products;
- expanding the "intellectualization zones" of labor;
- the "clustering" of production relations;
- paying more attention to the role of individual, motivational, psychological, social, and other such characteristics in the worker;
- reducing labor costs for the production of new products, as the cost of their development grows;
- changing the structure of production profitability in favor of high-capacity and high-productive products.

The most important modern production principles are the individualization of production and the *modularity* of high-tech production, for example, of machine tool construction, aircraft construction (civil and military), heavy machinery, etc. Individualizing production and establishing contact between the producer and the individual consumer makes sense in the context of modern information and telecommunication technologies. Thanks to the Internet, many B2B and B2C communication platforms have formed, allowing for effective direct contact between customer and manufacturer. Add to this fact the development of fundamentally new technologies (virtual design, computer visualization, 3D printing, etc.), and individual, virtually *waste-free* production with near *instantaneous delivery* will soon be possible.

At the same time, the individualization of production also facilitates the easy transition to the *networked organization of not only business, but also of the material production process*. This makes it possible to quickly reconfigure how producers interact with sub-suppliers and subcontractors and outsourcers in general and create new channels of communication between them. As a result, it is possible to quickly adapt the product to the consumer's individual needs and just as quickly move on to new products for other customers, users, or markets. In turn, networked organization also contributes to the increasing individualization of production, as the effects of these processes snowball.

According to RAS studies, the economies of today's leading countries are based on the fifth techno-economic paradigm and are transitioning to the sixth, while Russia's economy is mainly in the fourth paradigm with some elements of the fifth (fig. 7).

Technological diversity of Russian industry

■■■ Russia
▨▨▨ Developed countries during this time

FIGURE 7. Comparison of techno-economic paradigms

The practical application of knowledge is one of the main characteristics of the fifth and sixth techno-economic paradigms. It is at this stage that the concept of the *knowledge-based economy* emerges. Scientific knowledge begins to occupy a growing share of value added. This is the origin of the term "innovation," which means not just novelty, but novelty created specifically through the application of scientific knowledge.

Today the world is on the threshold of the sixth techno-economic paradigm: the world of biotech, nanotech, robotics, VR technology, new medicine that will increase the length and quality of human life, and so on. The scope of the technologies that will become the basis for the economy of the future is only just coming into focus. For this reason, different countries are racing one another, making great efforts to be the first to transfer their economy to the sixth paradigm.

Its contours are only just beginning to emerge in the technologically developed countries of the world, primarily in the US, Japan, and China. According to expert estimates, if the current pace of technological and economic development continues, the sixth techno-economic paradigm will first form over the 2010s and 2020s and will enter maturity in the 2040s. There will also be a new *techno-scientific* and *technological revolution* between 2020 and 2025, based on developments that synthesize the achievements of the above-mentioned (and possibly some other) trends.

The mutual influence of nanotechnology, biotechnology, information technologies, and cognitive science—a phenomenon called *NBIC-convergence*— is particularly significant. Michael Roco and William Bainbridge introduced the term in their seminal 2002 report for the World Technology Evaluation Center (WTEC), *Converging Technologies for Improving Human Performance*.[33] It details the features of NBIC-convergence, its role in the development of the modern world, and its evolutionary and culture-forming significance. To visualize NBIC-convergence, the authors constructed a diagram of the network of intersections of the latest technologies. Analyzing scientific publications, the authors created a visualization method based on mutual citation and cluster analysis.[34] We can see the emerging technologies on the periphery of the diagram forming mutual intersections. At these junctions, the tools and know-how of one domain are used to advance the other. Moreover, scientists sometimes find similarities between objects of study in different fields.

Taking into account this mutual influence, as well as the interdisciplinary nature of contemporary science, it is possible to imagine, in the long term, the merger of NBIC into a single scientific and technological field of knowledge.

---

33 See M. Roco and W. Bainbridge, eds., *Converging Technologies for Improving Human Performance: Nanotechnology, Biotechnology, Information Technology and Cognitive Science* (Arlington: National Science Foundation, 2004).

34 Katy Börner, "Mapping the Structure and Evolution of Science," Presentation at the Symposium on Knowledge Discovery and Knowledge Management Tools at NIH, Bethesda, MA, February 6, 2006. https://grants.nih.gov/grants/KM/OERRM/OER_KM_events/Borner.pdf

This new field of study and practice will encompass almost all levels of material organization: molecular (nano), living (bio), mind (cogno), and informational (info).

The distinctive features of NBIC-convergence are:

- the intensive interaction of these scientific and technological fields;
- their corresponding synergy;
- their great breadth (from the atomic level of matter to the mind);
- identifying prospects for the growth of both individual and social technological capabilities.[35]

The technological trends now emerging as part of the sixth techno-economic paradigm and even beyond it entail a significant change in the level and structure of the prospective industrial product. The new industrial product will take less energy and material to produce, while its knowledge content will only grow.

A less energy- and material-intensive product allows for the greater satisfaction of human needs for a lower environmental price. This is all the more important because the development of production based on the fourth and even fifth techno-economic paradigms cannot overcome the economic backwardness of a considerable part of the Earth's population without leading to resource exhaustion and environmental destruction in the pursuit of economic growth. This threat is already becoming a reality, and therefore, only the transition to technologies that dramatically reduce the material- and energy-intensity of industrial production opens the way out of this danger.

While the role and importance of nonmachine technologies, like bioengineering, continue to grow significantly, the sixth techno-economic paradigm does not yet go beyond the industrial mode of production.

Some have argued that production equipment operating on nonmechanical principles—acoustic waves (ultra- and infrasound), electromagnetic fields, radio-frequency radiation, plasma, elementary particle streams—is not a machine per se, though this is fallacious. They claim that nonmachine equipment uses natural processes as "working organs" [rabochie organy], unlike machine equipment with artificial working organs. But the movement of electrons in wires that is produced by an electric generator is just as "natural"

---

35 V. Pride. "The Phenomenon of NBIC-Convergence: Reality and Expectations," in *Problems of the Effective Integration of Russia's Scientific and Technological Potential into the World Economy*, ed. V Pride and D. A. Medvedev, 97–116 (Moscow: LKI Publishing House, 2008). http://transhumanism-russia.ru/content/view/498/110/. (in Russ.)

as the mechanical action of a lathe cutter, composed of natural iron and carbon molecules, on a workpiece. And, indeed, if the cutter is replaced by a natural diamond, will the machine cease to be a machine?

Convergent (hybrid) technologies give a "second life" to the industrial mode of production, combining machine and nonmachine principles of acting on nature to create products that satisfy human needs with the least possible use of materials. Technology based on new types of machine technology (printers) integrated with information technology and virtualization (3D-printing) opens up a world of opportunity. This will likely lead to the spread of additive technologies and a reduction in the share of traditional manufacturing. Products will be assembled primarily by combining or building up materials layer by layer based on a 3D model, a process that is replacing traditional manufacturing, which processes raw materials with subtractive technologies (i.e., trimming, grinding, cutting).

There are also some traditional industrial technologies that can be classified as additive: casting, sintering, powder metallurgy. The possibilities of these technologies are now combined with the possibilities of 3D-printing. We may yet witness the creation of 3D-printers capable of printing entire buildings and structures, or at least their large building blocks. Additive technologies cover a whole range of technological techniques (extrusion and jetting, sheet lamination, photopolymerization, product synthesis from powder, direct point energy release) and use a variety of materials (plastics, new plastics, metals, composites, hybrid materials, materials for metal casting processes, ceramics, materials for testing, etc.).[36]

The question remains: how difficult is it to catch up to the sixth technological paradigm and, on top of that, come out on top in technological leadership? Russia is not in the best position compared to the real technological leaders of today. In the US, for example, the share of productive forces based on the fifth techno-economic paradigm is 60 percent; the fourth—20 percent; the third—less than 15 percent; the second—1 percent. The sixth paradigm accounts for about 5 percent.

Russia's economy is very technologically diverse, with more than 50 percent of technologies belonging to the fourth paradigm and 33 percent to the third paradigm. The share of technologies of the fifth paradigm is about 10 percent, while technologies of the sixth paradigm are still in their infancy. To enter the

---

36 For an overview of the possibilities of additive technologies see A. Prosvirnov, "The New Technological Revolution Is Passing Us by," ProAtom Agency, December 11, 2012. http://www.proatom.ru/modules.php?name=News&file=article& sid=4189. (in Russ.)

ranks of the *technological leaders* within the next ten years, we must develop production based on the sixth techno-economic paradigm and its share in output must be significant. But a technological leap is not all that is necessary. We must also upgrade all the components of modern material production: materials, labor, production, the application of knowledge, the organization of production. Only then will it be possible for Russia to enter the new industrial state: NIS.2.

9.3. From changes in technology to changes in the entire system of material production

In the new industrial state (NIS.2), the tendency of technological progress to grow exponentially will be of fundamental importance. This "acceleration of acceleration" will be one of the primary features of the imminent economic system of the future. The pace at which scientific advances are applied to industrial production and actualized in industrial products will grow quicker. This faster and more efficient process of technology transfer is already coming into focus, a sign of the new stage of development on the horizon.

The increasing role of knowledge-intensive technologies and their application in production, their accelerated rate of development and improvement, cause changes in the macrostructure of the economy. The second generation of the industrial economy is replacing both the classical industrial system, with its absolute dominance of industrial production, and the service society of the more recent past, in which service industries displace material production. The new industrial state will be informed both by the sectors that create the knowledge-intensive product and by the sectors that create that knowledge itself and shape the person capable of mastering that knowledge. Thus, the twenty-first century economy should be a complex that combines the following micro- and macrolevels:

- *high-tech material production,* which creates knowledge-intensive products;
- *science,* which creates the know-how;
- *education and culture,* which creates a knowledgeable person able to use that knowledge in production.

It is thus that the three main spheres of new social production, based on material production itself, are formed.

According to many well-known economists, including Buzgalin and Kolganov, the priority of economic development should not be in material production, but in the "creative sphere."[37] By this they mean education, science, and culture, relegating industry, construction, transport, agriculture, etc. to the "servants" who work for this creative class. As I see it, this model explicitly denigrates the role of the market and private production, while interpreting too broadly the functions of the state, civil society, and planning.[38]

Of course, the role of education and science cannot be underestimated, as I have repeatedly mentioned. But we should not forget that science is not only a producer, a sublimator, a processor of knowledge [dobytchik, sublimator, pererabotchik znanii]. The leading role of science is only apparent in its application to material production, where it acts as a vehicle for knowledge in the production process, and ultimately in the industrial product. It is for this reason that the speed at and efficiency with which scientific knowledge is transferred into industrial production is of fundamental importance. It is also for this reason that I have advocated for the closer integration of science, production, and education.[39]

Allow me to return to the genesis of the new industrial state after this brief detour into arguments over the priority of this or that sector. Under these emerging conditions, material production has a qualitatively new nature, different in its content and role from what it was in the classical industrial and so-called "postindustrial" eras.

Industrial production differs from classical production primarily in its content—new types of technologies, resources, and results—and in the fact that is closely integrated with science and education. It also differs from the "postindustrial" system in its "negation of a negation," i.e., in that it restores the defining role of material production itself, displacing pseudo-productive

---

37 See A. I. Kolganov and A. V. Buzgalin, "Reindustrialization as Nostalgia? Theoretical Discourse"; A. I. Kolganov and A. V. Buzgalin, "Reindustrialization as Nostalgia? Polemical notes on targets of an alternative socio-economic strategy"(in Russ.).

38 A.V. Buzgalin, "The Renewal of Russia's Economic System: The Need to Abandon Market Fundamentalism," *Problems of Modern Economics* 3 (2014): 53–55; A. V. Buzgalin and A. I. Kolganov, "The Russian Economic System: The Specificity of Property Relations and Intracorporate Management," *Problems of the Theory and Practice of Management* 10 (2014): 8–17. (in Russ.)

39 See S. D. Bodrunov, "Reindustrialization of the Russian Economy and Import Substitution Based on the Integration of Production, Science, and Education," in *Integration of Production, Science, and Education as a Basis for the Reindustrialization of Russian Economy: Proceedings of the Scientific Seminar "Modern Problems of Development,"* 26–51 (St. Petersburg: Institute for New Industrial Development (INID), 2015). (in Russ.)

services and intermediaries, as well as the artificial-virtual production of simulated goods.

I certainly do not mean to diminish the importance of services that serve human development and social needs. But we must restrict industries that do not produce goods that contribute to personal and social progress. I will consider below how to go about restricting those industries, but for now allow me to emphasize that these restrictions should not be legislative, but economically directed and socially formed, in the same way that we have limited smoking, alcohol consumption, etc.

The new industrial economy of the twenty-first century will also create a new type of worker. Toward this we must build on the culture of "professionals" of modern developed economies, though we must do this critically. The new economy will undoubtedly inherit the high level of professional education that we see in the information economy. Significant changes should, and have started to, take place on this front, too: *the main professionals of the new industrial production should not be managers, marketers, and financiers, but engineers, scientists, and engineers.* The contours of the industrial worker are, and have long been, changing. The new industrial worker is someone with a specialized secondary education and high professional qualifications that he or she is regularly improving upon. Under the new conditions of material production, scientists, engineers, and workers will become participants not only in the production process itself, but also in a process of lifelong education (Smolin and his colleagues have discussed this elsewhere).[40]

As a result of the changes in the content and structure of social production, the *main production link of the twenty-first industrial economy is a complex that integrates production, science, and education in a single reproductive process at the microlevel.* Such complexes could become the basis for production-science-education (PSE) clusters that connect manufacturing enterprises, research and development centers, and educational organizations within a single infra- and ultra-structure. We can see prototypes for these kinds of structures in the Soviet period (especially in their space and nuclear projects), foreign techno-parks [tekhnoparki], and in Silicon Valley and other such places where production, science, and education are integrated. Russia has recreated clusters like these in recent years.

I will return to these processes in due time, but for now I will consider the *changes in the system of economic relations and institutions* determined by the

---

40 O. N. Smolin, "Development of Human Potential as the Basis for XXI Century Modernization," *Economic Revival of Russia* 44, no. 2 (2015): 34–37. (in Russ.)

new content and structure of social production. This new economy, which sees the return of past features in a new capacity, creates new challenges for, on the one hand, market self-regulation and private property, and on the other, state influence in the economy.

Indeed, the individualization, flexibility, and knowledge-intensity of production, the widespread use of Internet technologies in material production and its continuous exchange, the increasing importance of individual professionalization—all this creates momentum for the development of small and medium-sized businesses and contributes to economic freedom. The personal experience, verve, and talent the entrepreneur-innovator play a fundamentally important role.

In this sense, the new industrial economy is a rejection of both the classical industrial era, which saw the rise of Ford's, Krupp's, and Benz's industrial empires, and the beginning of the late-industrial capitalist era, which saw the rise of Morozov's and other Russian entrepreneurs' industrial organizations. But the new industrial economy of the twenty-first century is fundamentally different from those eras. Contemporary challenges require that we develop many spheres of the social-state economic system, especially fundamental and applied sciences as part of the foundation of modern production, and the easily accessible professional and higher education as part of regular improvement of workers' qualifications.

We must also make it one of our main goals to develop complex, integrated production units (PSE clusters), and integrate production, science, and education on the macroeconomic level. We must address the problems that will arise as these structural adjustments take place in various economies. And it will be necessary to employ an active state industrial policy and long-term public-private investment to purge those hypertrophied intermediary sectors from the economy.

The state economic regulation of all sectors must be carried out with these factors in mind (as is already happening particularly in China).

The transition to the widespread construction and use of knowledge-intensive products imposes significant requirements on economic relations and institutions. The synthetic [sinteticheskaia] nature of such a product leads to many changes in the existing system of economic relations and institutions. In particular, proprietorship of such a product comes with certain rights, which covers both the material object itself and its intellectual component. It is no secret that, when it comes to high-tech products, the cost of developing the technology and protecting the IP rights is comparable with, if not higher than, the cost of the product's production. Hence, the paramount importance that IP issues will hold in the new industrial economy.

The new industrial economy needs a new perspective on market and government regulation and private enterprise and public ownership.

Part Four

REINDUSTRIALIZATION, IMPORT SUBSTITUTION, AND ACTIVE INDUSTRIAL POLICY

Chapter 10

Technological Leadership and National Security[1]

———————

Looking at Russia's current economic situation, I have to ask: will we be able to preserve not only opportunities for effective economic development but also, given current global economic and geopolitical trends, our country as a state entity, an economically self-sufficient territory, and a subject of international law? Here is a quote on this issue.

> We may consider economic security a certain economic state and state of productive forces that guarantees the independent, sustainable socio-economic development of a country, and maintains the necessary level of its national security, as well as the competitiveness of its national economy. These are the priorities for Russian economic security: the country's economic recovery; carving out its own independent economic course; overcoming its scientific and technological dependence on external sources; [. . .] taking measures to preserve and develop its scientific,

---

1   This chapter is based on a report from the All-Russian Conference "Innovative Development of Industry as a Basis for the Technological Leadership and National Security of Russia" (Moscow, May 20, 2015) and a presentation at the Abalkin Lectures: "Russia's Economic Growth Round Table" on the topic: "The Economic Security of Russia" (Moscow, February 10, 2016). (in Russ.)

technological, and productive potential; eliminating distortions in its economic structure to promote the accelerated growth the of production of science-intensive and high-grade products; reorganizing its economic structure and strengthening state regulation. We should also stress the importance of supporting leading scientific schools, accelerating the formation of the techno-scientific reserve and national technological base, and creating mechanisms to involve private capital in this process. [. . .] From a historical perspective, Russia has always been self-sufficient in its development. This is the only condition that will enable our country to become one of the world's centers of social and economic progress in the foreseeable future. The present moment is a turning point. Now Russia has the chance to eliminate the heavy socio-economic damage done during the crisis, and create the preconditions for sustainable development, one of the most important being the accelerated modernization of its industry.[2]

This is a fragment of an article I published in a collection by the RAS Institute of World Economy and International Relations, written at the request of the editorial board as part of the "Strategy for Russia's National Security" that was then under development. I also considered the problem of Russia's national security in the context of its economic security in my December 2005 report for a meeting of the Russian Security Council. Leonid Abalkin led the discussion and actively commented upon the report. Russia's current problems of economic security have indeed been discussed at the highest levels.

However, the research of many experts, their recommendations, and even the President's "Strategy for Russia's National Security," in the end "kudrinomics" [kudrinomika, after Aleksey Kudrin, the former Minister of Finance] prevailed. Despite the torrent of petrodollars that poured into our economy in the years before the 2009 crisis, virtually nothing was done to develop industry. After the crisis, too, little attention was paid to the development of the industrial base as the backbone of the economy, though the problem was discussed at various levels. For example, INID, together with the RAS Institute of Economics, prepared a report in March 2013 (Dmitriy E. Sorokin headed the working

---

2 S. D. Bodrunov, "The modernization of the defense-industrial complex and the provision of economic security of the state," *Year of the Planet: Politics, Economy, Business, Banks, Education* (Moscow: IMEMO RAS; Ekonomika, 2005), 107–112. (in Russ.)

group), which Ruslan S. Grinberg and I presented to the Federation Council. The report stressed the need to change our economic model and return to industrial development as a condition for national security.

The President himself has said more than once that the current model of economic development has completely exhausted itself, that we need to transition to another model and prepare for the next technological revolution, and generally that we must pursue technological development.

But the economy did not stray from its dead-end path until it "suddenly" became clear in 2014 that we have to catch up to the others in a very short time. Only now this task will be much more difficult than it would have been. At last, real measures are being taken in this direction.

Unfortunately, our economic inertia may be so great that we may not be able to step off our current path based on the liberal-monetary model. The risk of the traditional Russian approach—vigorously patching up holes instead of solving the problem substantively—is already in sight. Indeed, the measures that our authorized agencies sometimes take look more like patching up holes than strategic industrial development. The past year has highlighted the lingering illness of our domestic industry: no adequate plans for the development of the industrial base, in particular, of mechanical engineering. Our 2011–2012 strategies for industrial development, unsupported by financial-economic authorities and detached from trends of global development, crumbled before our eyes in 2013–2014.

For example, the automotive industry localization program folded: not only did General Motors leave Russia, but so did many companies of second- and third-level cooperation, which is even more detrimental. And it is not only due to sanctions that they left, but due also to other factors, including consumer demand. Almost 35 percent fewer cars were sold in 2015 than in 2014. Foreign cars, or those made from imported parts, are becoming too costly for the Russian consumer. And the localization program did not facilitate the construction of Russian factories that could have manufactured the necessary parts. Under these conditions, import substitution is nothing but wishful thinking. A similar situation is ongoing in the engine-building, machine tool, and aviation industries.

Inconsistency, lack of coordination, and other such factors have had a negative impact on these industries. And only when problems become critical are they addressed. Auto industry leaders asked for a preferential car loan program in 2014, but the government did not deliver on it until April 2015, when sales had already fallen by 42.5 percent. Customs delays of car parts from Turkey, just one example of the lack of coordination in the industry, have led to a half-year lag in production.

Now that developed economies are transitioning to the sixth techno-economic paradigm, the world's economic leaders will also be its technological leaders. As Russia is still in the fourth paradigm, with some budding elements of the fifth, catching up with the more developed countries should be one of the pillars of its economic development goals. Especially when it comes to critical technologies, Russia must not fall further behind lest its national security be threatened.

The primary parameters of an economic system are determined by the level of its advanced technologies, what is known as the *technological frontier*. According to the calculations of the Higher School of Economics, at its current pace of technological development Russia will reach the current technological frontier of advanced countries approximately by 2050. For this reason, we need to start (and have much discussed) the reindustrialization of the economy on a new technological basis. Russia must turn to an economic model based on advanced technological development. This new model will guide state institutions in solving our current problems. What's more, it will guide the strategic development of the Russian economy as a whole.

Economic and political authorities are today faced with the task of finding a *new model of economic growth*, or more broadly, a *new economic doctrine*.

Though I will not get into the numbers here, I will again note that domestic industrial production has been on the decline (see ch. 5). The outflow of capital from Russia presents yet another, separate problem: according to the Bank of Russia, capital flight amounted to 151.5 billion dollars in 2014, which is almost 2.5 times more than in 2013 (61 billion). This put additional pressure on the national currency (fig. 8) and market dynamics, curtailing domestic sources of long money for Russian companies. The Russian stock market declined (fig. 9) much more than other BRICS markets—an indirect but very important piece of evidence pointing to the inefficiency of the current economic development model.

As the Institute of Economics' Center for Macroeconomic Analysis and Forecasting reported (fig. 10): "The main risks are related both to problems that emerged after the 2008–2009 crisis and to new challenges. The former model of economic growth based on energy exports and rising oil prices has exhausted itself. The positive dynamics that emerged in 2011–2013 in the energy market did not lead to an acceleration of economic growth. But the negative dynamics of oil prices in 2014 undoubtedly influenced problems in balancing the budget, creating the preconditions for the national currency to grow significantly weaker, with the Russian ruble devalued much more than other 'commodity' currencies. The necessary structural and institutional changes in the current system of economic management are long overdue."[3]

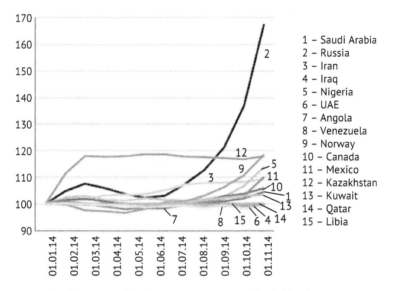

FIGURE 8. The dynamics of exchange rates against the dollar for oil-exporting countries in 2014

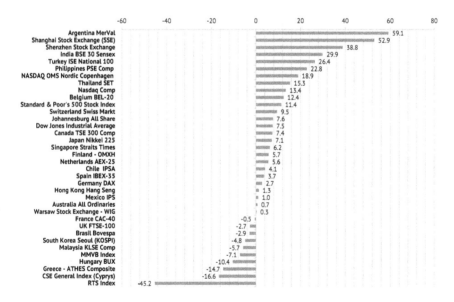

FIGURE 9. The dynamics of fixed assets in 2014

3   Institute of Economics at the Russian Academy of Sciences. *The Situation in the Russian Economy in 2014 and Forecast of Its Development in 2015–2016*. 2015. (in Russ.)

As is clear, there were problems in the Russian economy long before sanctions were imposed. The latter only exacerbated them and made obvious what experts had long been concerned about. I insisted, as early as in the mid-2000s, that we *abandon our current economic model and move towards economic modernization by restoring the industrial development.*[4]

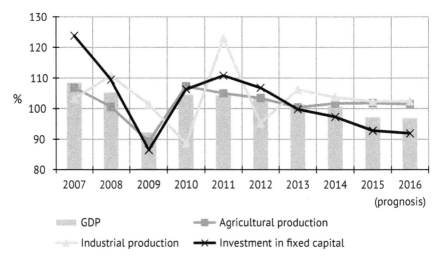

FIGURE 10. The dynamics of primary macroeconomic indicators, percent of the previous year

Reindustrialization based on high-tech development is the very heart of the economic model I am proposing.[5] I want to reiterate that I am not proposing that we restore the Soviet industrial system (though in some cases these

4   S. D. Bodrunov, "The modernization of the defense-industrial complex and the provision of economic security of the state," *Year of the Planet: Politics, Economy, Business, Banks, Education* (Moscow: IMEMO RAS; Ekonomika, 2005), 107–112. (in Russ.)

5   See, for example, S. D. Bodrunov, R. S. Grinberg, and D. E. Sorokin, "Reindustrialization of the Russian Economy: Imperatives, Potential, Risks," *Russia's Economic Revival* 1, no. 35 (2013): 19–49; S. D. Bodrunov, "Institutional Mechanisms of the Concept of Russia's New Industrial Development in the WTO Environment," *Russia's Economic Revival* 3, no. 33 (2012): 47–52; S. D. Bodrunov, "Reindustrialization. Roundtable at the Free Economic Society of Russia," *New Economic World* 1 (2014): 11–26; A. I. Tatarkin, "Sobering up after the market euphoria is delayed, but still happens," *"Gorod 812"* 32 (2014): 21–23; S. D. Bodrunov, "What is to be done? Imperatives, Opportunities and Problems of Reindustrialization," in *Collection of the Scientific and Expert Council under the Chairman of the Federation Council of the Russian Federation "Re-industrialization: Opportunities and Limitations,"* ed. S. D. Bodrunov and R. S. Grinberg, 14–25. (Moscow: Federation Council of the Russian Federation, 2013); S. D. Bodrunov, "Reindustrialization of the Russian economy: opportunities and limitations," *Proceedings of the Free Economic Society of Russia* 1 (Moscow, 2014): 15–46. (all in Russ.)

minimal steps are necessary), but that we renew the *technological* basis of material production, and that we do this with INID's economic vision. We must accelerate how quickly changes in the economic system take place, especially in the production process itself: its organization, technology, materials and equipment, the content of its labor, and its result, the product.

I will also reiterate that the task I have set forth here, to build a new technological industrial base, does not conflict with the tasks set forth by other economists: for example, to transform the material base of production via technologies of the fifth and sixth techno-economic paradigms,[6] via informatization, miniaturization, customization, and network-organized production,[7] via the creative potential of workers[8] (again, see ch. 9). My ideas do, however, oppose the tenets of a vulgar post-industrialism, which *prioritizes* nonproductive services, intermediation, and financial transactions. This kind of thought is misguided, the result of methodologies based on a static view of the economy, or even on a dynamic view of the economy that still does not take into account the changing dynamics of the system itself, the second derivative of its acceleration and deceleration, changing the very essence of the analyzed phenomena and processes and their interrelation.

The main objective of *reindustrialization* as an economic policy is *to restore the role and place of industry* in the Russian economy. In the process, *structural changes* must take place to *prioritize the development of material* production and the real economy on the basis of the *most advanced technologies*. This is the way to *modernize* Russia.

As one *result* of deindustrialization, Russia is badly integrated into the global labor market. In most basic sectors, Russia generally participates only at the beginning of value chains, which leads to technological dependence on more developed countries. We specialize in extraction, production, and supply to international markets of low value-added products: natural gas, oil, ferrous and nonferrous metals, potash fertilizers, etc. Russia's high-tech exports are mainly related to weapons and military equipment. Russia is also involved in the nuclear

---

6 S. Y. Glazyev, *On External and Internal Threats to Russia's Economic Security in the Context of American Aggression: Scientific report* (Moscow: n.p., 2014). (in Russ.)

7 M. Castells, *The Information Age: Economy, Societies, and Culture*, trans. and ed. O. I. Shkaratan (Moscow: MGU HSE, 2000). (in Russ.)

8 A. I. Kolganov and A. V. Buzgalin, "Reindustrialization as Nostalgia? Polemical notes on targets of an alternative socio-economic strategy"; V. A. Krasilshchikov, "Modernization and Russia on the Threshold of the XXI Century," *Problems of Philosophy* 7 (1993): 40–56; T. Sakaiya, *The Post-Industrial Wave in the West: An Anthology*, ed. V. L. Inozemtsev, 337–371 (Moscow: Academia 1999). (in Russ.)

industry, space technology, titanium production, though in the greater context, this output is small.

In the run-up to the 2012 election, President Putin highlighted Russia's *technological leadership* as an important condition for overcoming the current situation.

Experts now agree that the country's technological modernization of production is the biggest guarantee of Russia's competitiveness on the global stage. Speaking at the St. Petersburg Economic Forum in 2014, Putin said: "Russia needs a real *technological revolution*, a serious technological upgrade, we need to carry out the largest technological re-equipment [perevooruzhenie] of our enterprises of the last half century."[9]

We must first and foremost solve the problem of the depreciation of Russia's production capacity and fixed assets (fig. 11). According to Rosstat, by the end of 2013 fixed assets in various industries had depreciated by 40 percent to 60 percent. The share of fully depreciated fixed assets (fig. 12) in commercial organizations was 14.6 percent (in manufacturing it was 13.3 percent, and this figure has been stable since 2007).

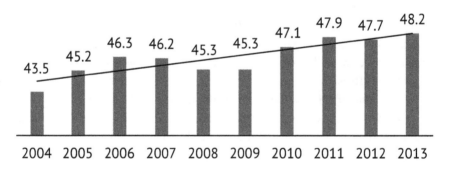

FIGURE 11. Fixed asset depreciation, %

Other sources provide even more alarming data: the depreciation of fixed assets in, for example, the electric power and gas industry is 60 percent, in oil refining it is 80 percent, and in the coal industry up to 90 percent.[10] In 2004, only 8.6 percent of industrial equipment was under five years old (for reference:

9 Website of the President of Russia, V. V. Putin, "Speech at the plenary session of St. Petersburg International Economic Forum," Verbatim record of the plenary session of the 18th St. Petersburg International Economic Forum. http://kremlin.ru/events/president/news/21080.0. (in Russ.)

10 See the Russian Energy Strategy until 2030.

in 1988, 33.7 percent was under five years old); 5.1 percent of it was from six to ten years old (in 1988, 29.1 percent was six to ten years old); and 51.5 percent was over twenty years old (in 1988, 12.4 percent was over twenty years old). Thus, during the reform years, the share of equipment more than twenty years old increased significantly.[11] And this means that technological breakthroughs in these industries are impossible; neither the equipment nor the specialists are there. The renewal rate of fixed assets (excluding small businesses) in Russia in 2013 was only 11.4 percent.

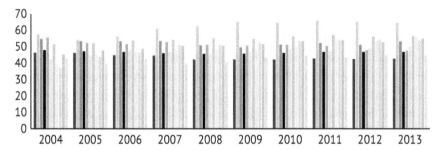

- agriculture, hunting and forestry
- fishery, fish farming
- mining
- manufacturing industries
- production and distribution of electricity, gas, and water
- construction
- transport and communications
- public administration and military security
- education
- healthcare and social services
- provision of other utilities, social, and personal services

FIGURE 12. Depreciation of fixed assets by type of activity, %

The coming technological revolution will unfold as an industrial revolution and will likely lead to the launch of a network of "smart," robotized, information-networked enterprises. They will be guided by virtual modeling with a high degree of individualization. Their products will be capable of self-improvement. And they will rely on integrated technologies: bioinformatics, additive technologies, etc.

---

11 A. Grazhdankin and S. Kara-Murza, eds., *The White Book of Russia: Construction, Perestroika and Reforms: 1950–2012* (Moscow: Librokom Book House, 2013). (in Russ.)

But will Russia be able to make the transition from the (predominantly) fourth techno-economic paradigm to the sixth all at once? Economists seriously disagree on this question. Oleg S. Sukharev, from the RAS Institute of Economics, believes that "any industrial programs, any systemic changes—as the logic of technology tells us—must be built up not according to [...] a logic of jolts, of jumping over some breakthroughs [...] in technology. There can be no leaps across generations of technology. Yes, it is possible to bridge a gap by borrowing [zaimstvovaniia], but the logic of technology does not assume any unreasonable leaps."[12]

Other scholars have a different view on the situation. For example, Glazyev notes that, "in order to successfully make a technological leap forward, lagging countries need to correctly assess the prospective developmental directions of the new techno-economic paradigm and, in anticipation, translate them into production on an industrial scale. Success is more likely when a country is ahead of the curve at the embryonic stage of the new techno-economic paradigm. The transition between dominant techno-economic paradigms is characterized by the formation of new 'technological trajectories' and new 'industry leaders,' and less time between the applied results of basic research and their implementation in the real sector of the economy."[13] According to Glazyev, the current stage of economic development is characterized by the "transition between techno-economic paradigms."

A government resolution from 2008—"The doctrine of Russia's long-term socioeconomic development up to 2020"—sets as its strategic goal Russia's transformation into a global economic leader. This innovative model of economic growth emphasizes the importance of new knowledge, which leads to new technologies, which leads to a new kind of production, with new equipment. Only those innovations that have lived an entire lifecycle—from the birth of the idea to its dissemination in economic practice and its transformation into a quotidian technology—can provide development with the necessary impetus.

Naturally, this requires a developed industrial base. It is no coincidence that countries that have developed their industrial potential and apply the most modern mechanical engineering lead in economic innovation. Mechanical engineering is the core of a national system's innovation: on the one hand, it

---

12 In The Russian economic system: the future of high-tech material production: Proceedings of the meeting of the Scientific Council of Lomonosov Moscow State University on the development of social economic theory and Russian model of socio-economic development (June 5, 2014) (St. Petersburg: S. Y. Witte INID, 2014). (in Russ.)

13 S. Y. Witte, *The strategy of the advanced development of Russia in the context of global crisis* (Moscow: n.p., 2010). (in Russ.)

demands steady technological innovation, and on the other, it contributes to the practical implementation of those innovations in the production process.

At the same time, the high-tech production of consumer- and investment-demand products may take place beyond the bounds of national borders (production outsourcing). But technologically innovative companies will still remain the proprietors of that technical knowledge; they will be the ones to integrate it into production, and thus receive innovation rents [innovatsionnaya renta]. In this way, the future economy offers a new environment for the development and *competitiveness* of the industrial base. In this new environment, the *scale of industrial potential*, its *innovativeness*, and its permanent technological renewal will play a paramount role in maintaining the ongoing development and competitiveness of a particular business and the national economy as a whole.

The task of *import substitution* is local: *institutionally*, in its *aims*, and to a large extent, in the *mechanisms* that allow it to happen. This task also coincides with the broader task of the *innovative reindustrialization* of the domestic economy.[14] If Russia can successfully implement an *import substitution* policy and *reindustrialization* strategy, and *modernize* its national economy, we will enter into the same *now-developing techno-economic paradigm* as the other developed countries, achieve *technological leadership*, and ensure our *national security*.

---

14 S. D. Bodrunov, *Theory and Practice of Import Substitution: Lessons and Problems* (St. Petersburg: Institute for New Industrial Development (INID), 2015). (in Russ.)

Chapter 11

Innovative Economic Development: Into NIS.2

As a matter of fact, Russia is regularly developing new technologies, but there is no significant progress in the main sectors of the economy. The number of new technologies developed annually remains approximately at the same level (fig. 13).

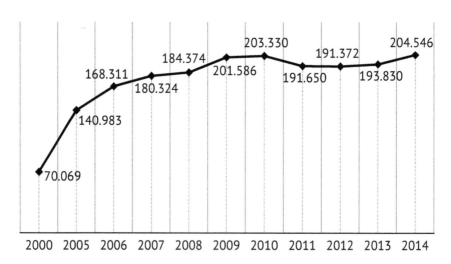

FIGURE 13. Number of advanced technologies used in industry in the Russian Federation by units

In general, despite *high scientific and technical potential*, entrepreneurial innovation is rather low and remains practically unchanged in recent years. The share of organizations that carried out technological, organizational, and marketing innovations in 2013 was less than 10 percent. The culprit here is the lack of effective mechanisms for *transferring* the existing potential into the necessary technologies, particularly industrial technologies. A system of special institutions—what the global community calls a *National Innovation System* (NIS)—is necessary to promote the generation, selection, development, and implementation of new ideas into innovative technologies.

An *innovation system* is generally defined as an *organizational-economic system* with the necessary *infrastructure* to lead scientific organizations in their commercial and social contributions to development; to lead industrial organizations in the constant upgrading of its production, technologies, organization, labor, and management via the previously mentioned developments; and to lead the authorities and civil society at large in the development of mass innovation. A national innovation system can also be defined as a set of individual institutions that both jointly and individually contribute to the development and dissemination of new technologies; together these institutions form a structure within which the government applies policies to stimulate innovation (fig. 14).

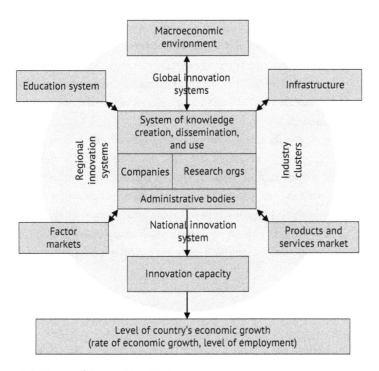

FIGURE 14. National Innovation System

K. Todd Freeman first used the term *national innovation system* was in 1987 in his study of technological policy of Japan. Two monographs on the topic came out shortly thereafter: *National System of Innovation*[1] and *Technical Progress and Economic Theory*.[2] Today's experts treat the concept differently than these first works, but most definitions have the same basic elements. In its basic methodology, NIS holds:

- competition based on corporate innovation and scientific development is the main factor of economic dynamics, as Joseph Schumpeter has argued;[3]
- knowledge has a special role in economic development;
- the institutional context of innovative activity is a direct factor of its content and structure.

The NIS can be seen as a complex system of institutions (legislative, structural, innovative), which ensures that the state maintains a certain level of innovation. In other words, the NIS is a set of interconnected organizations (structures) involved in the production and commercialization of scientific knowledge and technology within a country's borders. At the same time, the NIS is a complex of legal, financial, and social institutions that catalyzes innovation and has national roots, traditions, political, and cultural features.

As of late, however, an innovation system tends to be seen as a system of knowledge transformation. The INID takes exactly this approach. As I have mentioned, the key element of every basic element of social material production is knowledge (see ch. 1).

In essence, the NIS is a *system of interconnected institutions for creating, storing, and transferring knowledge and skills that shape new technologies*. From this point of view, neither reindustrialization nor the further successful development of modern production and industry is possible without the *deep integration* of production with education and science, both ideologically and practically. The *integration of science, production, and education* is also a *necessary organizational precondition* for the *practical implementation* of Russia's reindustrialization.

---

1   B. Lundvall, ed., *National System of Innovation* (London: Pinter, 1992).
2   G. Dosi, C. Freeman, and R. Nelson, *Technical Change and Economic Theory* (London: Pinter, 1988).
3   I. A. Schumpeter, *Theory of Economic Development* (Moscow: Progress, 1983). (in Russ.)

Knowledge is the main informational input that the innovation system receives from its environment. Within the system, this knowledge is *transformed* into new knowledge. Thus, knowledge is also the main output of the system. The process of knowledge transformation—including its acquisition, production, dissemination, ordering and standardization, application, and its management— is carried out within the NIS by various organizations. They include universities, research institutes, company R&D departments, technology transfer centers, standardization institutes, patent agencies, and government agencies involved in innovation policy.

In principle, the *Russian national innovation system* is similar those of developed countries. It has passed through several formative stages and today functions on the basis of federal laws, state decisions, and target programs, in particular the Strategy for the Innovative Development of the Russian Federation up to 2020.[4]

The main stages of development of the Russian NIS are:

- *the preliminary stage*: the Russian Fund for Technological Development was established in December 1991; the Russian Fund for Basic Research appeared in April 1992; the Foundation for Assistance to Small Innovative Enterprises in Science and Technology was established in February 2014;
- *the first stage (2000–2005)*: identifying and supporting deserving institutions, implementing specific projects; direct financing of the most important innovation projects of state importance, providing grants to small high-tech enterprises; creating the human resources basis of the innovation system, financing worker training and retraining;
- *the second stage (2005–2010)*: developing infrastructure for innovative activity and project tools for tackling tasks financed with the state budget using the Federal Target Program. Forming venture companies, special economic zones, technoparks, and commercialization centers: in 2005, business incubators were created; in late 2005, six special economic zones were established; in March 2006, the complex program on the "Creation of High-Tech Technoparks in the RF" was approved; in June 2006, the Russian Venture Company was established; in 2007, the "Nanoindustry Development Strategy" was

---

4 Strategy for the Innovative Development of the Russian Federation (approved by Order No. 227-r of the Government of the Russian Federation on December 8, 2011). http://minsvyaz. ru/common/upload/2227-pril.pdf. (in Russ.)

approved; in June 2007, "Russian Nanotechnology Corporation" was established;

- *the third stage (2010 to present)*: transferring the bulk of applied research from the Russian Academy of Sciences and industry-specific research institutions to universities: from 2008 to 2010, a number of national universities were singled out and received additional funding for development; in April 2010, a program for the state's co-financing of high-tech industries was established; in August 2010, a list of companies to receive state support to develop innovation programs was drawn up and approved; at the end of 2010, various technological platforms launched; in spring 2012, innovative territorial clusters were created.

The main actors of a NIS are the state, the scientific and educational innovation complex, the system of infrastructure investment reproduction organizations, business structures, and market infrastructure institutions (fig. 15).

The state, as a key element of the national innovation system, provides comprehensive support for economic innovation processes, their priorities, and their coordination. Though the main institutions of innovation have already been created in Russia, the Russian *system's biggest problem is a lack of demand for innovations*. From 2000 to 2010, share of industrial production organizations that carried out technological innovations decreased from 10.6 percent to 7.9 percent and amounted to 8.9 percent by the end of 2013. At the same time, the volume of innovative goods, works, and services increased from 4.5 percent in 2009 to 9.2 percent in 2013, but this number is still much lower than that of the global leaders of innovation.

The Achilles' heel of the Russian NIS is its low efficiency, caused by an inconsistency of interests among its various participants and their lack of mutual dependence. The system is also hampered by a lack of proper economic motivation, and a proper system for indicating the results of innovative activity across its various organizations and institutions.

The Russian NIS

1. Institutions for elaborating and implementing state policy on innovative economic development (Ministry for Economic Development of the Russian Federation; Center for Strategic Research; system of state procurement; Ministry of Education and Science of the Russian Federation; Interdepartmental Commissions on Scientific and Technical Policy; Ministry of Finance of the Russian Federation; Gosbank of the Russian Federation).

2. Institutions of knowledge production and dissemination (Russian Academy of Sciences; branch academies; national research universities; system of secondary and higher professional education institutions; postgraduate professional education institutions, postgraduate studies, doctoral studies; state innovation corporations - "Rosnano", "Skolkovo").

3. Institutions for infrastructural support of the innovation process (technoparks; technopolises; information and technological centers; information and production complexes; science cities; business incubators; technology transfer centers).

4. Market institutions for the commodification of innovative products and services (Venture Innovation Fund, regional venture funds; venture companies; marketing companies; information centers; leasing companies; insurance companies; centers and agencies for the protection of IP rights).

5. Legislation. The regulatory base for innovation (Federal Law "On Science and State Scientific and Technical Policy"; Civil Code of the Russian Federation, part 4; Strategy for the Innovative Development of the Russian Federation up to 2020; strategies for socio-economic development of Russian regions, developed and adopted by the subjects of the Russian Federation; general federal and sectoral regulations governing the innovative activities of enterprises and organizations).

6. Organizational and industrial integrated business structures - subjects of the innovation process (transnational companies; international strategic alliances; consortia; cross-border clusters; financial and industrial groups; scientific and technical alliances; public-private partnership institutions; state corporations; industrial clusters, free economic zones (technological, industrial-innovative, etc.); globally integrated companies; small and medium-sized business).

FIGURE 15. The Russian NIS

There is an obvious need to develop a new methodology for assessing the effectiveness and efficiency of the Russian NIS and its components based on a systematic approach. We must double down on the innovation renewal of Russian industry, create the prerequisites for Russia to achieve global *technological leadership* in certain fields, and form effective mechanisms for the *transformation of innovation potential* into new, market-demanded technologies.

Another problem for the Russian NIS is the *lack of a developed market of innovative products, services, and technologies*. Indeed, a major problem is the undeveloped intellectual property market. Together with the Russian Institute of Intellectual Property, the INID conducted an analysis of more than one hundred fifty federal, regional, and industry-specific strategies and programs of innovative development by industry. Our analysis found that the majority of these strategy documents failed to consider the development of the intellectual property market at all, though it is one of the driving forces of innovative development.

Based on these facts, it is clear that the technological modernization of the Russian economy is impossible without a large-scale transfer of foreign technologies. Russia already spends 140-165 billion dollars annually on foreign technologies. Due to financial and political constraints, however, Russia cannot access the full range of necessary technologies. Consequently, there is legitimate doubt about our goals of technological modernization. On January 13, 2014, the Chairman of the Government of the Russian Federation approved the Forecast of Scientific and Technological Development of the Russian Federation until 2030.[5] According to the government, technological forecasting should pursue new technological solutions, Russia's *technological leadership*, and *its technological independence*. The Forecast suggests prioritizing areas where Russia can achieve technological advantages, and thus prioritizing where resources go and what specifically to borrow from abroad. Promising areas of scientific and technological development in the Russian Federation include: information and communication technologies; biotechnologies; medicine and health care; transport systems (including aircraft and shipbuilding); space technologies and systems; materials (including nanotechnologies); technologies for smart environmental management; energy efficiency.

Again, I want to reiterate that its *knowledge-economy innovativeness* is what sets apart today's industrial production from the industrial production of yesteryear, when active industrial policy was first widely and successfully applied. The task at hand is not just checking off a list of new technologies but ensuring the continuous innovation of these technologies.

The innovation of new technologies has always existed in industrial production, regardless of the society system in which it took place. But since the end of the twentieth century, the flow of innovations has become

---

5 Materials concerning the Long-Term Forecast of the Scientific and Technological Development of the Russian Federation until 2030. GU-HSE website. http://prognoz2030. hse.ru/. (in Russ.)

uninterrupted. It is now *imperative for effective production* to continuously update product lines and develop *new technologies.* Continuous innovation now defines production. The research, transfer, introduction of technologies has become an integral element of the production system and a part of production process. The interrelation of scientific and production structures in the framework of industrial activity—like *technology transfer,* for example—is a necessary part of the industrial process. Ensuring the flow of innovations at the national level means that R&D will become a large and important branch of the national economy. The flow of innovations will also contribute to the NIS, which will push innovation at every level of the national economy.

The state program on the "Development of Science and Technologies"[6] is designed to create a competitive Russian R&D sector capable of ensuring the technological modernization of the economy. The plan is to finance this program with 1.187 trillion rubles between 2013–2020. The program's main objectives are to finance scientific and technological breakthroughs for their further use by the relevant departments, and to support interdisciplinary research, has led to promising results in science and technology of the recent decades. Toward these ends, the financing of scientific activity is steadily increasing. The share of federal budget expenditures on science is gradually increasing, as is their share in the GDP, though this figure remains rather low (0.5–0.6 percent) (fig. 16).

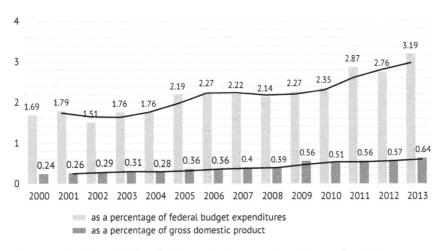

FIGURE 16. Federal budget funding of science, and its share in the GDP

6 Site of the Ministry of Education and Science of the Russian Federation. http://минобрнауки.рф/%D0%B4%D0%BE%D0%BA%D1%83%D0%BC%D0%B5%D0%BD%D1%82%D1%8B/2966. (in Russ.)

But the state's measures develop the national innovation system and to finance scientific research remain clearly insufficient. The number of organizations that carry out scientific research has decreased significantly (from 4099 in 2000 to 3605 in 2013), while the number of economic entities and the GDP itself is growing. It is becoming less attractive for companies and organizations to carry out research (fig. 17). According to Rosstat, this kind of work is carried out more and more by specialized research organizations that are not sufficiently close to the production process. This trend suggests the continued disentanglement of science and production, which only slows down innovation.

For the Russian economy to occupy a worthwhile niche in the global labor market in the coming decades, we must devise, develop, consolidate, and implement a systematic strategy. The Russian Academy of Sciences is developing just such a strategy—the "Conceptual Framework for the National Technological Initiative (NTI)"[7]—by order of the President, on the basis of his Address to the Federal Assembly of the Russian Federation on December 4, 2014. The Russian Venture Corporation (RVC) has begun to develop the roadmap for the NTI, which includes the input of some seven hundred fifty experts.

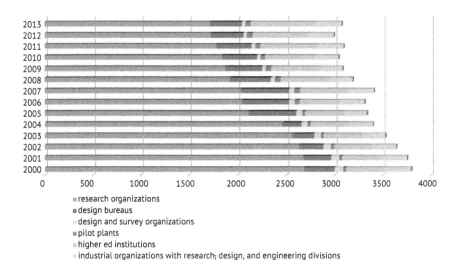

FIGURE 17. Structure of participants in scientific activities

---

7   Site of the Russian Academy of Sciences. http://ras.ru/viewnumbereddoc.aspx?id=69fa7c74-4033-4215-b908-911a87acf803&_Language=ru. (in Russ.)

A working group of the RAS (of which I am part), headed by the Deputy President of the RAS Vladimir V. Ivanov, developed a draft of this document. It includes the following requirements for a country to be one of the technological leaders of the coming decades:

- a diversity of scientific research modalities;
- a knowledge-intensive industry based on its own technology;
- education focused on training creators [tvortsov];
- business as the main investor of research and development;
- a business sector that is an active participant in societal development.

Russia needs to take on a number of tasks in order to become one of those *technological leaders*:

- modernizing of production facilities;
- supporting and creating incentives for innovative activity enterprises;
- financing R&D toward the development of new technologies;
- training highly qualified personnel of different levels: workers, scientists, teachers, and managers;
- actively developing innovation infrastructure designed to help unite science and business.

Only when the technological level of the Russian economy is on par with that of the leading countries will it be possible to meet the goals stated in this draft document.

Chapter 12

Industrial Policy as a Tool of Reindustrialization, Import Substitution[1]

12.1. Import substitution and export restructuring: The international experience and the Russian situation

Western sanctions on Russia have created the need for import substitution, a situation that we should take advantage of and use to stimulate reindustrialization (table 15). These sanctions target mostly military-industrial complex enterprises, which produce both military and civilian products, actively participate in innovative and technological industrial development, and cooperate with civilian production facilities, research laboratories, design bureaus, etc.

---

1 This chapter is based on a report by S. D. Bodrunov at the international scientific conference on the "Promotion of industrial development in the era of economic crisis," specifically from the session on "Import substitution and other reindustrialization strategies," May 14, 2015. (in Russ.)

TABLE 15. Russian companies subject to sanctions in 2014 (sample)

Company	Business profile
Kalashnikov Concern JSC	Manufacturer of automatic and sniper combat weapons, sporting and hunting weapons, machine tools and instruments
Academician A.G. Shipunov Instrument Design Bureau JSC	Developer of anti-tank missile systems, air defense systems, small arms, and grenade launchers
Military-Industrial Corporation 'Scientific-Production Association of Mechanical Engineering' JSC	Designer of rocket technologies, including ballistic and cruise missiles, satellites and manned spacecrafts
Air Defense 'Almaz-Antey' Concern JSC	A group of companies that develops and produces means of air and missile defense
Concern 'Radio-Electronic Technologies' (KRET) JSC	Management company that includes companies that develop and produce electronic warfare systems and avionics equipment
Rosneft JSC	Ranks first in both Russia and the world in oil production, and Russia's third largest producer of natural gas
Concern 'Sozvezdie' JSC	Developer and manufacturer of communication complexes
'Uralvagonzavod' Research and Production Corporation JSC	Corporation that produces railroad, construction, and military equipment, including T-90 tanks
United Shipbuilding Corporation JSC	Russia's largest shipbuilding company, about 80% of the domestic shipbuilding complex is consolidated in it
United Aircraft Corporation (OAK) JSC	Holding company that unites about 30 companies of the RF aviation industry, including: Sukhoi, Irkut, Tupolev, Yakovlev Design Bureau, MiG, etc.
RT-Stankoinstrument JSC	Holding company established for the integration of production and scientific and technological enterprises in the field of machine tool products
RT-Chemcomposite JSC	Holding company that develops and produces polymer composite materials and products

Source: http://tass.ru/ITAR-TASS website.

These sanctions disrupted the framework, built during the post-reform years, for how Russia participates in the global division of labor. As a result, sustainable development without a developed industry became much more difficult, confirming experts' fears about the risks of deindustrialization.[2]

In 2014, President Putin singled out import substitution was one of the main ways forward for Russia's economy. Speaking at the 2014 St. Petersburg Economic Forum, Putin said: "I consider it necessary to quickly explore opportunities for competitive import substitution in industry and agriculture."[3]

These are the main goals of import substitution:

- ensuring Russia's national (economic and technological) security;
- achieving technological independence in critical areas of science and technology;
- assisting in forming a trade surplus;
- creating and cultivating companies to be national leaders and conquer the global market.

Import substitution policy can also have positive ripple effects in other spheres, particularly in employment growth, and consequently, reduction of unemployment and improvement of living standards. It can activate scientific and technological progress; raise education levels; strengthen national economic and military security; raise demand for domestically produced goods (what Keynes calls "effective demand"); and expand production capacities, especially in high-tech and innovative industrial enterprises.

More and more economists, both theorists and practitioners, agree today that the priority development of high-tech material production, integrated with R&D and education, should become the basis for import substitution and export restructuring. But practice lags far behind planning. Thus, according

---

2 See, for example, R. P. Mgoian, "Financial Instruments of State Support for High-Tech Industries," *Proceedings of St. Petersburg State University of Economics* 84, no. 6 (2013): 122–125; V. A. Plotnikov, "Innovative Activity of Russian Industrial Enterprises as a Factor of Economic Security," *Bulletin of Belgorod State University; Series: History, Political Science, Economics, Informatics* 13 (2012): 5–10. I. V. Gerasimov, "Innovative development of machine building division of SC 'Rosatom' in WTO context (by the example of CJSC 'AEM-technology')," *Proceedings of St. Petersburg State Economic University* 3 (2014): 80–82; and others. (all in Russ.)

3 Website of the President of Russia, V. V. Putin, "Speech at the plenary session of St. Petersburg International Economic Forum," Verbatim record of the plenary session of the 18th St. Petersburg International Economic Forum. http://kremlin.ru/events/president/news/21080.0. (in Russ.)

to Deputy Minister of Industry and Trade Sergey Tsyb, "import substitution [. . .] is possible only if adequate spare production capacity is available."[4] But the Russian economic recession in the fourth quarter of 2014 saw the under-utilization of production capacities at 30–40 percent and over-employment in industry at 15 percent.[5] Moreover, in many strategic industries the share of import consumption exceeds 80 percent, which poses a potential threat to national security as a whole.[6]

If we *implement a consistent import substitution strategy*, we will minimize the negative effects of economic sanctions. This strategy should then become a *central element and way forward for Russian economic policy as a whole, especially industrial policy.*

Equally important is that we develop new directions for the production of exports: machines and equipment, technologies, know-how, educational services. Together with foreign countries, including Asian and Latin American countries, we could also develop long-term programs for integrating production, science, and education (i.e., PSE clusters).

Note that numerous countries have implemented strategies for economic growth via import substitution: Brazil, Argentina, Mexico, South Korea, Taiwan.[7] They used the following tools to stimulate import substitution:

- protectionist measures, in particular, state subsidized price reductions for domestic products;
- restrictions on imports of industrial products;
- investment in the modernization of industrial enterprises using state funds from the sale of import-substituting products.

In Brazil, the import substitution policy ("Plano Brasil Maior") was initially aimed not so much at limiting imports, but at stimulating exports. The program guaranteed national producers-exporters a partial tax refund and the opportunity to use a special state fund to finance exports. Additionally, Brazil created globally competitive manufacturing industries, especially in the aviation sector (Embraer), as well as in machine-building and shipbuilding.

---

4 Y. Voronina, "A cure for addiction," *Rossiiskaia Gazeta*, August 5, 2014. http://www.rg.ru/2014/08/05/zameshenie.htm. (in Russ.)

5 S. Y. Glazyev, *On External and Internal Threats to Russia's Economic Security in the Context of American Aggression: Scientific report* (Moscow: n.p., 2014). (in Russ.)

6 Voronina, "A cure for addiction."

7 See, in particular, Khoros, V. G. and V. Malysheva, eds, *The Third World: Half a Century Later* (Moscow: IMEMO RAS, 2013).

Together these factors allowed Brazil to increase its economic growth rate and become one of the most dynamic economies in the world.

South Korea also had a positive experience with its import substitution policy. The country used import substitution not as an independent growth strategy, but as a transitional policy to strengthen the national economy and create strong export potential. They called this strategy "export-oriented import substitution."

In most countries, import-substitution growth strategies have led to an increase in exports (table 16) and in the share of high value-added industry.

In Russia, *import substitution is not a de facto priority of the government's economic policy.*[8] Although exports and imports have been growing steadily since 1999, the ratio of imports to exports fell from 2.3 times in 2000 to 1.57 times in 2012. In the export structure, the share of mineral products increased from 42.5 percent in 1995 to 72 percent in 2014, while the share of machinery, equipment, and vehicles decreased from 10.2 percent in 1995 to 4.5 percent in 2014. Machinery, equipment, and transport vehicles are the main imports: their share increased from 33.6 percent in 1995 to 48.3 percent in 2014, while the share of equipment halved from 28 percent in 1995 to 14 percent in 2014.[9] And though economic modernization and reindustrialization have been on the agenda since 2008, and many enterprises have updated their fixed assets, expanded, and built new constructions, Russia has not seen the rise of numerous competitive industries, and demand for domestic products remains insufficient to stimulate production.

---

8   S. Y. Glazyev, *On External and Internal Threats to Russia's Economic Security in the Context of American Aggression: Scientific report* (Moscow, 2014). (in Russ.)

9   Official Rosstat website: http://www.gks.ru/bgd/regl/. (in Russ.)

TABLE 16. The dynamics of GDP, GDP per capita, exports and imports (2010–2012)

Country	GDP dynamics, %			GDP per capita, USD			Share of exports in GDP, %			Share of imports in GDP, %		
	2010	2011	2012	2010	2011	2012	2010	2011	2012	2010	2011	2012
Argentina	9.1	8.5	0.9	11460.38	13693.7	14679.93	17.50	17.79	15.80	15.04	16.14	14.06
Brazil	7.5	2.7	1.0	10978.26	12576.20	11319.97	10.87	11.89	12.59	11.90	12.62	14.03
Belarus	7.7	5.5	1.7	5818.85	6305.77	6721.83	54.28	81.13	81.34	67.89	83.07	76.73
Kazakhstan	7.3	7.5	5	9070.65	11357.95	12120.31	43.96	49.47	47.60	29.21	27.75	30.33
Mexico	5.1	4.0	4.0	8920.69	9802.89	9817.84	29.87	31.25	32.64	31.07	32.50	33.75
Russian Federation	4.5	4.3	3.4	10709.77	13324.29	14090.65	29.22	30.27	29.59	21.14	21.73	22.26
USA	2.5	1.8	2.8	48357.67	49854.52	51755.21	12.32	13.53	13.52	15.79	17.19	16.89
EU countries	2.0	1.6	-0.4	32381.81	34920.83	32917.26	40.19	42.90	43.18	39.32	41.90	41.41
Developing countries in Europe and Central Asia	5.9	6.2	1.8	6177.36	6852.42	6907.21	37.73	42.03	36.22	41.29	46.60	40.93
Developing countries in East Asia	9.7	8.3	7.4	3885.29	4699.64	5187.39	35.20	35.00	33.51	31.31	32.29	31.04
Developing countries in Latin America and the Caribbean	9.7	8.3	7.4	8611.928	9539.82	9404.30	22.16	23.47	23.73	22.75	24.12	25.09

Source: http://www.worldbank.org/. Website of the World Bank

Moreover, technological exchange is slowing down in Russia. The number of advanced production technologies used in the manufacturing industry is decreasing. The number of developed production technologies is growing, but for the most part these technologies, which are new for Russia, do not allow for competitiveness in foreign markets (table 17).

TABLE 17. Creation, acquisition, and use of advanced production technologies in the Russian manufacturing industry (2010–2013)

Indicator	2010	2011	2012	2013
Number of advanced manufacturing technologies developed	864	1138	1323	1429
Number of production technologies developed that are new for Russia	215	320	320	374
Number of fundamentally new advanced production technologies	16	18	16	24
Number of advanced manufacturing technologies used	135945	118021	119182	121103
Number of new technologies acquired	11832	23236	12050	9989

In one of his speeches at the State Duma of the Russian Federation, Minister of Economic Development Aleksei V. Ulukaev said that the import substitution program should develop in three directions: diversifying imports, diversifying exports, and developing new production capacities. To this list I would also add modernizing production facilities, which would enable the aforementioned diversification, and possibly increase exports of Russian products. At the same time, I would prioritize the reconstruction of Russian industry on a new technological basis—the re-industrialization of the Russian economy.

The government is first focused on the task of rapidly substituting imports in sectors that may soon become critical for the "first-order" economy: the consumer sector, health care, the provision of important social objectives. Next on the agenda is solving the problems of certain strategic industries, primarily providing them with resources and defense security. Equally important is preserving unified a communications sector: telecommunications, communications, data networks, including in the financial sector, etc. The federal budget for 2015–2017 allocates more than thirty-five billion rubles for these purposes. The Ministry of Industry and Trade is preparing an import substitution program, which will not only allocate additional funds toward this end, but also will also adopt new administrative and organizational measures, and put to use the federal contract system, and tariffs, customs, and tax regulation. The Industry Support Fund, created by the Ministry of Industry and Trade, will allocate eighteen billion rubles for these purposes over the next three years. Starting in 2015, together these various plans should ensure an annual increase in the production of Russian goods and equipment by thirty billion rubles. Though these measures should be fully supported, we should not forget the dangers of confused priorities, a lack of clarity about the volume, timeline, and evaluation of results, and of distributing money based on the principle "to each his own" [vsem sestram po ser'gam].

For an effective import substitution policy, we must restore the structure of domestic industry and recreate those basic production niches that were replaced by foreign manufacturers during the years of deindustrialization, leading us to today's problems.

Take the basis of technological independence: the machine tool industry. Today we produce twenty-five times less machine tools than in 1991, while the need for them is acute, despite the decline in industrial production, and satisfied almost entirely by imports. Other basic production sectors are also important: microelectronics, advanced oil and gas equipment (horizontal drilling, hydraulic fracturing, etc.). Financial investments here are not enough. There must be strong state support of other forms—a concentrated effort to prioritize these sectors, set up key projects, set clear goals, and make organizational decisions that will have a long-term impact. Private entrepreneurs must also be protected because modern industries are, as a rule, created by private business.

We must strengthen protectionist policies for domestic producers: create direct incentives for their technological progress, stimulate investment in the modernization of production facilities and technologies, and reasonably and gradually limit the import of industrial products. We must also change the financial circumstances of production companies: changes in the mechanisms of state aid, longer and cheaper credit, and so on. Changes in administrative practices with regard to industry and entrepreneurship in general must also take place: decriminalizing entrepreneurial activity, legislatively restricting "gray" imports, delineating the legal status of modern industrial structures like industrial parks, clusters, etc.

When reindustrialization has been discussed in the recent past, the discussion always starts with the question: where to start? But now there is no question at all about where to start. By starting with import substitution, we can restart the country's reindustrialization. This process should proceed step by step, layer by layer, from the simple to the complex. In this context, the local and global goals of reindustrialization are already clear, as are its priorities and implementation mechanisms. The Russian economy's potential is currently insufficient to support an import-substitution industrial policy. The Soviet Union, unlike Latin American countries, had a developed industrial sector, and though traces of it may still be found in Russia's economy today, it plays a much smaller part in the country's GDP than it did in the past.

12.2. How to implement reindustrialization and import substitution

Research and international practice show that successful reindustrialization, including export-oriented import substitution, requires at least two policy priorities:

1. a *supportive economic environment*: available resources, fewer administrative barriers and bureaucratic pressure, tax breaks for industrial enterprises, preferential long-term lending, better protection of investments and assets, of investors' rights and property, etc.;
2. an *active state industrial policy* aimed at the priority development of key areas of material production (primarily science-intensive high tech), as well as science and education.

An *active industrial policy* broadly implies:

- a *suitable monetary and credit policy on the part of the Central Bank*, and a *suitable fiscal policy on the part of the Ministry of Finance*, both of which would ensure the financing of industrial and agro-industrial development to the necessary extent;
- *stimulating domestic demand* for the products of industrial enterprises, including through subsidized prices and a government order system;
- *long-term measures* to attract long-term investments;
- *preserving economic openness* (with the exception of defense and civilian safety industries); developing methods of cooperation with foreign partners: technological exchange, scientific cooperation, and codeveloping advanced production technologies;
- *state support of the export* of competitive industrial products.

Successfully tackling the above tasks requires an active industrial policy, public-private partnerships (PPPs), selective protectionism, and international NGO cooperation.

We should not forget the risks involved here, the most important of which include:

1. Those "sterile" economic conditions meant to aid the development of Russian industrial enterprises—state support and lack of competition with leading foreign manufacturers in the domestic market—may make *Russian industrial enterprises less competitive.* As a result, quality management may decrease, leading to lower product quality but higher prices. For example, because Russian suppliers could not provide a competitive price-quality ratio, foreign rather than domestic components were used in the development of the Sukhoi Super-Jet 100. The production of these aircrafts is now facing difficulties because of the ongoing sanctions and the depreciation of the Russian ruble. The main way out of this predicament is through the development of domestic innovation,[10] targeted applied research and its implementation in industry, which requires the tighter integration of science and industrial production.

2. *The economy as a whole may see lower efficiency rates* if products and technologies by national manufacturers are inferior in competitiveness (price, quality, assortment) to foreign analogues. This situation is taking place in the development and production of oil and gas extraction equipment in nonstandard geological and climatic conditions. The deterioration of, for example, domestic medical technology or medicinal products may lead to a significantly lower quality of life. A policy of industrial import substitution without a competent systematic approach to its implementation (including continuous monitoring of the dynamics of industrial development) may lead to a worse economic situation overall. This is a systemic risk that is determined by the inefficiency of the institutional context.

3. *The national budget may become overburdened.* Implementing an import substitution policy as part of a reindustrialization strategy will require significant state investment. For example, the state has allocated three

---

10 A. N. Tsatsulin, "Approaches to the economic analysis of complex innovation activity," *Proceedings of St. Petersburg State Economic University* 80, no. 2 (2013): 12–21.

trillion rubles from 2011 to 2020 for a federal program to develop the military-industrial complex. If the economic situation continues to worsen and the planned budget numbers cannot be met, the government will have to choose: reduce spending on social programs or suspend funding for import substitution measures. Corruption may consequently rise. Opportunities to lobby for this or that expense over another when funds are limited may tempt state officials and state corporation representatives.

4. *The technological backwardness of Russian industry* at the global level may also present a risk. During the long process of import substitution, there is the risk that imports from economically developed countries may be replaced with affordable imports from Asia, Latin America, and the EAEU. Not only will this slow down industrial development, but it may also heighten Russia's technological lagging-behind (Russia is as many as forty to sixty years behind the developed economies of the world). In the short term, import substitution is aimed at replacing foreign products with domestic analogues. Essentially the goal is to copy foreign products and technologies that already exist on the market. And this means a permanent technological lag. We can overcome this risk by advancing domestic research, technological and design schools, and the technological base at large, which requires intensified efforts to support science and education and their integration with production.[11]

Note that political will alone, even if backed by the necessary financial resources, is not enough to implement reindustrialization via import substitution. The complex and ambitious task of revitalizing high-tech material production requires world-class science, education, and cultural production that Russians will be proud of, and foreign citizens will be drawn to.[12]

---

11 See V. A. Krasilshchikov, *Catching up with the Past Century: Russia's Development in the 20th Century from the Perspective of Global Modernization* (Moscow: Russian State Library, 2010). (in Russ.)

12 S. D. Bodrunov, "The Integration of Science, Education, Production and the New Industrialization of Russia," *Vedomosti*. 215 (November 19, 2014): 17. (in Russ.)

Chapter 13

Imperatives, Opportunities, and Challenges of Reindustrialization[1]

Today Russia is going through one of the most difficult periods of its post-Soviet history. We are facing new geopolitical and geo-economic challenges, largely unexpected for a large part of the Russian establishment and state administration. And it is in this context that Russian economists and political authorities have come face to face with the challenge of finding a new model of economic growth and, more broadly, a new economic doctrine for Russia.

There are many works devoted to the search for a new model of economic growth,[2] and most of their authors believe that it is necessary to radically renew

---

1 The chapter was based on a report from the meeting of the Scientific and Expert Council under the Chairman of the Federation Council of the Federal Assembly of the Russian Federation on March 28, 2013 and a report from the Plenum of the Russian Economic Society on December 11, 2013.

2 See S. N. Pshenichnikova, "Investments and Economic Growth in Eurasian Countries," *Proceedings of the St. Petersburg State University of Economics* 83, no. 5 (2013): 14–26; S. D. Bodrunov, R. S. Grinberg, and D. E. Sorokin, "Reindustrialization of the Russian economy: imperatives, potential, risks," *Economic Revival of Russia* 35, no. 1 (2013): 19–49; A. I. Popov and V. A. Plotnikov, "Choosing a New Model of Development and Modernization: The Basis for the Transition to the Innovation Economy," *Proceedings of St. Petersburg State Economic University* 2 (2012): 197–209; A. E. Karlik and M. A. Osipov, "The state and prospects of Russian macro-economic development in the context of the theory of economic growth taking into account the crisis phenomena," *Economic Sciences* 57 (2009): 12–18; A. I. Popov, "Neo-industrialization of the Russian economy as a condition for sustainable development,"

the existing system of economic institutions rather than make simple cosmetic changes.[3]

Reindustrialization must be at the heart of any new paradigm of Russian economic development (see ch. 7). The term "reindustrialization" is a topic of ongoing discussion in the scholarly community. The studies mentioned above use the terms "new industrialization," "new industrial development," "neo-industrialization," but despite the similarity of these concepts, each term reflects different aspects of the complex phenomenon of reindustrialization. If *industrialization* is traditionally understood as the process of transferring the economy to industrial production, the *main purpose of reindustrialization* as an economic policy is to restore the role and place of industry in the national economy as its basic component and prioritize the development of material production and, more broadly, of the real economy. This should be done on the basis of a new techno-economic paradigm, which will be achieved by tackling a set of related economic, technological, legal, and organizational tasks within the larger framework of Russia's modernization. As A. I. Amosov noted, the concept of reindustrialization "emphasizes the restoration of industry destroyed in the process of deindustrialization" of a previously industrialized economy, a process that occurred for various reasons (I will discuss the reasons in the Russian case of deindustrialization below). On the other hand, the term "innovative reindustrialization" emphasizes the innovative side of this process of reindustrialization, and the term "new industrial development" emphasizes the developmental process itself.

Though I am certainly taking into account the peculiarities of the above terms, I will stick to the term "reindustrialization" as an umbrella term that encapsulates both the positive development of this process and its orientation toward innovation. At the same time, we must understand that reindustrialization is only one means of achieving the innovative modernization of the Russian economy and ensuring the dynamic socioeconomic development of the country. That is, reindustrialization must measure up to the goal of realizing the

---

Proceedings of St. Petersburg State University of Economics 3 (2014): 7–12; . Tatarkin, "Sobering up after the market euphoria is delayed, but still happens," *"Gorod 812"* 32 (2014): 21–23.

3   S. D. Bodrunov, "What is to be done? Imperatives, Opportunities and Problems of Reindustrialization," in *Collection of the Scientific and Expert Council under the Chairman of the Federation Council of the Russian Federation "Re-industrialization: Opportunities and Limitations,"* ed. S. D. Bodrunov and R. S. Grinberg (Moscow, 2013); S. D. Bodrunov, "Reindustrialization of the Russian economy: opportunities and limitations," *Scientific Proceedings of the Free Economic Society of Russia* 1 (2014): 15–46. (all in Russ.)

goal of socioeconomic development in its shape, content, stages, mechanisms, etc. and become an indispensable tool of this process.

Different approaches exist to the concept of new industrialization. I will give two examples of definitions that reflect the most popular approaches.

For President Putin, industrialization means "the intensive development of Russian industry through large investments in the development (including foreign purchases) of new technologies and equipment, [which can happen] through the reorganization of the recipient of these investments—industry as a whole and its basic elements and subjects."

At the same time, according to Academician Evgeniy M. Primakov, new industrialization is primarily defined by: the diversification of the *economic structure* toward an increase in the *manufacturing industry's share* in the economy; *human resources* with the necessary *qualifications* to make this happen; the *modernization of the financial system* in order to support reindustrialization; the development of channels of *cooperation between science and production*; and the *system-wide import of high-tech*, a) through foreign purchases, and b) through incentivizing investment in Russian industry *under the condition of technology transfer*.

Reindustrialization means tackling several, related major challenges:

1. restoring or modernizing production capacities that were lost or became obsolete in the process of deindustrialization;
2. implementing innovative industrialization programs and projects;
3. transitioning to a new stage of industrial development, taking into account the peculiarities and technological challenges of industry in the coming decades. Reindustrialization as a way out of recession and as the basis of a new model of economic growth is a global trend.

The United States seems to understand how the current crisis came about and the dangers inherent in the seventeenth-century Dutch scenario. Now they have embarked on a reindustrialization plan based on two basic ideas: a) implementing an energy strategy to make energy resources more available and affordable (primarily for industry), and b) encouraging the "onshoring" of manufacturing industries.

To close the gap with the US and ensure a rapid transition to the fifth techno-economic paradigms (with flowering elements of the sixth), Russia must tackle two similar challenges as part of a new industrialization: a) making the resource base relatively cheaper, and b) upgrading manufacturing facilities and modernizing industry as a whole.

The Decree of the President of the Russian Federation of May 7, 2012, No. 596, "On the long-term state economic policy," defines the targets and tasks of reindustrialization. It is particularly important to set targets to address two interrelated key problems: increasing financing for reindustrialization (no less than 25 percent of GDP by 2015 and up to 27 percent by 2018); creating and modernizing twenty-five million high-performance jobs by 2020.

13.1. Prospects and resources for Russia's reindustrialization

There is no doubt that the scale of the challenge before us is impressive. Taking into account all of the above, can a policy of reindustrialization be successful in Russia? Glazyev points out that a crisis in mature industries gives a better chance to those lagging behind to catch up. In a crisis, the capitalization of firms with advanced technologies decreases, and the option of acquiring these technologies, for example, by acquiring a controlling stake, buying out technologies, etc. becomes more realistic. Moreover, as leaders in high-tech equipment develop fewer needs for said equipment, it becomes more accessible to countries that are catching up. For example, in the 1970s, South Korea actively purchased equipment and technology from Japan's shipbuilding industry when it needed to reduce its overcapacity.

In order to successfully make a technological leap forward, lagging countries need to correctly assess any prospective developmental directions and, in anticipation, implement new technologies in production at the beginning of a new techno-economic paradigm. As already noted, the current stage of economic development is characterized by a "*change of the dominant techno-economic paradigm.*"[4] It is during this period that new technological trajectories and new economic leaders are made.

Russia still has a chance to join the technological leaders of the world, despite its current problems. We must correctly calculate out capabilities, take into account our limitations and possible risks. The first question here is whether Russia has the *financial resources* necessary for reindustrialization. If, according to the Presidential Decree No. 596 of May 7, 2012, investment in

---

4 "Strategy for the economic development of Russia. Based on the materials from the All-Russian discussion held by the State Duma Committee on Economic Policy and Entrepreneurship, the Department of Economics of RAS, the Russian Trade and Financial Union, and the Russian Economic Journal. Reports at the extended sessions of the State Duma Committee on economic policy and entrepreneurship," *Russian Economic Journal* 7 (2000). (in Russ.)

reindustrialization should reach 25 percent of the GDP in 2015 (and 27 percent in 2017), then if we take into account the Ministry of Economic Development forecast in 2015, investment in the real economy should be increased to twenty trillion rubles. For comparison, under the state program "Development of Industry and Improving Its Competitiveness," approved by the government at the end of December 2012, the average annual amount of financing up to 2020 is about four hundred forty billion rubles. Of course, the state program does not include all the investment projects necessary for industrialization, and the Presidential Decree did not refer exclusively to state investments. And yet the figures still show that we need to considerably increase the amount of funding for investment projects and programs related to industrialization, the modernization of manufacturing, and other basic sectors of the real economy. According to the calculations, such a large-scale increase in investment requires a significant reorientation of both corporate and state monetary and credit resources.

We must formulate a monetary policy that is up to the task of reindustrialization. The current level of monetization of Russia's economy (below 50 percent of the GDP) and credit saturation (only 35 percent of the GDP) does not allow for sustainable economic growth. If the cost of market credit resources for key industries is higher than the rate of profitability, lending for industrial development is practically impossible. We can achieve a significant effect by softening monetary, budgetary, and fiscal policy, reducing the cost of borrowed capital for industry, implementing measures to reverse the trend of massive capital exports from Russia, etc.

It is necessary to expand the credit system for financing structure-forming modernization programs and select sectors of the national economy. Toward this end, we can create an index fund with household deposits in Sberbank before 1991, which have depreciated due to inflation. But we must listen to the Russian people and accordingly limit the use of this index fund to:

1. replenish pension capital;
2. build mortgage capital to finance social mortgages (for those who need to improve their housing conditions);
3. acquire shares in a special state investment fund for the modernization of the national economy.

At the same time, using credit to finance priority investment projects implies the restriction of "financial freedom" in order to reduce the risks of financial destabilization. This will require, firstly, significantly higher quality investment projects and, secondly, more transparency about the flow of capital in general and foreign exchange funds specifically.

We must also abandon our battle to bring inflation to 3–4 percent, which is supposed to attract investment (including in technology sectors) by reducing the rate on loans. But this battle with inflation will only cause us to lose sight of our investment objectives, and losing the domestic market will only increase inflation.

A policy to reduce the gap between export and import capital can also provide more financial resources for reindustrialization.

When considering how to finance reindustrialization and which sources to use, the prospect of using financial reserves is controversial. The Reserve Fund and, to a lesser extent, the National Welfare fund are seen as our only reserves in case of crisis, though I argue that this approach is incorrect. On the basis of this debatable approach, the budget will see the expansion of the Reserve Fund from 2.8 trillion by the end of 2012 to 4.7 trillion by the end of 2015. In other words, two trillion rubles will be removed from economic turnover and will not contribute in any way to innovative modernization. The assumption is that the National Welfare Fund will also increase to 2.8 trillion rubles. There are also the reserves of the Deposit Insurance Agency, the Housing Construction Financing Agency and, finally, the Pension Fund (about 2.5 trillion rubles). In total, the government's financial reserves amount to about twenty trillion rubles. According to available estimates, this is three to four times more than was spent on overcoming the crisis of 2009.

The continued accumulation of excessive financial reserves seems inadvisable and, indeed, more dangerous for the economy than insufficient reserves. An abundance of financial reserves only tempers the consequences of the monetary crisis to an extent. Real and reliable protection against the crisis comes only in the form of economic modernization.

We should consider expanding lending opportunities for reindustrialization projects by transferring part of the state's international reserves to the Development Bank. This seems a rational solution, as they do not bring much profit as it stands (the highest return in 2008 was 4 percent in dollar assets and 5.57 percent in euro assets; the lowest in 2012 was 0.33 percent in dollar assets and 1.09 percent in euro assets).

There will certainly be objections to the plan I have laid out here. But allow me to note that the *risks of continued deficits are negligible compared to the risks of a primitive production structure, dilapidated infrastructure, technological backwardness, mass poverty, housing shortages, and other problems for which there is insufficient money.*

Reducing the level and changing the structure of tax exemptions will result in a massive reserve for financing reindustrialization. According to the Ministry of Finance, tax incentives cost the budget 1.8 trillion rubles a year (almost 3 percent of the GDP in 2014); almost 95 percent of them are income, value added, severance, and corporate property tax benefits. At the same time, there are no significant benefits for industry. At the local level, industry is being cut down everywhere. For example, the St. Petersburg City Council has cancelled property tax benefits for industrial enterprises. These benefits had been granted after a new cadastral land value, which exceeded the market value, became the basis for the tax. On the other hand, those who do not need benefits are the ones who receive them: trade, oil, and gas, etc. Reestablishing order in this sphere and redistributing privileges toward industry will create one of the most important financial reserves for reindustrialization.

Russia has one of the lowest nominal rates of profit tax; in Europe, this number is around 40–45 percent. Their real rate of profit tax is comparable to Russia's: 20–22 percent. Unlike Russia, however, European countries have an effective system for the targeted use of funds allocated for investment and innovation from tax-exempt profits. We should restore tax incentives for investors focused on modernization, despite arguments to the contrary about the potential abuse of differential incentives.

Meanwhile, Russia should be actively participating in international financial organizations, but without any illusions about actually influencing their projects and decisions. It is a given that those organizations will primarily represent the interests of the leading economic powers, which are hardly interested in turning Russia into an independent center of economic power.

It is important that the government take out foreign loans, because it can do so on better terms than private businesses can. International financial institutions, state institutions of other states, as well as large international private financial companies are all good options for creditors. The borrowed funds can go in special investment funds rather than the budget itself. While the budget finances ongoing government expenditures, special investment funds spend their funds on lending through special development institutions, like specialized banks or financial companies. In Japan and South Korea, state cofinancing of such projects was provided through the state Development Bank.

However, foreign direct investment (FDI) is not, and cannot be, the main source of Russia's large-scale modernization. Recall that in 2008 Russia received 27.03 billion dollars in FDI, less than 10 percent of the total volume of investment in fixed assets, of which only 4.5 percent went to the high-tech sector of Russian industry, 12 percent went to mining industry, and 23 percent to wholesale and retail trade.

In general, it is difficult to imagine why foreign investors should increase their investment in the least attractive sectors of the national economy when domestic business avoids doing so. We must make the manufacturing sector more attractive for foreign investors, first and foremost in mechanical engineering, by lowering domestic prices for energy, metal, and plastics, which account for 70 percent of costs in the automotive, construction, and agricultural equipment manufacturing industries. However, as a result of free pricing [svobodnoe tsenoobrazovanie], we have already cost our cost advantage in metals, and matching domestic prices for gas and electricity to global prices will not lead to beneficial results. Governmental investments play the decisive factor in attracting corporate capital. Foreign investors are unlikely to invest in the Russian economy if the state does not do so.

We should use international economic institutions as platforms to delineate our vision of how to transform the global financial system and international trade in goods and services. At the same time, we must avoid making commitments that may hinder the modernization of the Russian economy.

Transforming Moscow into an international financial center deserves special attention. The global financial system produces crisis after crisis, and for a new financial center to become a barrier against, rather than a conductor of, these crises, we must develop regulations to encourage real investors instead of speculators.

Many economists believe that Russia has the necessary tools to stimulate cash flow for the country's reindustrialization and modernization. Academician Viktor V. Ivanter argues that the state's and energy sector's reserves, as well as expanding credit, can be used as financial resources for investment and development.[5] He correctly suggests that the very fact of using these reserves will lead to the return of substantial capital to Russia, which boosts investment.

If we accept the proposals I have detailed here, which consolidate the opinions of many Russian economists on the topic of reindustrialization, then the financial and investment opportunities to implement reindustrialization are sufficiently clear.

---

5   V. V. Ivanter, "The new economic policy," *Russia's Economic Revival* 22, no. 2 (2013): 7–12. (in Russ.)

13.2. Reindustrialization: how to overcome systemic imbalances

There are large structural imbalances in the Russian economy that play a significant part in the country's irrational direction of cash flow and weak position in the world economy. As a result, Russia's socioeconomic development largely depends on the state of the global market for energy commodities. The "Main Guidelines of the Government up to 2018" state: "The non-oil-and-gas deficit now stands at 10.5 percent of the gross domestic product, while its safe level is estimated to be half that. At the same time, its reduction will curb public demand and contribute to a slowdown in economic growth."

Due to its lagging mechanical engineering industries, Russia, one of the world's leading producers of energy resources, is far from being a leader in the production of advanced technological equipment for prospecting, producing, and processing oil and gas resources and other raw goods. Its fuel and energy complex evinces low levels of technological and economic performance indicators when compared to leading economies.

Mineral products made up 53.8 percent of exports in 2000, machinery, equipment, and transport vehicles—8.8 percent; in 2005, 64.8 percent and 5.6 percent respectively; in 2011—71.1 percent and 5 percent. At this rate, Russia is predicted to become an energy appendage of the global economy, but only one part of Russian territory participates in the energy economy. Due to a number of geopolitical and economic circumstances, the Russian Federation *may turn* from a subject into an *object* of global relations, with all the corresponding consequences for its statehood.[6]

To avoid this fate, Russia needs a comprehensive industrial policy to restore lagging industries through technological development and make them technologically independent. *The essence of the task before us lies in the development of domestic industrial-technological chains for the production of both industrial and consumer products.*

Despite the obvious losses in scientific and technological potential, Russia is still able to overcome its economic deterioration and tackle the task of modernization head on. On this topic, I cannot agree with the widespread opinion that our country is so far behind others in mechanical engineering

---

6   "Following this scenario," noted Putin in his speech at an extended session of the State Council "On Russia's development strategy up to 2020" (February 8, 2008), "we cannot ensure neither the security of the country, nor its normal development; I say without exaggeration that we'll endanger its very existence." Presidential Website. http://kremlin.ru/events/president/transcripts/24825). (in Russ.)

that it is easier (cheaper and faster) to buy products abroad than to develop technologies and produce domestic products of a similar or even higher quality. Of the fifty to fifty-five macro-technologies that form the basis of the fifth techno-economic paradigm, Russia has seventeen (including nuclear, space, and aviation technologies, some nano- and biotechnologies, some oil and gas production and refining technologies, and some types of weapons, chemical, energy, and transport machinery).[7]

In assessing the challenges ahead, we should look back at the experience of the twentieth century, which demonstrates the possibility of launching massive projects even with a battered engineering base.[8]

The examples of Japan and Germany in the 1950s and China in the 1980s–1990s are also instructive. These countries were able to restore (or in China's case, establish) their own mechanical engineering industries fairly quickly and become global leaders (or in China's case, very important) in industry.

The geopolitical position of a country predetermines the self-sufficiency of many industries, even if it is more economically advantageous to rely on the international division of labor. The priority of Russia's reindustrialization policy should be to create a core of self-development: a set of industries that produce tools to create high-tech equipment for other key industries vis a vis economic security. It is no less important that such productions are able to reproduce themselves. The examples of the US, Japan, and Germany, where these industries are import-independent, demonstrate as much. And countries aspiring to be economic leaders are following the same path.

For this reason, we should support the State Program for Industrial Development, which states that the priority of the machine tool industry's development is creating "import-substituting resources for machine building, which include dual-use technologies, and are most in demand by strategic organizations of the mechanical engineering and defense-industrial complexes." Such a complex is *necessary* to maintain armed forces equipped with weapons systems capable of protecting Russia's geopolitical and economic interests. Here

---

7 This does not mean abandoning the use of imports. It is necessary to overcome this "hopeless backwardness" and to build a competent foreign economic policy that takes into account all aspects of this problem.

8 It is not a question of replicating this experience in the modern context, but of the fundamental solvability of the task.

we cannot rely on imports. The task at hand requires the development of our own production base.[9]

The sub-program for the machine tool industry states that, "the direct participation of state corporations, joint-stock companies with state participation, and other legal entities (public and scientific organizations, as well as state nonbudgetary funds), is not provided for." *In light of the above,* this position is cause for concern. The program also suggests that the domestic machine tool industry's share in the domestic market is sufficient, which is also doubtful. For example, metal-cutting machines is expected to double by 2020 (in comparison with 2011) but will amount only to 12 percent. Practically no growth is planned for forge-pressing machines: 6.7 percent in 2011, and 7 percent in 2020.[10]

13.3. We need a breakthrough in innovation

Russia needs a real breakthrough to modernize its industrial material base. A sharp increase in innovation is critical. We can gauge the success of Russia's economic and technological modernization, for example, by the share of innovative enterprises in the economy and the volume of innovative products (fig. 18). The Strategy for the Innovative Development of Russia up to 2020 is aimed precisely at their growth, and the goal is to catch up to the economic leaders in those sectors of the economy where there may be competitive advantages. According to the document's target goals, the share of industrial enterprises implementing innovations should increase four to five times by 2020 (as compared to 2010), the share of innovative products in the total volume of industrial output should increase by five to seven times, and the share of Russian high-tech products in the total volume of global exports should increase by eight times.

---

9 This is evident in the information cited in the mass media about denying imports on CNC systems for 5-axis parts processing. US, EU, and Japanese import contracts with Russia stipulate a ban on the unauthorized use and transfer of knowledge-intensive machining equipment as a prerequisite for licensing exports of dual-use technologies (e.g., the machinery must be equipped with GPS location control sensors or mandatory Internet connections). It is thus clear why S. Ivanov, as the First Deputy Chairman of the Government, at a meeting on the problem of domestic machine-tool manufacture (in Ivanovo in July 2007) noted that the "provision of the Russian machine-building industry with domestic machine-tools of the most knowledge-intensive categories is a matter of national security."

10 According to published expert estimates, approximately 70 percent of the equipment produced by Russian machine tool factories consists of imported units and parts.

It is worth mentioning that similar plans were outlined over the past decade: the Guidelines of the Long-Term Socio-Economic Development of the Russian Federation, which was developed by the Ministry of Economic Development and Trade in 2000 and covered the period up to 2010. The second section of this document was devoted to the modernization of the economy and regarded the innovativeness of economic development (which was to become the standard between by 2007–2010) as the deciding factor of modernization.

Though the project was never adopted due to a variety of reasons, all the subsequent three-year plans adopted over the following decade set the same objectives: the Basic Policy Guidelines of the Russian Federation for the Development of the Innovation System to 2010 (adopted in 2005); and the Strategy for the Development of Science and Innovation in the Russian Federation to 2015 (adopted in 2006).

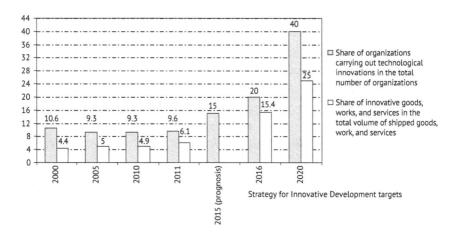

FIGURE 18. The dynamics of innovation in industry

But just how realistic is the strategy's planned leap in innovation? To answer this question, it is necessary to identify the reasons why past measures have not yielded results.

The state must actively support investment in innovation, but this is *not enough* to build an effective industrial policy. There are limits to the state's ability to modernize the economy. Both the Russian and foreign experience show that the state, if it concentrates its resources in specific areas, can provide for targeted breakthroughs in innovation, particularly in sectors like space, nuclear, aviation, and rocket production. But it is the state of the economy as a whole, not of individual industries, no matter how big and important, that guarantees innovative economic growth. And the economy as a whole must develop primarily through the wide use of technical, technological, organizational, managerial innovations, and the latest scientific knowledge in the relevant fields. This knowledge may be produced in fields where the state is actively involved, too. But the state itself is not able to provide for all these developments due to the limitations inherent in centralized decision-making on the economy.

Only if a sufficiently significant number of entrepreneurs takes up the task of technological innovation will modernization be possible. In Russia, however, neither the state nor big business is doing enough work to stimulate demand for innovation. Though the Russian economy and leading economies spend a similar amount of state funds (in percent of GDP) on research and development, Russian entrepreneurs are spending much less than their foreign counterparts. As a result, on the whole Russia allocates significantly less funds for R&D (table 18).

Barriers to innovative development in the Russian economy exist on both the macro and micro levels. Problems at the macro level include: brain drain of scientific personnel; low level of IP protection; high cost of credit; imbalanced distribution of state resources (corruption, kickbacks, etc.); insufficient cooperation between the state and the private sphere in funding projects, etc. These problems are widely known.

TABLE 18. Knowledge-intensity and scientific output of some national economies in 2004

Country	GDP per person employed, thousand dollars	Share of spending on R&D in GDP, %	Current competitive capacity index	Share of high-tech products in exports, %	Share in global exports of high-tech equipment, %
USA	73.1	2.64	2*	28.2	16.3
China	7.2	1.0	46	16.7	4.6
Germany	56.0	2.50	13**	15.3	4.8
France	56.5	2.20	27	19.4	3.4
Russia	18.0	1.24	70	3.1	0.2

* In 2006 – 6th place
** In 2006 - 8th place

Economists have paid less attention to problems at the micro level, at the level of industrial enterprises. Unlike many of my colleagues, who consider problems at this level to be insignificant, I believe that even if we create an ideal environment at the macro level, we cannot boost innovative industrial development without effective, innovation-minded managers and executives; without companies with experience in innovation, a developed management system, and the appropriate infrastructure, etc.

Note that there are also problems at the national level: sub-optimal and underdeveloped infrastructure for innovation, technological transfer, and IP management. Comparing Russia's situation with China's in this regard is particularly instructive (table 19).

China's success is largely due to its strategy "Toward an innovative economy through the intellectual property market," which is rigidly managed by the state through a centralized system of IP committees that goes down to the municipal level. This system helps reduce administrative barriers in developing the national IP market. Kazakhstan has implemented a similar strategy. Its Intellectual Property Committee, housed in the Ministry of Justice, has taken over all IP issues. This committee also has subdivisions down to the municipal level (table 20).

TABLE 19. Intellectual property (IP) management

China	Russia
"Towards an Innovation Economy via the Intellectual Property Market" strategy (adopted in the mid-1990s)	Work began on creating IP management mechanisms (2010)
System of government: unified - intellectual property committees (vertical - from Beijing to the district center)	No single government body for management, and no unified policy; management at the federal level - more than 20 ministries and departments; in some regions IP management issues are in the jurisdiction of "economic," "industrial," and/or "scientific" committees/departments
Number of IPs (per year): up to 30 thousand patents per municipality	Number of Ips (per year): 44.6 thousand patents (in 2011) for the whole RF

TABLE 20. State management of intellectual property in the CIS*

CIS country	Governmental agency
CIS	Interstate Council on the Issues of Legal Protection and Enforcement of IP (since 14.08.2011) - all OIP, IP Council under the EurAsEC Integration Committee
Russian Federation	Rospatent plus 20 federal agencies (27.03.2013 - MES supported the project to create a single IP Ministry). Government Commission on Economic Development and Integration (IP sub-commission)
Republic of Kazakhstan	Committee on Intellectual Property Rights under the Ministry of Justice of the Republic of Kazakhstan - all IPR, structures up to the municipality, Commission on Protection of OIP Rights
Republic of Armenia	IP Agency (since 2002) - all IPs, IAC on combating violations in the realm of IP (2009)
Republic of Azerbaijan	Copyright agency, State Committee for Standardization, Metrology and Patents
Republic of Belarus	National IP Center at the SCST (since 2004) - all IPs; Interdepartmental NMS on IP education (since 2005); Commission on Protection of Rights and Combating Violations in the Sphere of IP at the Council of Ministers of the Republic of Belarus
Kyrgyz Republic	State Service for IP and Innovation under the Government of the Kyrgyz Republic - all OIP, IAC to combat violations in the realm of IP, State IP Fund
Republic of Moldova	State IP Agency under the Government of the Republic of Moldova
Republic of Tajikistan	National Patent Information Center (NPIC) at the Ministry of Economic Development and Trade
Turkmenistan	Patent Office under the Ministry of Economy and Development (1.03.2013 - Decree of the Government on establishment of the State IP Service - all OIP)
Republic of Uzbekistan	IP Agency (since 2011) under the Cabinet of Ministers of RU - all OIP, Republican Commission to Combat Anti-counterfeit trade
Ukraine	State IP Service under the Ministry of Education, Science, Youth and Sports - all OIP, Coordination Council on combating IP infringements, IP Research Institute of the National Academy of Legal Sciences of Ukraine

*Data: RNIIS, Moscow

Entrepreneurial innovation does not only depend on a robust and well-functioning national innovation system with all its corresponding institutions. What drives an entrepreneur to modernize his business? Economics has long known the answer to this question: *competition*.[11] Innovation is one of the most effective tools of competition, though it can be very expensive to achieve. For an entrepreneur to seriously consider new techniques and technologies, the cost of their implementation must be lower than the cost of labor. The cost of technologically upgrading existing production is not economically feasible with cheap labor.[12]

We must also take into account the scale of poverty in Russia today. As table 21 demonstrates, the share of the population earning an income below the poverty wage decreased by 2.5 times from 1992 to 2011. The poverty wage itself decreased from 50 percent to 30 percent of the average per capita income. Accordingly, if in 1992–2000 people who earned less than 50 percent of the average income per capita were classified as poor, today those who earn less than 30 percent of the average income per capita are classified as poor. The share of those who earn less than 50 percent of the average income per capita has not changed since 2000 and amounts to nearly 30 percent of the population. Over 70 percent of the poor were employed in the economy in 2011; about 10 percent were pensioners. Moreover, the cheapest labor force is employed in those industries responsible for economic modernization (table 22). As long as this situation persists, it is difficult to expect entrepreneurial interest in innovation.

---

11 "The capitalist who applies the improved method of production, appropriates to surplus labor a greater portion of the working day, than the other capitalists in the same trade. [. . .] This same law, acting as a coercive law of competition, forces his competitors to adopt the new method." Karl Marx, *Capital*, Vol. 1(Moscow: Progress Publishers, 1977), 223. Marx refers to the 1720 edition of "The Advantages of East-Indian Trade to England": "any invention, tool, or machine, which allows one to use fewer hands and, consequently, to produce more cheaply, makes others compete, either to use the same invention, tool, or machine, or to invent something similar, so that all are on an equal footing and no one can sell more cheaply than his neighbor." *The Advantages of East-Indian Trade to England* (London: J. Roberts, 1720), 67.

12 The first Russian political economist I. T. Pososhkov noted this fact. In a manuscript intended for Peter I (1724), he noted that "not giving full nutrition for the Russian people's desire and diligence for craftsmanship suppresses and does not allow good art to multiply." I. T. Pososhkov, *Book on scarcity and wealth* (Moscow: "Economics Newspaper" Publishing House, 2001), 248. Note that "good art" at the time meant craft-industrial activity, i.e., in modern parlance, low income did not stimulate modernization.

TABLE 21. Indicators of poverty

Year	1992	1998	2000	2010	2011
Share of population with income below the poverty line, %	33.5	23.4	29.0	12.5	12.7
Poverty threshold, % to average per capita cash income	47.2	48.8	53.0	30.7	30.8
Share of population with income less than 1/2 of the average per capita cash income	26.5	~32	~29	~29	~29

Note: the average per capita income in 2011 was 20.702.7 roubles/month.

Cheap labor is not the only thing standing in the way of entrepreneurial interest in innovation. The fact is that innovations are a risky means of competition, something that both economists[13] and businessmen[14] know. It is no surprise that innovative entrepreneurial development requires the wide distribution of derivatives, which insure against investment risks. Obviously, an investor is unlikely to invest his own funds directly into innovations given their well-known feasibility statistics.[15] If cheaper and more reliable means of competition are available, it only makes sense that an entrepreneur would choose those over innovative means.

---

13 "The far greater cost of operating an establishment based on a new invention as compared to later establishments arising *ex suis ossibus*. This is so very true that the trail-blazers generally go bankrupt, and only those who later buy the buildings, machinery, etc., at a cheaper price, make money out of it." Karl Marx, *Capital*, vol. 3, 74.

14 As Victoria Livshits, founder of Grid Dynamics (Silicon Valley, US), points out, in the US "there is a statistic that out of ten good initiatives one will become very successful. Two will survive and seven will go bankrupt. And ten projects didn't just come from the street, they were the best of the best." Quoted from E. Bilevskaia, "The Kremlin will assess risks," *Novaia Gazeta*, August 11, 2010. (in Russ.)

15 Another issue is that these same financial instruments, "penetrating" into other areas, were the catalyst of the latest financial and economic crisis.

TABLE 22. Average monthly accrued nominal wages by type of economic activity, % of the average for the Russian Federation

Years	1995	2000	2005	2011
Average monthly wage, roubles	472.4	2223.4	8554.9	23.369.2
By type of activity:				
Extraction of energy resources	2.6 times	3.1 times	2.7 times	220.8
Financial activities	1.5 times	2.3 times	2.6 times	238.7
Manufacture of machinery and equipment	80.3	88.8	97.9	97.5
Production of electrical, electronic, and optical equipment	76.0	90.1	96.1	100.0

13.4. The cadres of reindustrialization

One of the imperatives of reindustrialization is investment in human capital and an active human resources policy. There is a plan to create and modernize twenty-five million high-performance jobs by 2020. Let us consider two important aspects of this problem:

- the professional qualifications and socio-demographic background of the personnel involved in industry; opportunities for their retraining and professional development;
- the problems and prospects of training new personnel for industry.

Specialists, especially those of working age, continue to leave the industrial sector to this day. The average number of employees in the Russian economy decreased from 1990 to 2009 by eight million people; in industry, this number decreased by 9.5 million people. Mechanical engineering industries suffered most of all, with nine to ten million people employed in 1990 and less than three million at present. Thus, the number of those employed in mechanical engineering as a whole decreased by about seven million people, including the number of production personnel, which decreased by 2.5 times; in certain types of mechanical engineering, there was an even worse decline (Table 23).

TABLE 23. Decrease in industrial production personnel (IPP) in industry and mechanical engineering

Type of activity	1990	1995	2004	Decrease in the number of SPTs, times
All industry, million people	21.0	16.0	11.9	1.8
Engineering, million people	8.0	4.9	3.2	2.5
Including by type, thousand people:				
• diesel engineering	68	40	21	3.2
• mining and mining equipment	75	49	31	2.4
• materials handling	86	70	40	2.2
• railroad	153	114	85	1.8
• for the electrical industry	545	346	252	2.2
• chemical and petroleum	280	191	241	1.2
• for the machine tool and instrument industry	279	169	88	3.2
• instrumentation	748	388	170	4.4
• for the automotive industry	814	706	566	1.4
• ball-bearing	113	75	47	2.4
• tractor and agricultural equipment	512	280	86	6.0
• road construction, and utilities	163	105	87	1.9
• for light industry, food and household appliances	198	139	73	2.7

This results in older personnel and more and more unfilled vacancies. Over the entire post-Soviet period, the number of employees has grown only in the extractive industries, energy industry, and iron and steel industry, while the number of production personnel in mechanical engineering has shrunk drastically. Over the reforms years (1990–2012), the number of people employed in mechanical engineering decreased by almost 90 percent: by August 2012, 851 thousand people remained in these enterprises, while in 1990 there were eight million people. Even relatively successful enterprises face the problem of aging of personnel. There is a demographic gap at play here: we lack in a qualified and reliable core of middle-aged workers. The core has shifted to older workers, who are left to train young workers as much as possible.

Less successful companies with low competitiveness on the labor market are experiencing severe staffing shortages.

The labor shortage has lately been exacerbated by layoffs due to economic crisis, industrial restructuring, and the introduction of technologically automated labor. It is no coincidence that the Strategy of Industrial Development in Mechanical Engineering highlights "the risks inherent in the discrepancy between personnel qualifications and the necessary qualifications for the program's implementation, and in the actual absence of a qualified labor force in industrial enterprises."

Meanwhile, reindustrialization requires that we provide industry with qualified personnel.

We must increase the number of people employed in microelectronics, modern machine tool construction, and other industries working toward the production of new types and models of technical equipment. To ensure the development of high-tech operations, six to seven million new high-tech jobs need to be created in the mechanical engineering industry as a whole. Additionally, the share of spending on R&D should be increased to 2.5–3 percent of the GDP, which will provide design, engineering, and other such organizations with more than a million new jobs.

In total, seven to eight million new jobs should be created in mechanical engineering and R&D, and another seventeen to eighteen million new jobs should be created in industries that use the products of the former two industries as they transition to new technologies. The fact remains, however, that a lack in human resources is holding back the technological modernization of Russian industry.

We must address the following problems that are holding us back in restoring our machine-building and metalworking industries:

- discrepancies between the interests of employers, employees, and the state in modernization;
- the loss of personnel of working age, the aging workforce, and the difficulty of retraining it;
- the decline in young people's motivation to work in industrial production;
- low wages in existing production; underestimating its complexity as it transitions to new technologies;
- the inconsistency in extra pay for employees working in new capacities; low compensation levels for nonstandard working conditions;

- the lack of training for specialists to work with new equipment in industrial production;
- the breakdown in the training and retraining system for specialists, enterprises, and higher-ed instructors;
- when developing training programs, we must take into account the radical newness of production technologies in advanced countries.

It is impossible to provide industrial enterprises with specialists without restoring an adequate personnel training system, one that includes postgraduate training and technological know-how. We must also create a system to retrain university instructors with the participation of industrial specialists well trained in new technologies and products.

The HR departments of industrial enterprises report that the education system does not provide an adequate number of specialists for their needs. If the workers that they hire have no experience in a similar industry, they need to be retrained, or retrain themselves. Nevertheless, the spread of universal higher education has partially compensated for the failures of the lower school system and has created a good basis for mastering the modern workplace.

In any case, the success of reindustrialization will be largely determined by the quality of both state and corporate personnel policy. Consequently, financial methods of state regulation should be combined with entrepreneurial costs for specialist training and retraining. And though employers are dissatisfied with state efforts in personnel training, they have not been very active themselves in training workers. According to Rosstat, the share of expenditures on in-house training in total labor costs over the past two decades has remained at a catastrophically low level: 0.3–0.4 percent. According to PriceWaterhouseCoopers' annual analysis of personnel management efficiency, which looks only at the large and successful companies that make up the most prosperous segment of the Russian labor market, Russian in-house training costs are about half as high as they are in the EU.

The increasing imbalance between the results of professional education and the needs of industrial enterprises is forcing employers to take action. Two initiatives exist toward this end: that of the Russian Union of Industrialists and Entrepreneurs (RSPP) and that of Business Russia (Delovaya Rossiya). In the context of these initiatives, industrial enterprises are ready to cooperate with the state in reforming this system at all levels: from developing educational and professional standards, to providing universities with additional funding, equipping classrooms, laboratories, and workshops, developing corporate methods of modular training, used to fine-tune the skills of university graduates in the workplace, and personally participating in the educational process. It is clear that we must develop a public-private partnership in training personnel capable of reindustrializing the Russian economy.

The modern technological base requires not just *a highly qualified worker, but a creative worker.* Such workers demand a high quality of life, the satisfaction of which implies the vibrant improvement of education, culture, health care, and material conditions at large. In this context, the calls to "tighten the belt" for the benefit of the next generation are inappropriate: in such conditions, workers can be *neither a source nor a conduit for innovation.*

Without industrial development that ensures the reproduction of national human potential adequate to the tasks of new industrial development, economic and sociopolitical imbalances are inevitable, leading to economic stagnation and social conflict.

13.5. A focus on technological priorities

Now that there is a growing understanding of the need for broad economic modernization as the basis for sustainable growth, our inability to launch this process of modernization is becoming more and more evident. The domestic economy has found itself in a structural-institutional trap: it has failed to effectively respond to rising domestic demand by increasing investment. A lack of goal setting in economic policy led us here. Without a holistic vision of Russia's economic prospects before us, we have failed to launch the necessary modernization of its main sectors.

Delineating an effective reindustrialization policy implies three tasks: 1—identifying priorities; 2—establishing algorithms for their implementation; 3—concentrating resources in priority areas to ensure the achievement of our objectives.

Determining the priorities of reindustrialization requires that specialists from different branches of knowledge work together. In recent years, these priorities have changed several times (table 24).

TABLE 24. Changes in the priorities of scientific and technological development

Priority areas	1996	2002	2006	2009	Areas of technological breakthrough
Basic research	+	–	–	–	–
Information and telecommunication technologies	+	+	+	+	+
Production technologies	+	+	–	–	–
New materials and chemical technologies	+	+	–	–	–
Living systems, medicine (life science)	+	+	+	+	+
Transportation technologies	+	+	–	+	–
Energy and energy conservation	+	+	+	+	+
Ecology and environmental management	+	+	+	+	–
Space technologies and systems	–	+	–	+	+
Nanosystems industry	–	–	+	+	+
Military-industrial complex, nuclear technologies	–	+	+	+	+
Security and counterterrorism	–	–	+	+	–

Sources: Ministry of Industry and Science of the Russian Federation,"Main directions of state scientific and technical policy for the medium-and long-term," 2000.
(In accordance with the order of the Government of the Russian Federation of October 27, 2000.) (IC-P 829 269); Priority directions for the development of science, technology, and techniques in the Russian Federation (Pr - 843 dated May 21, 2006); and the List of Critical Technologies of the Russian Federation (Pr - 844 dated May 21, 2006); Priority areas for the development of science, technology, and engineering in the Russian Federation (Presidential Decree No. 899 dated July 7, 2011).)

Since today's economy is characterized by highly dynamic technologies, we must adjust our priorities accordingly. The frequent turnover in priorities, however, indicates our lack of goal setting in national economic policy. We must set priorities not only at the macro level, but at the level of individual sectors. These priorities should be specified in the various structure-forming [strukturoobrazuiushchie] projects we take on. Implementing them effectively will ensure a compound large-scale, inter-industry effect.

In practice, we should reduce our reindustrialization policy to the basics: state-sponsored investment projects to increase the capacity of priority industrial enterprises, which will act as engines of sustainable economic growth. Determining the footholds of these investment projects will require a large-scale inventory of our technological potential. This inventory will make it possible to determine how to implement our priorities and how to identify the necessary resources to make our goals reality.

The structure of Russian industry is organized around capital in the fuel and energy complex (primarily gas, electricity, and oil). The manufacturing industry, especially machinery and equipment construction, is on the periphery of this structure. Russia lacks big, international-level mechanical engineering corporations capable of operating in the global market. With such a structure in place, Russia's manufacturing industry cannot be competitive with the leading foreign industrial corporations, which are integrated into transnational financial-industrial groups.

As I have noted, it was only in the second half of the 2000s that the government began to take measures to concentrate assets and restructure some engineering industries into state corporations and joint-stock companies with governmental supervision to adapt them to globalizing commodity markets. (These include aircraft, shipbuilding, and defense-industrial complex industries like the Rostech State Corporation). The consolidation of machine tool building assets under OAO Rosstankoprom also began. But restructuring industrial potential into state corporations is a task with a narrow focus, related mainly to the preservation of the country's defense industry potential. The system-wide effect of this move on industry at large is rather small. And, as in Soviet times, the Russian defense-industrial complex remains organizationally and economically isolated from the civilian sector of technologically intensive mechanical engineering, which hinders the opportunity for technological transfer. Unlike raw material corporations with a high share of exports, the domestic mechanical engineering complex (except for some export-oriented defense-industrial sectors) has no opportunity to increase investment via external financial markets (long-term loans, IPOs), leading to its low level of competitiveness. To improve the situation, we must restore applied science, design, and engineering, which are, in fact, on the verge of extinction. We must develop a special program to revive applied science and R&D, based, perhaps, on forming a system of national research universities (though they should not be pitted against the scientific centers of the RAS).

It is typical that in the *new version of the "Strategy-2020,"* there is *no mention made of the priorities of industrial development* in the chapter devoted, namely, to industrial development. The Russian government still seems to lack an effective approach to industrial policy. The government's economic ministries continue to practice the old radical-liberal approach, which suggests that the state *should ensure the active development only of transportation infrastructure and minimize its participation in projects aimed at the modernization and diversification of industrial potential.* It is also no coincidence that the "Strategy-2020" prioritizes the overall institutional environment but foregoes an active industrial policy. Moreover, there is no specific vision for the long-term transformation of domestic mechanical engineering in the section on the country's most important sectoral complexes.

Russia has yet to develop a system for independently evaluating the priority areas of its industrial potential, and for selecting priority projects for state support. Governmental functions are unclearly distributed between three ministries: the Ministry of Industry and Trade, which drafts concepts and development programs for individual industrial sectors; the Ministry of Economic Development, which is in charge of investments in the budget and selects targeted development programs, i.e., creates the economic conditions for their implementation; and the Ministry of Finance, which draws up a general plan for allocating budgetary expenditures.

After eighteen years of negotiations, Russia entered the WTO with an unstructured and uncompetitive industry. Its accession to the WTO does not simplify things. The government was forced to hastily develop special programs to support various sectors of domestic industry, with dubious effects. Membership in the WTO increases competitive challenges for domestic producers but does not create opportunities to increase their competitive edge. Countries with highly competitive manufacturing industries benefit from WTO membership the most, as they gain access to a more favorable export regime through the organization.

Russia also faces other foreign economic problems. International experience demonstrates that there are several conditions for industrial breakthroughs: the "spillover" [pereliv] of advanced foreign technologies into the national economy by purchasing foreign equipment; the selective import of products and services that carry information about technological innovations; the imitation of foreign technology and design based on purchased samples (reverse engineering); the purchase of intangible technologies (industrial designs, patents, licenses, know-how). This list should also include the *transfer of full or partial production of complex finished products from other countries; the establishment of research centers and design bureaus by transnational corporations in countries that are recipients of foreign direct investment (FDI); and the training of local workers employed in branches of MNCs.*

The Soviet experience is also useful here. To accelerate industrialization in the 1920s–1930s, the Soviets consistently increased the share of machinery and equipment in their imports. In 1930, the share of manufacturing equipment in total imports was 46.8 percent. During this period, the Soviet Union became the largest importer of mechanical engineering products. In 1931 the USSR accounted for 30 percent of total global imports of machines and equipment (without cars); in 1932 this number jumped up to about 50 percent. In 1938, when the backbone of Soviet industry had mostly formed, the share of machinery imports in its total volume decreased slightly, but still remained very high at 34.5 percent.

The former Soviet republics carried out the large-scale construction of new industrial enterprises primarily using equipment imported from abroad. It is in this manner that the Russian machine tool industry was formed, including its first specialized industrial factories: Frezer, Kalibr, Red Proletary, (Krasniy proletariy), and others. Large tractor-building enterprises in Stalingrad and Chelyabinsk used imported equipment, as did the Moscow and Gorky automobile plants. Power plants under construction were nearly 90 percent powered by imported electric generators and steam-power units. Metallurgical plants, including the Magnitogorsk, Kuznetsk, and Chelyabinsk combines, all under construction at the time, also received their necessary equipment from abroad.

Due to the degradation of domestic mechanical engineering, many types of machinery and equipment are either not produced in Russia or are of low quality and not in great demand. For this reason, imports play an important part in the revival of the Russian manufacturing industry. According to calculations by the RAS Institute of Economic Forecasting, domestic production can contribute only to 44 percent of the renewal of fixed assets in the Russian economy.[16]

---

16 V.V. Ivanter, ed., *The innovative and technological development of the Russian economy* (Moscow: Max Press, 2006). (in Russ.)

The possibilities of importing remain poorly used toward the restructuring of the domestic economy. Today, importing is primarily aimed at the satisfaction of current consumer needs. In 2011, the share of consumer goods in imports, according to Rosstat, was 36.7 percent, while the share of investment goods was only 21.3 percent. This preference for consumer imports is especially clear when we compare the Russian to situation to that of countries with similar problems. According to UN Comtrade (2007), consumer goods, including food and beverages, accounted for 5.6 percent of imports China's imports, 10.6 percent of Brazil's, 5.2 percent of India's, and 11.3 percent of Mexico's. Meanwhile, the share of production machinery and equipment in their imports was: 43.8 percent, 26.6 percent, 19.1 percent, and 31.8 percent, respectively.[17]

In short, *Russian imports are not yet* an effective tool for accelerating our scientific and technological progress, modernization of production, and technological potential.

The share of machinery and equipment in imports should be increased by one-and-a-half to two times if they are to become an effective tool of economic modernization.

The insignificant volume of foreign nonmaterial technologies that we purchase is yet more evidence of the fact that we are making insufficient use of our import opportunities. In 2011, Russia spent about 1.9 billion dollars on foreign nonmaterial technologies (0.5 percent of its total imports of goods and services).[18] By comparison, in 2011 the US, a leader in technological development, spent 34.8 billion dollars on foreign technologies, Japan spent 19.2, Singapore spent 19.4, Switzerland spent 16, and China spent 15 billion dollars.

There is yet a more serious problem at play here: the *unfavorable* structure of already purchased technologies. Engineering services (37 percent) and trademarks (22 percent) dominate in this sphere; they are mature technologies

---

17 Since 2009, UN Comtrade has not published this data. It is difficult to compare Rosstat and international statistics because the grouping of goods in the domestic and international statistics markedly differs. According to our calculations on the basis of UNCTAD data, in 2011 the share of machinery and equipment (excluding automobiles) in Russian imports is 27.1 percent; China 31.4 percent; Brazil 26.8 percent; India 16 percent; and Mexico 36.9 percent. If office and telecommunication equipment are excluded from the machinery and equipment group, the shares of machinery and equipment by country are as follows: Russia - 20.8 percent; China - 25.2 percent; Brazil - 20 percent; India -11.9 percent; Mexico - 24 percent. As for consumer goods, it is difficult to calculate their share according to international statistics.

18 The WTO estimates our technology imports differently ($6.1 billion in 2011) but does not cite its structure. See: International Trade Statistics 2012. WTO. www.wto.org.

with relatively low profitability. The share of patents, licenses, and know-how related to the development of new processes and types of products is only 9 percent.

Russian entrepreneurs prefer to buy foreign machine and equipment technologies to increase the technological level of their production. Even without the most advanced technologies, they can simplify and accelerate the renewal of production. However, international experience demonstrates that in some cases imported licenses and know-how are much more profitable. In addition to saving foreign currency, license agreements usually provide the buyer with valuable know-how, assistance in improving licensed products, and sometimes in selling them in foreign markets. Moreover, such an agreement may become a launching pad for new domestic developments. According to experts, more than half of the world's engineering products in the mid-2000s were produced under license agreements.[19] Note that Japan, South Korea, Singapore, and other states overcame their technical and economic backwardness thanks to licenses and know-how. Russia should also adopt this practice of importing advanced, mostly intangible technologies.

The relatively small volume of Russia's (soft and hard) technological imports is due to their low demand by domestic enterprises. The majority of Russian enterprises, with weak competition in the domestic market, does not see the need for the systematic renewal of their products and equipment. An unfavorable investment climate, coupled with lack of incentives for innovative development, also has a negative impact on the volume of imported foreign technologies.

There is also an insufficient use of clean technologies in Russia, due to a lack of experience with such technologies, and a lack of structures to ensure that the licensed idea is faithfully reproduced. To tackle these problems, we must complete and improve our national innovation system. This means reviving industry institutes, design bureaus, and pilot plants, which were all severely affected by the economy's *systemic transformation*. These institutions have especially important functions, including not only scientific R&D, but also the study of advanced foreign technologies, which allows us to keep abreast of foreign scientific and technological progress.

The state should systematically support the import of technologies to Russia, both as direct purchases of investment equipment, licenses, and know-how, and as more

19 Pride, V. "The phenomenon of the NBIC convergence: Reality and expectations," in *Problems of Effectively Integrating Russia's Scientific and Technological Potential in the World Economy*, ed. V. Pride and D. A. Medvedev (Moscow: LKI Publishing House, 2008), 35. (in Russ.)

complex forms of cooperation, such as turnkey projects, joint R&D ventures, and manufacturing with foreign firms.

To improve the current investment climate, it is necessary to restore tax incentives for investment. We must also take measures to simplify the import of foreign industrial equipment, for example, by reducing import duty rates for such equipment to zero for five to seven years, even though this is not stipulated by the WTO. This practice was common before the economic crisis. But as a member of the Customs Union, Russa cannot manipulate duty rates on its own, and must rely on the oversight of the Eurasian Economic Commission.

As part of its general scientific-technical and industrial policy, Russia must adopt a policy to stimulate the import of investment equipment and technologies. This policy should determine, on the one hand, the priority technologies and types of equipment to be developed in-house, and on the other hand, the technologies and equipment whose import should be stimulated by special measures. The policy should take into consideration existing domestic development and the general outlook of scientific and technical progress on the global level. It should be developed together with the users and creators of domestic technology, so that neither the domestic R&D sector, nor domestic industry, nor the technological safety of the country as a whole would suffer.

13.6. The new model of economic and institutional development

Implementing a national strategy of economic reindustrialization critically depends on the state's ability to solve all of the above problems in industrial policy by combining different measures. The quality and efficiency of this industrial policy is determined by the quality of the state institutions and procedures working toward it: the quality of the state's modernization priorities, its projects for investment, its lending schemes, and its control over the targeted use of resources.

Russia still lacks an effective system for developing strategy documents that define the prospects for the development of the main sectors of the national economy and industry. "Strategy-2020" did not sufficiently flesh out the development of individual economic and industrial sectors. Plans for different sectors were developed late in the process, and only a few industries received due attention, while most others were left without long-term programs of modernization that complemented one another. Consequently, there is no comprehensive system to select and evaluate modernization projects and the development of industrial complexes. The existing project is not sufficiently systematic in its approach; its different parts are not connected at the inter-industry level according to resources and budget planning.

As a result, there is still no transparent and clear system for the technological support of major industrial development. It is not clear who shaped the technological priorities of development (i.e., critical technologies) and how; what their expertise is; and how these priorities are linked to the development of the relevant sectors. It seems as if the disparate elements of this policy are the result of lobbying and serve mainly as a tool of access to the federal budget. The general lack of transparency of the Russian business sector only aggravates the situation: who are the real owners of these businesses and what are their real costs and profits?

It is important not to confuse cause and effect when we discuss the low quality of Russian public administrative institutions. The fact is that the functional quality of an institution is the result of its experience, which is accumulated by solving the relevant tasks. Contemporary Russian institutions were formed as the Soviet system was dismantled, capital quickly accumulated, and the state drastically reduced its involvement in the economy. These initial circumstances largely determine both the mentality and the professional level of very many civil servants.

The performance level of the state apparatus clearly cannot improve on its own, or by special campaigns to "clean it up." The quality of stare institutions will begin to improve when the nature of the necessary tasks changes, when there is a transition from regulatory and distributive functions to creative ones.

Reindustrialization is only possible in the *context of modernized institutions*. Most experts believe that a poor institutional environment is the main constraint on Russian economic growth. The effect of institutional changes is comparable with, and may even exceed, the effects of fiscal and monetary stimulus measures.

Increasing investments to the required volume is only half the battle. We must also change why entrepreneurs might be motivated to invest in reindustrialization. It is a well-known fact that in today's Russia the key to successful business is close cooperation with the authorities. It is not a question of the partnership between the state and a business, but of government representatives getting their way. It does not matter whether an official is guided by his or her idea of public benefit or by self-interest. What is important is that there is an institution, usually informal, that allows one to act a certain way. Such is the specific Russian approach to the nationalization of relations of appropriation [ogosudarstvleniya otnosheniy prisvoeniya]. Effective modernization is impossible without overcoming this seemingly steady system.

Entrepreneurs[20] and top representatives of the economic authorities[21] confirm this fact. The President has also spoken on the topic: "Costs for businesses can fluctuate: you can pay more or less depending on how much certain people within the state system 'favor' you. The rational thing to do for an entrepreneur in this case is not to comply with the law, but to find patrons, to negotiate. But such a 'negotiated' business will, in turn, try to suppress competitors and clear is place on the market, using the capabilities of the affiliated officials [...] instead of improving the economic efficiency of their enterprises."[22]

The issue is not that the market is not sufficiently competitive; the issue is in the means of competition. We must create such conditions that Russian entrepreneurs will be forced to use technological modernization as their main tool of competition. Destroying monopolies in order to develop competition is also necessary, but insufficient on its own. We must change how the products of entrepreneurial activity are appropriated. The main problem today is raiding [reiderstvo], i.e., taking away, unfairly appropriating, from the entrepreneur the result of his business: his income, the business itself, his hopes and dreams.

Both the struggle against raiding and calls for innovative development will be unsuccessful as long as the redistribution of property rights is more financially attractive than the actual development of property. Compensatory measures, like credit-investment tax incentives or state-private co-financing, are not significant enough to reduce the risks inherent in pursuing innovation. A more effective way to make innovation an attractive means of competition is through institutes that, in turn, make other (noninnovative) means of competition riskier.

The way that state property was privatized in the 1990s still ripples through the Russian economy today. That process led to an uneven, low-legitimacy system of property relations of the means and results of production, which in turn led to the ongoing nationalization [ogosudarstvlenie] of economic life today. In the 1990s, under the slogan of denationalization, an extremely primitive "renovation" of property relations took place, guided neither by economic science nor international experience. The result was the emergence of a class of

---

20 See the speech of the vice-president of "Business Russia" A. Galushko at the Business Forum of the real sector enterprises "Modernization," September 14, 2010. (in Russ.)

21 See the speech of Minister E. S. Nabiullina at the conference "Competition in Russia: how to create a favorable climate for business development" (Moscow, November 26, 2010); and the speech of Deputy Chairman of the RF Government, Finance Minister A.L. Kudrin at the VIII Krasnoyarsk Economic Forum on February 18, 2011. (in Russ.)

22 V. V. Putin, "We need a new economy," *Vedomosti* (January 1, 2012). https://www.vedomosti.ru/politics/articles/2012/01/30/o_nashih_ekonomicheskih_zadachah (in Russ.)

inefficient proprietors, in the national-economic sense.[23] In the early twentieth century, Vasiliy V. Rozanov wrote that, "all property in Russia has grown out of property that was 'borrowed,' or 'gifted,' or 'robbed' from someone. There is very little *self-earned* property. And because of this, [self-earned property] is not robust or respected."[24] Now, Russia's past has to come back to haunt it, as Rozanov's statement holds true today, too.

As a result, whatever the state (i.e., its representatives) might do to curb entrepreneurial freedoms, even anything that contradicts the law, finds support from the public, especially if done under the slogan of protecting the interests of "ordinary people." Hence the profound discrepancy between the law and law enforcement in Russian socioeconomic life.

Privatization itself is not the same as denationalization. Historical experience demonstrates that the only reliable mechanism of economic denationalization is the constant and active effort of the institutions of civil society. These institutions are capable of limiting selfish entrepreneurial interests on the one hand, and governmental overmanagement on the other. In a socially oriented economy, these institutions have an essential role in regulating a society's economic life. Thus, it is not surprising to see formerly socialist countries pay attention to the development of these institutions as they move away from a socialist mode of the organization of social production.

The institutions of civil society emerge as a result of changes in people's thinking and behavior. For this reason, we cannot confuse policies for developing civil society's institutional system with state measures for developing nonstate (social) structures. These policies can lead to the emergence of quasi-civil relations. The task of the state is to create a socioeconomic and political atmosphere that eliminates administrative, economic, social barriers to the social activity of citizens and to the development of a material economic base.

If we can solve this institution problem in the process of modernization and instill confidence in the entrepreneur, then he will begin to develop his business in earnest and bestow his good fortune to his fellow countrymen and to his society. He will have no reason to take his business abroad. It is at that point that we will see real investment in innovation in Russia. To use mathematical terms, this is the base set of necessary and sufficient conditions. The entrepreneur is the main driving force of modernization, and the main task of the state and society

23 A similar situation has developed in a significant part of the post-Soviet space. See Y. Kindzersky, "Deformation of the institute of property in Ukraine and problems of forming an effective owner in an ineffective state," *Questions of Economics* 7 (2010): 123–134. (in Russ.)
24 V. V. Rozanov, *Solitary Thoughts* (Moscow: Politizdat, 1990), 37. (in Russ.)

is to motivate him in a positive direction. I would summarize the situation as follows: if an entrepreneur is interested in doing business on Russian soil, we have modernized the economy. This outcome must be promoted through means both economic and noneconomic.

In conclusion, I would like to note the following: reindustrialization as we imagine it is possible only in the appropriate *institutional environment, which encourages production and its technological development.* Most experts believe that Russia's poor institutional environment is the main constraint on its economic growth and modernization, and that the effect of institutional changes would be comparable to or exceed the possible effects of fiscal and monetary stimulus measures.

We have an enormous opportunity before us, not only for industrialization, but for the development of our economy as a whole. But there is a systemic problem holding us back, and that is the current institutional environment for entrepreneurship.

Chapter 14

The Revival of Production, Science, and Education: The Primary Priority of Modern Industrial Policy

As I have stressed multiple times, successful reindustrialization is impossible without the *integration of production with education and science*: this is far from a new idea. But rarely are there calls today for the urgent undertaking of this task, which requires an urgent solution. Though some may object to this approach, I argue that the integration of science, production, and education in one system is a prerequisite to implement the necessary modernization projects in Russia's economy today. To analyze the links between production, science, and education, we must use a systematic method, which will allow us to distinguish the systematic qualities of our objects of study, their interrelations, and their interaction with external factors. Both domestic and foreign economics use this approach.[1]

I will begin with a look at the past, at the experience of the 1950s to the early 1970s.

---

1   See, for example, Y. Kornai, "The Systemic Paradigm," *Questions of Economics* 4 (2002): 10–12; G. B. Kleiner, "Systemic economics as a platform for the development of modern economic theory," *Questions of Economics* 6 (2013): 4–28; G. B. Kleiner, "What kind of economy does Russia need and why?" *Questions of Economics* 10 (2013): 21. (in Russ.)

14.1. Lessons from national history: A critical approach to the Soviet experience

The Soviet Union has much to teach us about the integrated development of high-tech production, science, and education. The USSR carried out many large-scale high-tech projects, which actively promoted "clustering" around new industrial production: auxiliary industries, educational organizations, and other such structures formed around new production. This practice bettered the general culture and the technical culture of production and aided in the territorial development of the country.

Major scientific and technological projects (nuclear, space, compute production, and many others) accelerated socioeconomic development, resulted in our global leadership in many areas, stabilized the entire socioeconomic system, and reduced the risks of its development. Russia still benefits from the industrial and technological know-how acquired in various fields during the Soviet period. All of the successful projects of the time were carried out with the close cooperation of basic and applied science, education, and material production.

As new industries quickly developed in the USSR, they faced the problem of personnel shortage, which they solved thanks to the organizational connection between education and production at the micro-level. Toward this end, in the 1920s the Soviets began to create factory schools, and later, vocational schools and technical colleges. These educational institutions worked for the needs of specific industrial enterprises and used their material and technical base for the necessary training, integrating vocational education and industrial production.

The next logical step was to include higher education in this chain of training and production. Since 1959, the largest and most technically advanced industrial enterprises have been actively establishing higher-ed facilities to training highly qualified specialists from among the employees of the basic enterprise and similar enterprises. It is in this way that higher ed was closely integrated with the production-technological process. Students generally received training in three to four production skills: first they were trained to carry out the duties of a foreman or technician, and then in their senior year of study, to become an engineer, designer, or researcher for a factory laboratory. During their studies, these students were also employed at the relevant enterprise, meaning that they were steeped in the culture of industrial production from the moment they stepped foot into school.

The history of the Soviet nuclear project is especially instructive here. For its implementation, specialized universities and related research institutes were established with the participation of prominent physicists such as Pyotr Kapitsa, Lev Landau, P. Skobeltsin, Igor Tamm, and many others. At the end of the 1940s, the Moscow Engineering and Physics Institute and the MGU Faculty of Physics and Technology (later called the Moscow Institute of Physics and Technology) were established. The MGU physics department organized a nuclear physics research institute (initially called NIFI-2). In 1949, the Matter Structure Branch (later the Nuclear Physics Branch), consisting of five departments, was formed in the Department of Matter Structure.[2] Similar measures were taken to implement the space rocket program, the electronic computer program, etc.

Major national scientific and technical projects ensured the integration of their many parts under one framework. Numerous examples exist: thermal and electric railroad traction; semiconductors in the radio-electronic industry; mass large-panel housing construction; and many more. Resources were highly centralized, and they were managed by the state, which facilitated the smooth operation of these industries.

This integration method also had its *downsides*: low efficiency of material resources use and overstretched human potential; departmental barriers and conflicts of interest; excessive centralization of decision-making; and a secrecy that hindered the spread of modern scientific and technological innovations beyond the defense sector.

By combining science and production organizationally at the microlevel, the USSR made an attempt to curb the latter problem, which especially affected the application of scientific and technological developments in production. The establishment of research and production associations (RPA) toward this end was successful. The country's first RPA "Pozitron," established in March 1969, produced electronic components and special equipment for the Ministry of Defense and was the first in the country mass produce small-size color TVs and video recorders.

In the transition from experimental or small-scale production at research institute pilot plants to mass production at the given enterprise, much time was spent coordinating scientific and technical issues. To solve a problem, one often had to turn to the employees of the branch ministry. When the

---

2   M.I. Panasiuk, E.A. Romanovsky, and A.V. Kessenikh, eds., "Initial stage of nuclear physicist training at Moscow State University in the thirties to the fifties," in *History of the Atomic Project*, 2nd ed. (Moscow: Russian Christian Institute for the Humanities, 2002), 491. (in Russ.)

"Pozitron" RPA was established, it was headed by a scientific research institute with a pilot plant. The association was made up of the Central Design Bureau of Technology and Equipment (TsKBTO) with its own pilot plant, and production companies with subsidiaries outside of Leningrad. The general director of the association was also the head of the institute and its pilot plant. The first deputy general director was the scientific head of the association and chief engineer of the research institute. The deputy general director on production simultaneously served as the chief engineer of the pilot plant, while the deputy general director on mechanization was the director of the TsKBTO and its pilot plant.

During the Kosygin reforms, RPAs operated on a self-supporting basis [khozraschet], partially using commodity-money relations. Pozitron's business accounting was distinctive in that it excluded mutual supplies from turnover, reducing the volume indicators of output, but increasing the output rate significantly. The volume of production of some products quadrupled during the first six months of operation.[3]

Despite significant positive results, RPAs were unable to overcome the institutional and economic obstacles associated with the Soviet model of planned economy to ensure high rates of scientific and technological progress. The problems of the Soviet planned economic system, seriously exacerbated in the 1970s–1980s, showed the need for qualitative changes in the economic system as a whole.

To summarize the Soviet experience, I will note the following features of that system as they relate to our goal of reindustrialization:

- the development of *large integrated structures* that organizationally unite science, education, and high-tech production via networks.[4] These structures should be more flexible, less hierarchical, and less bureaucratic than in the USSR. It is equally important to take into account the market criteria, incentives, and motives (cost reduction, monetary incentives, etc.) that go into their establishment and functioning;
- the development of *large-scale long-term state programs*, which, in contrast to the directive planning of the Soviets, should instead be

---

3   Socialist Industry 109.234 (May 12, 1970). http://statehistory. ru/2681/Pervoe-v-SSSR-nauchno-proizvodstvennoe-obedinenie-Pozitron/. (in Russ.)

4   O. O. Vatunina and Y. V. Vertakova, "Creating a sectoral integrated structure to increase the investment attractiveness of industry," *Microeconomics* 1 (2010): 174–80.

indicative, based on a system of flexible indirect incentives and checks (taxes, loans, etc.), combining private and state resources;[5]

- the *ideological and political support of the given programs*, which motivates their actualization by positively shaping the general societal and professional attitude towards reindustrialization.

Resources were highly centralized and clearly managed by the state. Such was the institutional environment in which Soviet modernization projects took place. Today these preconditions for efficient modernization no longer exist. We must create new economic policies toward this end that take into account the current state of Russia's institutional environment.

Another downside of the Soviet system was its overreliance on direct administrative pressure to solve critical issues. Unfortunately, this is also a sin of modern bureaucracy. This mode of manual control is unproductive because it leaves open the question of the economic efficiency of any given decision. Moreover, the integration of production, science, and education cannot be effective without stable institutions that ensure horizontal links between these spheres, wherein the direct participants of a process transmit their decisions to the top and receive instructions from above.

Unfortunately, no one paid any heed to the positive or negative lessons of the Soviet experience in 1991.

14.2. The positive and negative experiences of post-Soviet Russia

I want to draw attention to the failures of 1990s market fundamentalism. This period clearly demonstrates that a self-regulating market does not work without certain material, institutional, and macroeconomic prerequisites. The development of science, education, and production suffered significantly because we abandoned active state regulation.

As the reforms started, the attitude toward science, especially fundamental science, changed: now science was a nonproductive expense. Its financing fell, the wages of scientific workers did too, both absolutely and relatively as compared to other sectors. A period of massive brain drain began, as qualified personnel

---

5 A. G. Gruchy, "Uncertainty, Indicative Planning and Industrial Policy," *Journal of Economic Issues* 18, no. 1 (1984): 159–180.

in R&D fled abroad. In the early 2000s, the number of PhDs from the USSR working in the US was comparable to that of PhDs who remained in Russia.

It was not only fundamental science that suffered. In the course of privatization, the number of internal research organizations continually fell. Fundamental and applied science were cut off from each other, and production no longer had the support of applied science.[6]

The link between education and production also broke. Purely commercial criteria were imposed on higher education as its budgets were greatly reduced. Higher ed started to produce more and more lawyers, economists, and managers, but with a smaller and smaller qualified teaching force. Technical specialties lost their prestige. The number of students that enrolled just for a diploma as a ticket to the labor market increased considerably.[7] Meanwhile, there was a huge drop in the training of skilled workers, as private business rushed to relieve itself of the burden of training their workers in vocational schools (now colleges). Their complaints today about the lack of skilled workers is the direct result of their own actions back then.

But the main problem was the degradation of production itself. Production was curtailed in the real sector of the economy, and its technological level fell accordingly, leading to smaller demand for R&D and training. Such an environment does not generate demand for innovations or a highly educated labor force.

The disintegration of production, education, and science, coupled with a market fundamentalism that stressed spontaneous self-regulation, had a negative impact on the Russian economy. The situation in the machine tool, civil aircraft, instrument engineering, high-tech rolling, and other industries makes clear the industrial stagnation we face today (table 25).

As the real economy adapted to the reforms, production fell, and its technologies became primitive. Machine tool production dropped from almost seventy thousand units per year in 1991 to a little over three thousand in 2012 (more than twentyfold). The Soviet machine tool industry was a major global player: from 1984 to 1990, over forty-five thousand units of machine tools and press-forming equipment were exported to the Federal Republic of Germany alone.[8]

---

6   The Director of the Institute of the United States and Canada, for example, has written about this. See S. Rogov, "Lack of demand for science—a threat to the country's security," *Nezavisimaia Gazeta*, February 8, 2010. https://www.ng.ru/ideas/2010-0208/9_science.html (in Russ.)

7   See A. I. Kolganov, "Institutional and Organizational Problems of Russian Universities' Participation in the Innovation Process," in *The University as a Link in the National Innovation System* (Moscow: Max Press, 2011). (in Russ.)

8   A. Mekhanik, "Machine tools for a new way of life," *Expert* 7 (2013): 50–56. http://expert.ru/expert/2013/07/stanok-dlya-novogo-uklada/. (in Russ.)

TABLE 25. Russian production of certain types of machines and equipment, in units

Product range	1990	1995	2000	2005	2006	2007	2008	2009
Bridge cranes (including special cranes)	2943	370	638	729	554	936	748	442
Machine tools	74171	18033	8885	4867	5149	5104	4847	1882
Woodworking machines	25439	11192	10232	4489	4412	5102	4130	1800
Forging presses	27302	2184	1246	1533	2106	2700	2747	1266
Spinning machines	1509	133	8	16	13	25	31	12
Looms	18341	1890	95	95	173	89	43	13

Output in the high-tech civilian aircraft industry also declined noticeably (table 26).

TABLE 26. Production of civil aircrafts in Russia (1991–2013)

Year	1991	1992	1993	1994	1995	1996	1997	1998
Russia	66	83	72	25	19	11	12	9
Other CIS states	114	124	45	32	19	12	21	4

Year	1999	2000	2001	2002	2003	2004	2005	2006
Russia	10	10	7	7	10	11	10	14
Other CIS states	3	1	3	3	6	9	10	3

Year	2007	2008	2009	2010	2011	2012	2013	
Russia	12	17	12	13	19	22	32	
Other CIS states	3	5	3	7	8	8	4	

Source: http://superjet100.info/wiki:prod-by-type. Site for the Sukhoi Superjet 100

In 2012, Russia sold 307 industrial robots, while Germany sold 14,500. The number of in-use robots per ten thousand workers was 396 units in South Korea, 332 in Japan, 273 in Germany, and in Russia only two.[9]

Even agriculture, a seemingly conservative industry, was not left untouched by this process of primitivization. Large economic organizations were destroyed, and a large part of production moved to private household plots. From 1990 to 1999 the area of household land use increased from 3.25 to 6.14 million hectares, and the average plot size from twenty to forty hectares. The share of households in agricultural production sharply increased in comparison with the share of enterprises. In 1990, enterprises produced 73.7 percent of agricultural output (in effective prices), and individual farms 26.3 percent; in 1998, 38.7 percent and 59.2 percent respectively; and in 1999, 40.3 percent and 57.2 percent. In 1999, household farms produced 92 percent of potatoes; in 2000, they produced 92.4 percent. The rise of such low-tech farmsteads is a sign of economic devastation, as Glaz'ev and Batchikov's *White Book* argues.[10] These processes took place against the background of the general decline of Russian agriculture: a reduction in cultivated areas and the number of cattle; a decline in the production of grain, potatoes, meat, milk (table 27).

TABLE 27. Indicators of agricultural production in Russia (1990–2000)

	1990	1999	2000
Number of enterprises at the end of the year, thousands	25.8	27.3	27.6
Number of employees in agricultural production, millions	7.5	4.4	4.7
Agricultural land, million hectares	202.4	152.7	149.7
Sown area, million hectares	112.1	73.0	69.1
Livestock (at the end of the year), million heads:			
Cattle	45.3	17.3	16.4
Pigs	27.1	9.5	8.2

(continued)

9 "Recent Statistics on Global Robot Sales," http://www.robotforum.ru/novosti-texnogologij/svezhaya-statistika-mirovyie-prodazhi-robotov.html

10 S. Y. Glazyev and S. A. Batchikov, *The White Book: Economic Reforms in Russia, 1991–2001*, (Moscow: Eksmo, 2004). (tables 27–31 are compiled according to this publication).

	1990	1999	2000
Production, million tonnes:			
Grain (at net weight)	113.5	47.8	55.7
Potatoes	10.1	2.0	1.9
Livestock and poultry (slaughter weigh)	7.0	1.6	1.7
Milk	41.4	15.8	15.5
Eggs, billion pieces	36.6	23.2	24.1
Wool, thousand tonnes	169	15	15
Average number of employees per company:			
Employees	322	188	170
Sown area of all crops, thousand hectares	4.3	2.7	2.5
Cattle	1756	615	574
Pigs	1050	325	273

Despite a significant increase in food imports, the decline of agriculture has led to a decline in per capita food consumption (table 28).

TABLE 28. Consumption of staple foods in the US and Russia (average per capita, kg)

	USA (1989)	RSFSR (1989)	USA (1997)	RF (1997)
Meat and meat products	113	69	114	46
Milk and dairy products (in terms of milk)	263	396	305	229
Eggs, pcs.	229	309	239	210
Fish and fish products	12.2	21.3	10	9.3
Sugar	28	45.2	30	33
Bread products	100	115	112	118
Potatoes	57	106	57	130

Meanwhile, the situation in the service sector was more of a mixed bag. While the demand for high-tech communication and IT services grew (as trade and financial market demand also grew), the demand, for example, for air transportation services fell sharply. The degradation of the Russian civil aviation industry is in no small part related to this fact. A report from the CIS Executive

Committee Inter-State Council for Anti-Monopoly Policies, titled "On the State of Competition in the Air Transportation Market of CIS Member States," notes: "Until the early 1990s, air traffic in the former Soviet Union was developing at a very high rate, and in 1989 its indicators were at the same level as those of developed countries. At that time there was about a fourfold reduction in both passenger traffic and passenger turnover. The main decline occurred in the early 1990s. From the end of the 1990s to the present time there has been a steady growth in air traffic. However, as of 2005, there is still a large lag in air traffic compared to 1990, about 1.5 times less."[11]

The profound decline of most high-tech industries in the 1990s becomes especially clear when we compare it with the much smaller losses in the production of raw materials and products with lower degrees of processing (table 29). For example, though steel production has seen only a small decline, the production of high-tech rolled products and other steel materials has declined many times over.

TABLE 29. Use of production capacities of industrial enterprises (%)

Production	1980	1990	1993	1997	2000
Steel	95	94	69	68	77
Machine tools	87	81	54	16	17
Tractors	98	81	42	8	19
Cement	91	93	62	36	44
Shoes	89	87	48	17	29
Washing machines	88	87	51	12	–

As material production has declined, transport and communal infrastructure has also suffered major loses (tables 30 and 31). The reforms of the 1990s led to a reduced production volume and *lower technological level* in the Russian economy. There was no enthusiasm for R&D spending and personnel training (table 32). And no efforts have been made for far too long to revive the former system that integrated science, production, and education, albeit with new institutions for the market economy.

---

11 Website of the Federal Antimonopoly Service. http://www.fas.gov.ru/analytical-materials/analytical-materials_21436.html.

TABLE 30. Commissioning of paved roads in different regions of the RF, in km

Region	1990	1994	1995	1996	1997
Moscow Oblast	641.1	207.9	226.6	64.5	5.4
Central Black Earth District	2419.4	581.8	532.9	379.4	167.8
Orel Oblast	539.9	80.7	55.9	1.3	3.0
North-western District	2200.1	150.5	109.0	40.7	57.9
Kaliningrad Oblas	140.5	14.0	15.6	6.9	–
Republic of Buriatia	279.9	17.9	27.6	8.9	3.9
Primorskii Krai	230.7	51.7	70.8	18.2	10.9

TABLE 31. Commissioning of water supply networks in the RF, in km

Region	1990	1995	1996	1997	2001
Russian Federation as a whole	7524.3	2647.3	1330.1	1513.6	1076.9
Central District	883.2	143.3	95.0	81.4	
Central Black Earth District	1229.2	223.3	136.8	97.9	
Voronezh Oblast	227.5	32.4	38.1	3.7	
Tambov Oblast	151.4	45.7	24.2	2.4	

TABLE 32. Production of skilled workers and employees in Russia, in thousands of people

Year	2005	2006	2007	2008	2009	2010	2011	2012	2013
Total output	702.5	679.7	656.0	604.7	537.6	580.5	516.7	483.5	436.0
Including by industry occupations	214.0	206.3	202.7	189.4	168.1	174.8	160.0	152.6	138.3

To summarize, I want to emphasize again that market fundamentalism only hinders our progress in solving the urgent tasks of import substitution, reindustrialization, and economic modernization. I agree with RAS Institute of Economics Director Ruslan Grinberg's conclusion that, "the negative results of the market transformation are more visible and obvious. They explicitly eclipse its successes. The problem is not only that the country has lost half of its potential during the reform years. Even worse is that the processes of the primitivization of production, the deintellectualization of labor, and the degradation of the social sphere cannot be stopped. To this we must also add the rise of mass poverty, which spread rapidly during those years of radical change."[12] However, few have paid heed to Grinberg's argument here in recent years.

The growth that we saw during the recovery of the 2000s did not, unfortunately, change much in this respect. Though a number of industries (including high tech) saw their production numbers rise, this growth did not compensate for the massive failure of the 1990s. In fact, in machinery and equipment production, the situation remained just as bad, and even got worse in some respects.

The knowledge that the only source of growth for the Russian economy is in innovative development came up against passive economic institutions and deeply entrenched macroeconomic policies that suited only the interests of the 1990s reforms. Efforts to reestablish the integration of production, science, and education have failed for this reason.

There were some attempts to solve this problem in the 2000s through ambitious bureaucratic projects. The state created state corporations specifically for this purpose: Skolkovo, Rosnano, Rostekhnologii, etc. Unfortunately, these state corps spent state money inefficiently even recklessly, leading to significant criticism.[13]

It seems paradoxical that foreign nations have managed to successfully integrate production, science, and education in the same way that the Soviets did, while post-Soviet Russia has failed to do the same. Take, for example, the US military-industrial complex, knowledge-intensive production in MNCs, or the close link between fundamental science education and applied research education in Scandinavian countries. In Russia, we seem to put to poor use both our own Soviet experience and foreign experience in this sphere.

A number of the leading industrialized countries have placed the integration of production, science, and education at the forefront of their economic policies. In Japan, for example, the scientific and technological cooperation between these three spheres has led its state innovation policy for many years. Since the mid-1990s, Japan has adopted a number of legislative acts to strengthen relations between the private sector, science, and the state. In 1995, the "Law on Science and Technology" passed, providing state financial support for university research. In 1998, the "Development of Technology Licensing Organizations (TLO)" law passed, which allowed companies to benefit from university research; intermediary organizations between universities and industrial

---

12 R. S. Grinberg, "Russia: Economic Success without Development and Democracy?," *Russia's Economic Revival* 2 (2005): 11. (in Russ.)

13 A special study on this topic is A. A. Sokolov, "Influence of rent-seeking behavior on investments of Russian state corporations," (PhD diss., Russian Academy of Sciences, 2013). http://www.cemi.rssi.ru/news/cemi/sokolov.pdf. (in Russ.)

enterprises were specially created toward this end. In 2000, the "Law on Support for the Development of Manufacturing Technology" passed, allowing the academic staff of public universities to create private companies in order to ensure the practical application of research in industrial production. One of the main objectives of universities in Japan became to support the development of production technologies. And in 2002, the major "Intellectual Property" law passed, which defined the means of cooperation between industry, science, and the state toward economic development through the use of research results.

In according with current legislation, Japan is also actively implementing programs to develop the scientific and technological cooperation between industry, science, and government.[14] The Americans' successful example has led the Japanese to implement the same kinds of programs. The US has been able to significantly improve its competitiveness in biotechnology and information and communications technology (ICT) through such programs.

Germany provides another good example. Some of the German government's major initiatives and projects include:

a) integrating science, education, and industry via:
- state support of innovation clusters with the participation of small and medium-sized enterprises and scientific organizations (projects of the Otto von Guericke Association of Industrial Unions);
- implementing targeted innovation projects in the new federal states;
- developing new instruments for financing promising innovation clusters;
- the federal contest "The best innovation cluster in Germany," organized with the participation of universities and institutes;
- improving models of public-private partnership in the development of innovative activity;

b) improving how scientific personnel are trained and involving them in research.

The integration of production, science, and education is a strong trend throughout the modern global economy: projects to create and strengthen technological cooperation between business and science in the US and industrialized European countries began in the mid-80s to early 1990s. In the US, the Bayh-Dole Act and other legislation have played an important role in this regard.

---

14 Gruchy, "Uncertainty, indicative planning and industrial policy."

We should consider, though critically, both the Soviet and foreign experiences when we implement our import-substitution policy as part of Russia's reindustrialization strategy.

Note that there have been some positive developments in Russia as of late when it comes to the integration of production, science, and education. Some examples include the activities of FSUE Krunichev State Space Research and Production Center, the Aerospace Equipment Group, and others. More specifically, the Krunichev Center established a large, integrated company for the development of heavy launch vehicles, as part of the greater strategy on the development of the space rocket industry, and in accordance with the FTP "Reforming and developing the military-industrial complex (2002–2006)," approved by the Government of the Russian Federation on October 11, 2001, No. 713. The most important task of integration is two-fold: to preserve the production, scientific, and technical potential of the enterprise and to ensure the fulfillment of state orders. On February 3, 2007, President Putin signed the decree "On the Khrunichev State Research and Production Center. On February 3, 2007, Russian President Putin signed the decree "On the FSUE Krunichev State Space Research and Production Center." The center has begun to integrate with a number of leading Russian technical universities, recruiting students to work at the center's enterprises and design bureaus.

Similar micro-level projects are underway, creating innovation clusters, building technology transfer networks,[15] technology hubs, etc. Unfortunately, there are also negative examples of this trend in Russia. The country does not have a system, nor does it have a long-term working strategy, for the integration of production, science, and education at the macro level. Tasks are solved mostly manually on a case-by-case basis, and corruption is widespread.

14.3. Possible solutions toward the reintegration of science, education, and production

The development of new high-tech material production requires that we bring new theoretical ideas to concrete technologies, then to be implemented in mass production. Toward this end, we need: 1) *fundamental and applied science;* 2) *people capable of developing and implementing new technologies, which is impossible without quality universal life-long education.* RAS Academician Boris Kashin

---

15 A. S. Osipenko, "Technological transfer in the system of industrial innovation development," *Russia's Economic Revival* 39, no. 1 (2014): 83–88. (in Russ.)

and Corresponding Member Oleg Smolin have long emphasized both of these requirements,[16] though not all economists support this approach.

But policy imperatives alone are not enough. To solve the problems necessary for the reintegration of production, science, and education, we must consider how these three sectors function in today's economic context. There are three main points to consider here:

1. *The twenty-first century economy is driven by human creativity, which we must develop with education as a key production resource.* Economists have always known that the human being is one of the main factors of production, or, in Marxist parlance, the main productive force. In today's economy, however, humanity increasingly acts not only as a labor force with certain qualifications, performing standard functions at the machine or on the assembly line, but also in a new capacity. The creative potential of humanity plays the main role in the twenty-first century economy. To develop human creativity, we need accessible education that lasts throughout life. Smolin especially emphasizes this kind of education as a prerequisite to economic revival.[17]

2. *Without developing fundamental research, it is impossible to create new technologies and innovations.* These are the most expensive and competitive goods of the global economy, and their production determines the competitiveness of the national economy, as well as national security.

3. *Production is the base of today's economy; it structures education and science, and it is where their potential is applied.* There are two sides to the

---

16 "First of all, it is necessary to develop a roadmap for Russian economics, so that the latter can address well-defined tasks and their solution. On the other hand, it is necessary to raise the status of the Russian economist. And to not be guided by fictitious indicators, developed by incomprehensible Western experts, on the quality of his scientific work," writes B. S. Kashin. He continues: "The impression is that the authorities are not interested in the opinion of professional economists. Apparently, they only need an entourage of 'expert' representatives to legitimize decisions that they have already been made. It turns out that economics is separate from the sphere of managerial decision-making. Moreover, these two groups are sometimes hostile to each other. We can say that there is an anti-scientific approach to decision-making in the sociopolitical and economic spheres." B. S. Kashin, "The philosophy of innovation parasitism," *The Free Press*, December 13, 2011. http://commpart.livejournal. com/15221. html. (in Russ.); Smolin emphasizes: "Until the education system is restored, Russia will remain a third-world country. Either we change our economic course, or the national security of our country, its integrity, its future will be threatened." O. N. Smolin, Speech at the Moscow Economic Forum, 2014. http://me-forum.ru/media/events/plenary_discuss_I/. (in Russ.)
17 O. N. Smolin, *Education for All* (Moscow: Prospect, 2006).

main priorities of twenty-first century economics: science, education, and culture on the one hand, and material production on the other. An ineffective economic policy may upset the balance between the two, such as when investment in production leads to a decrease in investment for science and education. But this imbalance is resolved when education, science, and culture work for the progress of material production. And material production develops not by taking money away from social institutions, but by involving more qualified workers and newer technologies, which necessitates exactly those social institutions.

I have outlined why we must integrate these three spheres into a holistic, long-term development program. What steps can we take toward this goal?

Taking into account both domestic and international experience, and the theoretical provisions outlined above, we can formulate some *recommendations toward the reintegration of production, science, and education.*

Firstly, the material and technical base for integrative PSE projects must tackle the following, much-discussed problems:

- training creative personnel, specialists, and professionals in the education system;
- using scientific research and experimental development based on fundamental science;
- implementing new technologies up to the creation of industrial samples;
- organizing the mass serial production of such products in domestic enterprises.

Secondly, in today's Russia we should focus primarily on the revival of high-tech reserves (mainly in the defense sector). Programs for the comprehensive development of new technologies and new products should be limited in scope and to areas that promise the greatest economic impact.

Thirdly, the economic mechanisms of this project should be composed of: market incentives, like financing through state orders, long-term loans, and guarantees; public-private partnerships; long-term state programs; and an active industrial policy that links market mechanisms with state investments state enterprises (including educational and scientific).

Fourthly, this plan will need organizational and legal support, which we should provide via special institutions for long-term development (ensuring the development and implementation of strategic programs, active industrial and structural policy, etc.). Their successful operation requires that we reduce administrative barriers in the financial, credit, tax, and customs systems and expand state support in the field of patenting, certification of technological processes and products, etc.

Integrated PSE clusters should play an important role both gradationally and legally: from open networks to complexes with a common program working toward a common long-term goal, with united financing and coordinated management. The specific tasks and prerequisites of any given project will determine which of these options to use.

Chapter 15

NIS.2 as a Social System

—————

I have considered the second generation of the new industrial state (NIS.2) mainly in terms of technological progress, the growth of material production's knowledge-intensity, and the structural and technological shifts necessary to make it happen, which are ensured by a policy of reindustrialization. My task is not to delicately detail the coming transition to NIS.2, to paint an epic canvas of the second generation of the new industrial state. Nevertheless, allow me to point out the main outcomes of technological progress, which will shape future economic and superstructural relations. Only then will all these theoreticals about NIS.2 gain some concreteness.

The possibility of Russia's transition to NIS.2 is inextricably linked to its reindustrialization, based on advanced technological modes that allow for the development of knowledge-intensive material production. Reindustrialization will lead not only to changes in economic policy, but in economic relations, institutions, the public sphere, ideology, social psychology, etc.

Formulating the question in this way allows us to study not only the consequences of Russia's reindustrialization, but the consequences of the imminent global technological revolution, which will start in the most developed and dynamic economies. The totality of these shifts will lead to what I have termed the second generation of the new industrial state: NIS.2. The coming society will be new not only in its technological base, but in its entire social system. The changes coming in the social system are themselves the inevitable consequence of changes in technology and production relations.

When it comes to the post-industrialists, their study of the interdependence between the social system and technology/production is, unfortunately, wrought with primitive technological determinism. Their interpretation is one of automatic changes in the social fabric born directly of technological innovation. Take, for example, their contention that the ability to own a personal computer eliminates all ownership of the means of production, since everyone can be an owner, and thus all former relations based on the unequal ownership of the means of production, on concentration of capital, etc., melt away. No less than three decades have passed since this line of reasoning began, but it remains what it was in the first place: an empty fantasy.

The changes born of technological progress are not automatic, not at all without a struggle against old economic and social forms that seek to legitimize and perpetuate themselves, despite the imperatives of the new conditions of production. We must also take into account the relative inertia of social structures.

Nevertheless, that old principle of the materialist approach to history is by no means obsolete: changes in the technological and economic base of society will, in one way or another, compel all other spheres of social life to progress in accordance with economic necessity. The same example of the personal computer, if we take a closer, more critical look, will reveal that the ownership of such a computer and the access to the information and telecommunications networks that it provides do indeed have the potential to bring about very profound social change. But it is not enough just to have a personal computer and Internet access to make that change happen. For that change to come about, firstly, the information and telecommunication revolution must unite with the main production activities of the majority of the population, catalyzing the steep rise in the knowledge-intensity of material production and the finished product. Yet, despite the extensive functions of the computer and the Internet, as of now they are primarily a means of entertainment, shopping, and everyday communication in one's personal life, while at work they are a means of routine business communication. Secondly, even a real revolution in the level of people's involvement in knowledge-intensive production processes (including the personal computer) creates only the need for economic, institutional, and social restructuring. But that restructuring does not come without struggle; it requires that we search for new, more appropriate social forms, which are not handed to us in a ready-made.

This fact does not mean, however, that change is postponed to some indefinite future. Change is already underway. Its first signs, and a sense of its prospects, have already appeared in the work of some economists. After several decades of neglect, the idea of an "integral" or "convergent" society is again making a comeback. But the proponents of this idea have yet to go further than the original concept, of the convergence of the two systems: the socialist and the capitalist. This convergence theory is born of the desire to combine the best of the two systems and rid them of their vices.

Some of the most well-known proponents of the convergent (or integral) theory include Galbraith, the Russian American sociologist Pitirim Sorokin, the American economist Walt Rostow, the French economist François Perroux and philosopher Raymond Aron, the Dutch economist Jan Tinbergen, the American political scientist Zbigniew Brzezinski, and our own Andrey Sakharov.

According to Sorokin, the capitalist and socialist systems will unite into "a single integral, social, cultural, and personal system in the human universe, which will include the majority of their positive values and will be free of the serious defects of each type."[1] He goes on to say that, "in the future, the dominant form of society will be neither capitalist nor communist, but rather an intermediate form, an integral type between the capitalist and communist orders and ways of life. This new type will have a unified system of integral cultural values, social institutions, and personality types, significantly different from capitalist and communist models."[2]

Galbraith's approach to the convergence theory is somewhat more complex. As he understands it, combining elements of capitalist and socialist relations into a single social organism is possible because both systems are based on a similar mode of production. He also sees great danger in the direct confrontation of these two systems and wants to avoid it. "Convergence begins with modern large-scale production, with heavy requirements of capital, sophisticated technology and, as a prime consequence, elaborate organization. [. . .] Convergence between the two ostensibly different industrial systems occurs at all fundamental points. This is an exceedingly fortunate thing. In time, and perhaps in less time than may be imagined, it will dispose of the notion of inevitable conflict based on irreconcilable difference. [. . .] To recognize that industrial systems are convergent in their development will, one imagines, help

---

1 P. A. Sorokin, "Mutual convergence of the United States and the U.S.S.R. to the mixed sociocultural type," *International Journal of Comparative Sociology* 1, no. 2 (1960): 143.
2 Cited from E. A. Tiriakian, "Pitirim Sorokin: My Teacher and Prophet of Modernity," *Journal of Sociology and Social Anthropology* 2, no. 1 (1999): 23. (in Russ.)

toward agreement on the common dangers in the weapons competition, on ending it or shifting it to more benign areas."[3]

Sakharov focuses more on the necessity of cooperation in addressing humanity's problems: "To summarize, convergence is the real historical process of the coming together of the capitalist and socialist systems as a result of oncoming pluralistic changes in the economic, political, social, and ideological spheres. Convergence is a necessary condition for solving the global problems of peace, ecology, social, and geopolitical justice."[4]

The idea of convergence attempts to take the best of both systems and combine it. It is based on the moral imperative of cooperation and takes as its starting point the fact that both the capitalist and socialist systems share a common industrial base.

Today, however, the concept of convergence has proved untenable. Though the socialist and capitalist systems did show some real signs of convergence— like market reforms in socialist countries, and the rise of the social state and state regulation in capitalist countries—these signs did not pay off and result in an "integral" society. And once socialism fell, the theory of convergence was replaced by talk of the "end of history" and the ultimate triumph of liberal capitalism. There have even been claims of a kind of "negative convergence," a fusion of the worst features of capitalism and socialism in the post-Soviet space. In 1993, the sociologist Nikolai B. Pokrovsky argued that "convergence today has led primarily to the mutual gravitation and integration of the irrational, dysfunctional structures of the US and former USSR."[5] Georgiy N. Tsagolov has written about this phenomenon in today's Russia.[6]

Today's interest in theories of convergence did not come out of nowhere. The current discourse on integral or convergent society attempts to guess at the general evolutionary line leading to this kind of society but does not sufficiently explain how modern conditions can sustain this evolution (and the previous theories certainly cannot satisfy us now). Contemporary economic conditions

---

3   Galbraith, 390–91.

4   A. D. Sakharov, "Convergence, peaceful coexistence." http://www.sakharov-archive.ru/Raboty/Rabot_70.html. (in Russ.)

5   Lecture by N.B. Pokrovsky, Associate Professor in the Sociology Department of Moscow University, at the anniversary session of the Society for the Advancement of American Philosophy at Vanderbilt University (Nashville TN, 1993). http://ecsocman.hse.ru/data/106/202/1217/006_Pokrovskij-brauning.pdf. (in Russ.)

6   See G. N. Tsagolov, "New Integral Society - Seventh Formation," in New Integral Society: General Theoretical Aspects and World Practice, ed. G. N. Tsagolov (Moscow: LENAND, 2016), 126. (in Russ.)

are far too different from those that existed when Sorokin or Galbraith were active. The coming NIS.2 presents us with new challenges.

The proponents of an integral society argue that such a society demonstrates higher economic efficiency and human development, and they are not wrong. Tsagolov emphasizes that dismantling the socialist system did not mean abandoning attempts to synthesize planned (socialist) and market (capitalist) regulators. And where their optimal combination is achieved, excellent economic results are obtained. He writes that, "both systems, each with a number of undeniable advantages, are quite 'objective' and have not come about by accident in human history. But both are internally contradictory, unstable, and require coordination and support. That is why the world's fastest growing and most harmoniously developing countries have adopted the integral system as the basis of their way of life."[7]

Those who argue that the prospects for an integral society are inextricably bound up with a new technological revolution are also correct. Glazyev emphasizes this fact. "The transition to a new techno-economic paradigm is underway, characterized by the wide application of nano- and bioengineering and information-communication technologies. Due to the rapid spread of new technologies that dramatically improve the resource efficiency and reduce the energy intensity of production, advanced countries will experience a long wave of economic growth. In order not to lag behind, Russia will have to look for solutions not only in science, technology, and production, and work out a new development strategy and socio-economic structure."[8]

The NIS.2 is not simply composed of the "best" features of capitalism and socialism; that would be wishful thinking untethered from science. Nor is its formation limited to the injection of capitalist elements into socialism. China may be an economically successful example of this, but the Chinese experience also shows the limitations of socioeconomic development limited only to the combination of well-worn socioeconomic regulations. China's combination of state regulation, market incentives, and free enterprise has led to great development. Now, however, China is struggling to make a technological breakthrough and establish its techno-scientific independence, a problem that cannot be solved by simply combining socialist elements with capitalist elements.

---

7   Tsagolov, "New Integral Society - Seventh Formation." 130, 126–28. (in Russ.)
8   S. Y. Glazyev, "From Market Fundamentalism to a Convergent Model," in *New Integral Society: General Theoretical Aspects and World Practice*, ed. G. N. Tsagolov (Moscow: LENAND, 2016), 69. (in Russ.)

The Scandinavian experience of integrating elements of socialism into a capitalist system has been equally successful—and equally limited. The Scandinavian model mitigates the tensions of capitalism by relying on highly skilled and well-paid labor with a high degree of social protection, which creates good incentives for development. But it has long been clear that this integration alone cannot provide for more developmental potential in the future. Finland is a good example here: it successfully applied this model to boost innovation in the 1990s, but found that by the end of the 2000s, the model had run out of steam and offered no new developmental prospects.

Does the interpenetration of socialism and capitalism have no future use? On the contrary, it does. But only if we do not limit ourselves only to borrowing from the past. *The convergence of the two systems can only be fruitful in the future if it is tethered to the evolution of the techno-economic paradigms of industrial society, and to the growing knowledge-intensity of material production.* This trajectory makes it both necessary and possible for new economic and social relations and institutions, and corresponding political and cultural forms, to emerge. Indeed, this process forces a society not just to incorporate old forms of capitalism and socialism into the fabric of productive relations, but to form entirely new relations that dialectically negate and synthesize these old forms. New socioeconomic relations thus emerge, irreducible to a mechanical mixture of capitalism and socialism. Rather, they use the achievements of past systems to meet the requirements of knowledge-intensive material production today.

In other words, the new society will not simply take from the current types of social order, whether capitalist or socialist. It will negate the contradictions of these orders to create new socioeconomic relations that go beyond the convergence of old forms.

For dozens of years (nearly a hundred, in fact), economists have been trying to cross a snake with a hedgehog, so to say. That is, they have been trying to combine communism and capitalism to form, what they call, an integral or convergent society. By this, I believe that they have in mind the same kind of social organization that I have put forth in the pages of this book. I argue, however, that the term convergence is not appropriate. Convergence means coming together [sblizhenie] *by external appearance.* For example, some mammals live in the sea, and though they may bear an outward resemblance to fish, typologically, in internal structure and physiology, whales and dolphins are indeed mammals. The same may be said of amphibians who live on land and, like land mammals, have limbs for movement on land. Convergence is evident in both cases. It is conditioned by external factors, i.e., the *habitat.* It leads to the need to adapt physically because of environmental pressure. Social development toward NIS.2

is not convergence; it is the environment itself transforming into something new, which inevitably leads to the transformation of all the "animals" that reside within, i.e., to the transformation of different social systems into a uniform [edinopodobnoe] system. The system base is the same, and the superstructure is similar to that of the "twins" [bliznyashchestvo]; of course, civilizational differences, national peculiarities, etc. will influence some dissimilarities for some time. We are witnessing not the convergence of two different systems, but the *germination* of a single new type of society emerging out of the old ones, on the basis of and as a consequence of a *single* path of development. This is the path of technological progress and the reformatting [pereformatirovanie] of the industrial mode of production. There are not and cannot be any different paths forward. The development of technology and science follows the same path; it *cannot* lead us to *different* sciences and technological solutions.

You might be wondering: why did different types of social order emerge in the twentieth century, given the single path of technological progress? They emerged precisely because we did not sufficiently develop technology and production, leading us to scarcity, competition, struggle, and appropriation— all of which will be negated in the NIS.2.

The terms "integration" or "integral society" are even more terminologically suspect than the label "convergent." To integrate is to combine. An integral is the sum of all parts, up to the smallest part. Will the future society combine all the parts, features, and peculiarities (even the vices) of today's society? Of course, not. What surprises me is not so much the terminological laziness of the past experts that I mentioned, but of the present-day specialists who work using only the most modern mathematical apparatuses and advanced methodologies. And if the term "convergent" points at least to something external to the process of building a new society, the term "integral" is in disagreement with the essence of that process. It would be easy not to focus on such terminological nuances, but as the saying goes, "as you call the ship, so it will float" [kak korabl nazovyosh, tak on i poplyvyot]. Terminological confusion leads only to theoretical confusion. In this case, the use of such terms does not clarify the essence of the process, but only misleads. It leads the researcher (and with him, the state) away from understanding and conceptualizing a new society. And most importantly, it leads him away from the *appropriate mechanism* to realize his ideas.

The term "integral society" is inaccurate because the new society will not be a simple combination of different elements of the former one. The term "convergent society" is also inaccurate, since it is not a question of an organism adapting to a new environment and developing attributes to stay in this environment while remaining essentially the same. I am talking about the formation of an entirely new organism, not about the same organism with some novel additional attributes. In this sense, the term "NIS.2" is correct, albeit conditional, because it reflects the essence of the process.

Here I must raise a difficult question, one which only political economy can answer. Is it really possible to combine in one organism different systems of economic regulation: market and planned, capitalist and socialist? Past practice has already given us the answer: sometimes this combination is destructive (perestroika, for example), and sometimes it leads to tremendous economic success (the NEP in early Soviet Russia, for example, or Yugoslavia in the 1950s–1970s, or China from 1979 to the present). There is no fundamental reason why two different economic regulators cannot, in fact, work in tandem. And political economy theory has already established the following answer to this question. Tsagolov writes that, "the market and the plan are not irreconcilable antipodes, but different ways of economic regulation. Problems and disproportions exist even when and where only one of them is in effect."[9] However, we must use political economy to understand in sharper detail: by what criteria is it possible to combine socialist and capitalist principles in such a way that the consequences are not destructive but constructive?

In fact, the necessary approach has already been outlined above. When we prioritize progress in knowledge-intensive material production, the combination of heterogenous elements produces positive effects. The need for progress shapes those heterogenous elements into a positive structure. What does this mean in more concrete terms?

The capitalist system as a whole is currently burdened by the conservative legacy of market fundamentalism. Its economic relations, institutions, and overall ideology developed when the free and competitive market was the alpha and omega of economic progress. Though those days are long gone, the legacy persists, and it hinders the development and application of new approaches. Unfortunately, influential social forces that benefit from this approach still cling to it (financial speculators, for example). Paradoxically, even one of the most successful of these speculators, George Soros, now sees market fundamentalism as a threat to the future of the capitalist system.[10]

Nevertheless, some of the features of market fundamentalism remain in demand as necessary conditions of continuous innovation: the principles

---

9 Tsagolov, 126–27.
10 George Soros, "The Crisis of World Capitalism: Open Society in Danger," trans. S. K. Umrikhinoi and M. Z. Shterngarts (Moscow: INFRA-M, 1999). (in Russ.)

of individual initiative, material success through meaningful results, acting precisely on the basis of market relations.

The socialist system suffered from the hyper-bureaucratization of its central planning,[11] and from the fact that individual interests were relegated to the background in favor of public interests.[12] Nevertheless, it predicted the need for the national, even global, coordination of economic activity and for human development as prerequisites for progress in knowledge-intensive industry.

As a result, in the postwar period various hybrid economic forms were explored. They combined the principles of individualism and socialism in some fanciful ways: from autonomous, self-governing brigades at the grassroots level,[13] to indicative planning and large-scale state scientific and technological programs at the national level.[14]

I will return to the previous issue, on the fact that the old does not automatically disappear in the new, and the road to new social relations lies through the contradictions of obsolete socioeconomic forms. When, in the past, the forward march of technological and economic progress created social tensions, they usually found resolve in a series of revolutions. The challenge is to anticipate the rise of such tensions and to ensure the smooth resolution of these inevitable contradictions.

The NIS.2 has the potential to be a conflict-free society (if we ignore conflicts of personality or of ideas). Why? Because the basis of any conflict is competition, particularly over resources, products, the results, or components of labor. As we move toward the NIS.2, *the need for resources will decrease while product availability and its ability to meet consumer needs will increase,* leading to

---

11 See, for example, the following analysis of the contradictions of the centralized planning system: A. I. Kolganov, "Project 'USSR': what could not be completed?" in *USSR: Incomplete project*, ed. A.V. Buzgalin and P. Linke (Moscow: LENAND, 2012), 171–179. (in Russ.)

12 Ibid, 180–181.

13 For the Soviet experience, see A. A. Rodionov, "The Role of the Production Brigade in the Development of the Social Activity of Workers," (PhD diss, Moscow, 1990). http://cheloveknauka.com/rol-proizvodstvennoy-brigady-v-razvitii-sotsialnoy-aktivnosti-trudyaschihsya#ixzz4GYIDMM7J. For the foreign experience, see E. N. Rudyk, *Industrial Democracy: Theory, Practice, Practice, and the Problems of Its Creation in Russia* (Moscow: Foundation "For economic literacy," 1998; *Society on the threshold of the 20th century: the market, firms, and man in an information society* (Moscow: TEIS, 1998): 66–73. (all in Russ.)

14 For the Soviet experience, see Kolganov, 170–72. For the foreign experience, see E. N. Veduta, *State economic strategies* (Moscow: Academic Project; Business Book, 1998); I. P. Lebedeva, "The role of the state in economic modernization," *Japan: The Experience of Modernization* (Moscow: AIRO-XX, 2011); P. Aghion, "Some Thoughts on Industrial Policy and Growth," OFCE Working Paper (Paris: Observatoire Francais des Conjonctures Economiques, 2009). (in Russ.)

a *lower level of competition*. This trend is at the heart of the second generation of the new industrial state. The basis for conflict will disappear.

This possibility grows as does the technological progress of the industrial mode of production. As the newest generations of technology are developing, humanity is not moving away from the industrial process, but inserting into it a controlled and guided natural process.

Using the power of information technologies, we can integrate industrial technologies (mechanical, physical, chemical, biological, etc.), combining them to solve ever more complex problems and to satisfy ever more diverse needs. A small device that fits in the palm of one's hand can now satisfy needs that, a few decades ago, were satisfied by the TV, radio, telephone, computer, or massive information storage, and at a much lower level at that. And that is only one example. Additive and nanotechnologies offer even more opportunities to meet virtually any need, with minimal resources consumed.

These trends debunk Stalin's thesis that more class conflict is natural as we move toward socialism: "The case has always been, and remains, that the advance of the working class toward socialism cannot happen without struggle and unrest. On the contrary, the advance toward socialism cannot but lead to the resistance of the exploiting classes to this advance, and the resistance of the exploiters cannot but lead to the inevitable exacerbation of the class struggle. This is why the working class must not be lulled into complacency by talk of the secondary role of the class struggle."[15] In 1937, he repeated with renewed verve the same thesis. "The more advanced we become, the more successful we become, the more the remnants of the defeated exploiting classes will become embittered, the faster they will turn to more pointed forms of combat, the more they will disgrace the Soviet state, the more they will grasp at the most desperate means of struggle when the previous means are doomed."[16]

However, modern trends demonstrate that the course of social progress leads not to more social conflict, but less. Precisely on the basis of technological progress, which is indeed the basis of the NIS.2, we will see the resolution of social contradictions in exact accordance with the known philosophical paradigm.

---

15 Joseph Stalin, "On Industrialization and the Bread Problem: Speech at the Plenum of the Central Committee of the VKP(b) on July 9, 1928," in *Essays*. Vol. 11 (Moscow: Gosgolitizdat, 1949), 171–172. (in Russ.)

16 Joseph Stalin, "On the shortcomings of Party work and measures to eliminate Trotskyist and other two-faced men," in *A Word to Comrade Stalin*, ed. Richard Ivanovich Kosolapov (Moscow: Paleia, 1995), 121–22. (in Russ.)

What changes will knowledge-intensive material production bring about in the social order to reduce social conflict? We cannot as of yet imagine the shape of the social structures of the NIS.2, but allow me to note some trends that are already discernable today. First of all, the growing role of knowledge and the increasing pace of technological innovation in material production will result in changes in social relations. An ever-increasing proportion of the population, with ever-increasing levels of education and qualifications will be involved in processes of technological and, as an inevitable consequence, social creativity.

This trend is social relations will correspond to the growing role of various kinds of voluntary associations and unions of people engaged in research, development, manufacturing, economic, entrepreneurial, managerial, educational, and ecological tasks, to name only some. These structures of civil society will develop and grow out of the basic activities of the population. The educational potential of the population will also grow, its fundamental basis will expand, and we will master our classical cultural heritage. As a result, the level of people's general competence will also grow, their ability to think and solve creatively a variety of production and social issues.

Politically, these changes will also entail a transition, from the current democratic system based on formal equality, limited mainly to periodic participation in voting for members of representative bodies, to a democracy based on competent participation in the day-to-day management of society. This will be a kind of meritocracy, based on those civil society structures that bring together people with relevant skills, who will develop and evaluate the decisions (and their results) of various branches of government (including the fourth estate).

There remains yet another unanswered question: what can we do in advance to make sure that these transitions are smooth and manageable, that they do not occur as spontaneous bifurcations fraught with social tension? To answer this question, we should pay attention to the Northern European transition to capitalism without large-scale revolutionary shocks, which were typical elsewhere in Europe, and their subsequent successes in innovative development.

Why did the development of Scandinavian countries result in a lower level of conflict during their transition to a new stage of social development? This transition cannot be called completely conflict-free: Scandinavian countries have also experienced peasant uprisings, urban rebellions, and conspiracies at the top. But Sweden, Norway, Denmark, Finland, and Iceland did not experience the same whirlwind of revolutions that the rest of Europe did. The struggle for social progress came about primarily through reforms, even if some painful social upheavals followed.

What draws my attention when I look at the history of these countries is their lower level of class conflict. Serfdom was relatively rare, sometimes completely absent. As a result, the peasantry preserved its traditional institutions of communal self-government, and it was legally represented in the legislative and judicial systems. That is to say, the peasantry had the opportunity to legally defend its interests. It was not always successful in this, but these circumstances laid the foundation for a historical tradition of social compromise as opposed to violent action.

The particular social structure of the Nordic countries also resulted in a system of diverse social unions and movements that protected the interests of their members. Another cultural tradition also shaped this practice: a relatively high literacy rate, first based on family instruction and education, later supported by the early introduction of compulsory schooling (in Sweden, for example, "people's schools" were introduced in 1842 and made compulsory in 1889).

The countries in question have transitioned to an innovative economy before, too. As far back as the nineteenth century, the Scandinavian countries have struggled for a leading position in the world economy. Unable to rely neither on rich natural reserves nor on plundering colonies, they chose the path of technological progress and skills development instead. They combined this approach with a high degree of social protection based on well-developed social structures.

Allow me to draw some conclusions based on the Scandinavian experience: the more developed are the political, economic, social, cultural, etc. institutions that make it possible to reconcile conflicting social interests in the course of social change, the more manageable and less painful these changes become. This trend supports the prospective development of knowledge-intensive material production based on the latest technologies, which in turn creates a creative, proactive, cultural person capable of social action. Moreover, the potential for solving social tensions and contradictions lies directly in the progress of knowledge-intensive material production, which will better satisfy people's diverse needs while using fewer resources. And this mode of production is a direct continuation and development of industrial production.

I would go so far as to say that the industrial mode of production is likely the most *ingenious* invention of humankind. It was the industrial mode of production that allowed us to provide for people's needs in an entirely new way. It solved the problem of the accumulation of material resources and their investment (not just consumption), Marx's "value used to produce surplus value." Industrial production transformed these additional resources into capital, info self-expanding value. Capitalism was born on this basis. The industrial mode of production gave birth to capitalist relations, a capitalist superstructure, and created capitalism *as a system* of socioeconomic relations. And the new generation of the industrial mode of production will generate new relations, create a new superstructure, and become the basis for a new type of society, which I have conditionally termed the NIS.2: the second generation of the new industrial state.

The nature of social relations in the second generation of the new industrial state will be fundamentally novel. Because of the practically unlimited opportunity to satisfy real human needs in the NIS.2, the prevalence of the appropriation (of labor, of property, of products) will fall. The basic contradiction in capitalism, according to classical Marxist thought, between the social character of production and the private mode of appropriation, will also fall to the wayside: production will become "separate" from man, and "appropriation" will become the simple act of satisfying one's needs without detriment to other individuals.

Experts believe, on the basis of global statistics, that the global economy has been in a constant state of deceleration for the last two decades, the exception being certain regions, such as China, which has developed not so much intensively as extensively. In terms of human needs, however, contrary to standard statistics irrelevant to real research, the situation is just the opposite: perhaps humanity is just now entering a golden age in this sense.

Consider the use value of any given product designed to satisfy specific human needs. Take a watch, for example. A watch satisfies the need to know the time. Twenty years ago, a watch cost somewhere around one hundred dollars. Around that same time, cellphones also appeared. The first cellphones cost around one thousand dollars. They were used to satisfy the need for communication on the go. Someone who needed to satisfy both needs at once had to spend a combined one thousand one hundred dollars to do so. Fortunately, technological development led to technological synergy. After some small time, new gadgets contained both functions: telling the time and mobile communication. And these new gadgets, thanks to technological development, also cost less to produce that single product that combined two functions. These gadgets cost, let's say three hundred dollars. Looking at these numbers statistically, as does economics, we see a dip in demand, as the price to satisfy the two needs has fallen by eight hundred dollars. From the point of view of standard statistical methods, that would lead to a decrease in GDP. One could argue that the number of people who would want to satisfy those two needs for three hundred dollars is much greater than the number of people who would do so for one thousand one hundred dollars. And that is all true. But the number of people willing to satisfy these two needs at all is limited. And the total demand for these two needs created by people in this new situation will, as this trend develops, sooner or later be less than the total demand of people who could satisfy the two for one thousand one hundred dollars. Since the number of consumers is physically limited, sooner or later this trend will lead to a fall in the statistical volume indicator. Thus, there is a fundamental divergence between how the situation looks from the accounting perspective, and how it looks from the human perspective, from the perspective of people's needs being met. If we take into account the enormous number of combined functions that make it possible to meet people's ever-increasing needs in new knowledge-intensive products, we see not a slowdown in economic growth, but a dramatic increase in the ability to meet people's needs.

The knowledge-intensive product is evolving: its ability to satisfy an ever-widening range of human needs is growing, as we see in the above example of the evolution from watches and telephones to smartphones, with a tremendous increase in the range of functions. Advances in technology have already made it possible to satisfy multiple human needs previously satisfied by different industrial products with just one single knowledge-intensive industrial product. This trend will only continue in the NIS.2. The possibility of meeting people's needs at higher levels may even outpace the growth of their needs. The real question is about the virtually untapped potential capabilities of new products: how do we activate their potentialities so that they do not go to waste?

In knowledge-intensive production, we see a reduction in the consumption of material resources per unit of "former" need, and an increase in the product's knowledge content. Lower production costs per unit of former need are responsible for this simultaneous rise and fall. A fall in demand for traditional materials and resources means a fall in the importance of raw materials in the new global industry. Though Russia has condemned the raw materials economy in words, it has continued to support it in practice, though it amounts to a dead-end developmental strategy given the above considerations.

The simultaneous fall in resource-intensity and rise in knowledge-intensity offers us the opportunity to better balance industry and environmental concerns. Concurrently people's needs will shift such that they are focused more on personal development than putting bread on the table and a roof above their heads. Indeed, when it becomes possible to easily satisfy the need for sustenance and shelter, the need to grow creatively through labor comes to the fore. The future economy will depend significantly on the "cultural" person, in the broadest sense of the word. Creating such a person plays a big role in moving us toward the NIS.2.

The development and integration of production, science, and education also play a big role in this goal, as I have made clear. But are people ready for such a turn of events? Even the mere fact of less competition for material and other goods facilitates the birth of a new historical community of people. Still—human nature doesn't change overnight. Isn't that right? Certainly right, but that is not the final word on the matter. Humanity is evolving. Even the individual changes over time or under the influence of given circumstances and education. And the main educator of humanity is culture, in the broadest sense of the word. What's more, it is culture coupled with material production that birthed humanity. And together with a new industrial production, these factors will birth the man of the NIS.2, who "stands above and next to production" [stoiashchego nad, riadom s proizvodstvom], and who takes part in predominantly constructive intellectual activity.

I could end on this major note, but there is one serious concern about the fate of humanity in the new industrial future that I have yet to discuss.

A huge number of people are finding themselves out of work as industrial development intensifies and new technologies are rapidly introduced. The question that stands before us is: where can they go? Allegedly, technological progress will leave millions out of work, leading only to more and more social tension. But there will be no great social tension or rupture. The transition to the NIS.2. implies what I have termed the "acceleration of acceleration": the rapid acceleration of the rate at which the product's knowledge content grows, leading to a new type of industrial production, that is, knowledge-intensive production. A huge number of people will be needed to ensure the success of this process, the ever-increasing production of knowledge. Recall how, in the nineteenth and early twentieth centuries, many experts also feared that the progress of industrial production, particularly in agriculture, would lead to unemployment in the countryside, leaving millions of peasants without jobs. But their fears did not come true, because those peasants moved to the rapidly developing industrial sector. So, too, will the workers from the previous industrial production, working with technologies from the previous industrial cycle, move into the knowledge production sector. More and more of these jobs will become available as knowledge-intensive production proliferates and enters into all spheres of production. This rapidly developing (or "accelerating") sector will absorb the bulk of people who may now or soon find themselves without work. These new workers will require intensive training or retraining, as also happened during the industrial era. The new industrial era also requires that we readjust our system for training and educating workers. How do we do this? If we take into account that in our transition to the NIS.2, knowledge is constantly being updated, then so, too, will workers need to constantly be trained, i.e., we must create a system of continuous training that follows the worker throughout his life ("education throughout life," as Smolin puts it).[17]

The constant growth of knowledge-intensive material production demands that new knowledge is constantly applied in technology, an essentially endless process. This fact opens up a wealth of opportunity to put people to work, people who lost their jobs in traditional industrial production or the service sector because of the growth of productivity. The termination of jobs in industrial production does not necessarily need to lead to the growth of the post-industrial sector but can and must satisfy the growing need for human resources in the development of new industrial production, specifically its intellectual component. We have the opportunity to create potentially endless employment growth by putting people to work in industries that produce and technologically apply new knowledge, and in industries that support this process (education, healthy living, culture, etc.).

It will not be easy to tackle this challenge. We need to solve a mass of research problems to ensure the necessary technological progress. And this may become difficult if the financial elite fears that it will lose its control over the economy. The financial elite bribes the topmost class of technological specialists by ceding a share of their profits to guarantee that this class does not expand. The financial elite is willing to sacrifice technological advancement to share its economic power only with the smallest possible circle of technological specialists, preventing them from becoming an established and influential social stratum. We can only overcome this imbalance by shifting the power from the financial elite to the technocrats, enabling the technological elite to mobilize sufficient social resources for its growth.

---

17 "From the idea of an elitist education, a separate system of education for the rich and the managerial class and another system of education for the rest, we must turn to the idea of education for all and education throughout life." O. N. Smolin, Education throughout life: Problems of the legislation and development of education: transcript of a meeting of the State Duma Committee on Education (July 5, 2012).

Conclusion

—

The Specter of NIS.2: The Materialization of its Essence

—

Today's global economic system is at a crossroads. Chasing the specter of a postindustrial society has only led to one illusion after another, mirages like those that appeared to the Jews as they wandered the desert. But a mirage is a mirage because there is no material object there. And the industrial mode of production is used to do just that, produce material objects for the satisfaction of our needs.

The second generation of the new industrial state not only preserves, but indeed develops the material industrial base. Industry has not disappeared, and could not disappear, as it still exists throughout different countries participating in the global economy. There was only a spillover of industrial capacity from one region of the world to another, and now those countries that lost their industrial potential face the need for reindustrialization. Even the American economy, still the strongest national economy today, demonstrates the deleterious effects of deindustrialization.

Our pursuit of an illusory postindustrial, crisis-free "new economy" has led to a global economic crisis, only emphasizing the risks of deindustrialization and the instability of the financial system. The interests of financial speculators now dominate the economy, placing virtual reality and fictitious needs over the interests of material production.

The global economy needs a reset. And this reset must be based on the paradigm of the industrial mode of production. The economic leaders of the coming era will be the technological leaders. Russia has started to make a U-turn in this direction, but our efforts are not sufficiently thought-out or focused. We lack a long-term economic strategy, and the necessary theoretical basis and practical program to carry it out. According to some estimates, today Russia lags behind the technological frontier, i.e., the level of the most advanced industrial technologies, by fifteen to thirty years, even more in some areas. If we want to assert a strong position in the global economy, our movement toward the NIS.2 must be even quicker than that of others. At the same time, we must be consistent and measured in our steps toward this goal, moving confidently to avoid the risk of harming ourselves by taking an adventurous leap forward.

The new production and technology characteristic of the NIS.2 will make it possible to meet increasing human needs more and more quickly and fully. Society has not yet invented any other way to do so than on an *industrial basis*.

Marx's transition "beyond material production," the "leap from the realm of necessity to the realm of freedom," is a philosophical paradigm, not a prescription for the development of economic practice. All human needs, including the development of man himself as a creator, a demiurge, need a *material basis*. Marx's words that the kingdom of freedom can only blossom on the basis of the kingdom of necessity are true for this reason. A "pure" reign of freedom is impossible, but it is possible to approach this goal by liberating and developing the creative powers of man *on the basis of knowledge-intensive industrial production.*

The technological progress of this kind of production opens the way for the development of real (rather than simulated) human needs and for their satisfaction with real goods (rather than simulacra). The expanding technological application of scientific knowledge, and the growing knowledge content of material production, determines the speed of change, the growing acceleration of the movement towards new possibilities of production. This acceleration is not based on a simple increase in the number of industrial products, but on the growing complexity of industrial products, which are becoming more and more knowledge-intensive, while at the same time less material-, energy-, and labor-intensive as a result.

By reducing our consumption of natural substances, materials, and energy per unit of human needs, we put less pressure on natural resources and avoid the risk of global environmental collapse. The more we use new knowledge in production, the more we expand the possibilities of this process.

Human society is on the threshold of a new technological revolution, which, like the previous ones, inevitably entails profound changes not only in material production and in the production of new knowledge, but also in society's entire socioeconomic system. The transition to the second generation of the new industrial state (NIS.2) is looming.

But historical events do not always come about at the time and place that we had dreamed they would. Establishing the NIS.2 will require a huge and carefully coordinated effort toward a *technological breakthrough*. It will require *accelerating innovation; reintegrating production, science, and education;* improving *Russia's economic and institutional systems* to ensure an *active industrial policy* aimed at *reindustrializing* our country on the most advanced technological basis. Only then will it be possible to talk about Russia's transition to the NIS.2.

What will this transition look like? Will it not cause so much social tension that it will result in a revolutionary rupture not only in the technological but also in the sociopolitical spheres? Keeping in mind the inevitable costs of this scenario, we must anticipate and manage the processes of socioeconomic development in order to make the inevitable changes as natural as possible. It is urgent that we develop a sound scientific basis not only for progressive technological solutions, but also for effective economic and social policies capable of carrying us to a new stage of development.

And if this book makes it possible to take even a small step in this direction, my work will have not been in vain.

Appendix 1

The New Industrial State: Production, Economy, Institutions[1]

_____

Since its establishment in 1997, the S.Y. Witte Institute for New Economic Development (INID) has been studying problems of industry, its role in the modern economic system, and trends in the development of the industrial mode of production. For more than five years of its nearly twenty-year existence, the INID has worked under the supervision of the Russian Academy of Sciences (RAS) Department of Social Sciences. As director of the INID, I am convinced that today there is only one efficient path forward for the global economy, of which industrial production is a central component. Allow me to substantiate this argument using the institute's research.

Fulfilling human needs requires some sort of *production process*, where certain *ideas*, *material objects* (materials, tools, technologies, including technological equipment), and *human labor* come together to create goods (i.e., *products*) designed to meet those needs. In addition to the material component, in every basic element of modern material production there is yet another key element without which production cannot take place: *knowledge*. Knowledge is necessary to organize the production process, to *objectify* it (to determine the content of an industrial product or service as an object of

_____

1 Based on a report from a meeting of the Economics Section of the Department of Social Sciences of the Russian Academy of Sciences on March 9, 2016.

labor), and to create and streamline the means of achieving the desired result (*materials* and *technology*). Moreover, *labor* is itself based on the knowledge, skills, and abilities of the worker.

I have studied the *product* in its capacity to fulfill human *needs*; human activity in the process of *production* (its many *components*); and the changes that humanity has gone through over the history of *conscious production*. My studies show that *quantitative changes* in material production (accumulated *knowledge* about the tools and methods of labor organization) lead to *qualitative changes* in the mode of material production, specifically to the *industrial mode* of production, at a certain historical moment. This change is followed by the *industrialization* of the economy itself.

The history of industrial development demonstrates that, despite the (still ongoing) changes in material production (including the reduction of its share in the GDP of developed countries, the information revolution, etc.), *material production remains the basis of the economy*, of its very existence. Material production is predominantly *industrial* production. It is owing to scientific and technological progress that industry can *meet the ever-increasing needs of mankind more and more fully*.

At the same time, it is true that a society's given *mode of production determines the structure of that society*. In specific, as the technological application of scientific knowledge becomes more prevalent and important, the more a society based on the industrial mode changes. All the major scholars, from Smith and Marx to Galbraith and Bell, have drawn attention to this fact.

Galbraith's *The New Industrial State*, published half a century ago, challenged the author's contemporaries to rethink the industrial economic system, especially that of the US. The decades that followed the book's release saw the rise of theories that overshadowed Galbraith's vision, but recent years have cast doubt on the conclusions that economists came to in the nineties, when the world became captive to the ideas of post-industrialism. In works like those of Daniel Bell and Alvin Toffler, the post-industrialists denied the central role of material production. Theories of the emergence of an "information economy" and an "information society" appeared and were then furthered by concepts such as the digital economy. The works of Sakaiya, Castells, and, in Russia, Inozemtsev became very popular. But the global economic and financial crises of the late nineties and of 2007–2009 have dampened the enthusiasm for these theories. The attempt to go beyond material production did not result in more efficiency, productivity, or wealth, but in more intermediation, especially financial, which had a big hand in the crisis that began in 2007.

Material production, however, has not disappeared. Because of society's *unconditional need* for an *industrial means* to meet its needs, what we at the INID have called *"industrial spillover"* [peretekanie industrii] has occurred: while post-industrialization has taken hold in the West, the Global South and the East have seen a powerful wave of industrialization. There, the share of industrial production has decreased dramatically, and the role and share of workers and engineers employed in the purely industrial sector of the global total workforce has grown.

Meanwhile, Western economies remain in thrall to post-industrialism, which argues that the necessary economic system for a post-industrial society is one in which business is based on services, capital accumulation is based on financial transactions, and the dominant mechanism for balance and growth is the free market itself, which must spread into society's every corner (what our very own Grinberg has termed "market fundamentalism".) This position has grown in dominance and is associated with a number of specific processes: The process of *financialization* has not only led to the expansion of the "vital activity" of financial institutions, but it has also led to a new model of economic regulation, property relations, etc. Investment priorities have especially begun to change, directed more and more away from production and toward financial transactions. Financial institutions have begun to seize control over property and basic property rights. And the financial sphere has quickly developed into one of the main sources (sometimes the main source) of GDP growth. These factors have led to financial bubbles and, in one way or another, to the global financial and economic crisis.

The post-industrial wave has led to industrial spillover: a massive drift of industrial production capacity from the West to the South and East, *accelerating the industrialization of first semi-peripheral, then peripheral countries*, which put together make up almost half of the world's population. Then there is the *growing geo-political and economic influence* and power of China, India, and the BRICS community at large, which have led to new challenges for the most powerful economic leaders. Meanwhile, many economies of the Global North (especially the US) are in the process of deindustrialization, leading to an entirely new factor in global geo-political and economic relations: *the West's production dependence on the South and East.* Add to this fact that China and then India will soon reach the modern frontiers of high-tech production, allowing them to shed their technological dependence on the West, producing yet another challenge that forces Western economies to think about the recovery of material production and the development of a new industrial economy.

Studies on the fundamentals of industry, its developmental patterns and challenges over the last decade confirm the inevitable transition to a new stage of human development, a *new generation of industrial society*, and even a *new type of social structure, significantly different from that of the late twentieth and early twenty-first centuries. I have termed this new social structure the second generation of the new industrial state* (NIS.2 for short). The NIS.2 and its economy will be a "negation of a negation," a dialectical sublation of both Galbraith's late industrial system and the post-industrial system of Bell and others.

In order to characterize the coming NIS.2, allow me to analyze some *important modern-day trends in the development of modern material production that alter both the process of industrial production itself* (its *materials, technology, organization, and labor*) and *its result* (the *product*).

As I have already noted, any product that is the result of production contains within it, in addition to its material components, an intangible element: knowledge, which is present in all the components of the production process. Along with its material basis, knowledge constitutes an *integral part* of the product.

Throughout society's historical development, the *relative share of knowledge* in all components of production and in the product itself has been *continuously increasing*, as the material share has been accordingly decreasing. It is this trend that determines the gradual *qualitative* change of both the *production process and the industrial product* that is its result, generating new possibilities in the satisfaction of human needs and forming new needs. This trend may also create the illusion of the possibility of their "non-material," "non-productive," or "non-industrial" satisfaction. But it is incorrect to conclude based on this trend that the *defining role* of material production is itself dying out. Another conclusion seems more likely: namely, that the knowledge-intensity of material production is *constantly* growing, and that on this basis *a new type of material production is emerging*.

The *knowledge-intensive technology* used in material production synthesizes the achievements of both industrial and information technologies. It is not theoretical posturing that has led to this critical synthesis, but the real practice of modern high-tech production. In this kind of production, operations and processes where the worker acts not as an appendage of a machine (like at a conveyor belt), but as a carrier of knowledge that is transformed into technology, begin to play a defining role. As Marx said, "man grows closer to production" and "relates to the production process as its controller and regulator."[2]

---

2   Karl Marx and Friedrich Engels, *Collected Works*, vol. 46, pt. 2, 213.

In this regard, a fundamentally *new type of material production* is born: knowledge-intensive production. Its main features are gradually revealing themselves:

- the intangible component of the product becomes more important and its share in the product grows; there is a continuous increase of information in the product and decrease of its material component; miniaturization, i.e., a tendency toward the reduction of energy, material and, capital that goes into production;
- a *paradigm shift* is happening in industrial production. Allow me to elaborate:
- production is becoming both broader and deeper in its processes (individualization, optionality, etc., plus more flexibility, modularity, standardization, etc.), ensuring that the product *maximally approximates the consumer's needs*, can be delivered almost instantaneously, but at the same time requires less labor-intensity and lower production costs. These factors of the NIS.2 radically alter the possibilities of meeting people's growing needs, not through a return to the handmade production of individual products, but through the development of the *industrial mode of production*;
- *network-model industry structuring*, replacing vertically integrated structuring;
- the use of *modern methods* of production and management (just-in-time, lean-production, etc.);
- environmental friendliness and *new sources of energy*;
- the development of *new technologies* in material production, transport, and logistics (nanotechnologies, 3D-printing, etc.);
- the basic technological paradigm of industrial production is itself changing; the role of the traditional manufacturing industry is shrinking due to the spread of additive technologies (the process of combining materials to create an object from a 3D model, usually layer by layer, as opposed to traditional, subtractive manufacturing technologies: trimming, grinding, cutting, etc.;
- the nature of *industrial labor* is also changing toward *knowledge-intensive labor* (management control, high-tech labor, unmanned technologies, automatization, etc.);
- the way that workers assimilate the knowledge and skills necessary to carry out effective production in the new system is likewise changing: the use of gadgets, chips, the internet, virtual and augmented reality technologies, etc.;
- and other changes are currently underway.

This new stage of industrial society's development (NIS.2) is characterized not only by an increase in industrial production, but an increase in the importance of technological innovation and in the share of applied knowledge and information. Indeed, one of the most important characteristics of the new economic system is this tendency to *continually increase the rate of technological change*: an "acceleration of acceleration." Consequently, *the rate at which scientific advances are directed into industrial production*, into its *processes* and *products*, is fundamentally important. Industrial production must undergo (and is, in cases, already undergoing) *continuous innovation*.

All these changes will lead to *changes in the economic macrostructure*, where the industries that *dominate* will be those that form an integral production complex to *create a knowledge-intensive product*. These will be industries that *produce the given product, create the knowledge* necessary to produce it, and *train the workers* capable of mastering and applying that necessary knowledge.

The new economy must combine (at the micro- and macrolevels) the following elements:

- *knowledge-intensive, high-tech material production*, which creates a knowledge-intensive product;
- *science*, which creates the know-how;
- *education and culture*, which create a person who not only possesses knowledge and is able to apply it in production but is also able to generate it.

The *foundation* of these three basic spheres *of new social production* is *material production* itself. (My argument here follows the principles of classical political economy.) Science becomes a *direct productive force*, and education "throughout life" becomes an *indispensable condition for the efficiency* of production.

Because of the changes in the content and structure of social production, the main production link of the new industrial economy will be a *new kind of industrial complex, which integrates production, science, and education* in a single production process both at micro and macro-levels. These complexes will form the basis for industrial clusters that combine these components in a single scientific-production process. For example, PSE (production-science-education) clusters include manufacturing enterprises, R&D centers, and educational organizations within the same infra and ultra-structure, though the various elements remain legally independent.

As the new industrial economy emerges and social production develops new content and new structures, new economic relations and institutions also pop up. The new industrial economy recontextualizes the positive features of past systems and gives them new life. At the same time, it also presents new challenges to the development of *market self-regulation* and *private property*, on the one hand, and *state influence on the economy*, on the other.

The tasks of our times include: the development of complex integrated production units; the macroeconomic integration of production, science, and education; the major restructuring of the economy; and overhauling hypertrophied sectors of financial intermediation. These tasks demand an *active state industrial policy* and *long-term public-private investments*. The state regulation of the economy must be structured such that it supports these tasks (a process that is underway in many countries, especially in China).

As we transition to creating and using knowledge-intensive products on a large scale, our economic relations and institutions must also go through some necessary changes. The synthesized (i.e., both intellectual and material) nature of the knowledge-intensive product causes many other changes in the system of economic relations and institutions. For example, the growing importance of the intangible component in the industrial product leads to a sharp increase in the importance of the recent idea of *intellectual property*. *In knowledge-intensive production, the intangible, intellectual component will become the dominant one.*

The modern Russian economic model is rooted in theories of post-industrialism, market fundamentalism, and liberal monetary capitalism, which have led to the distortion of our national economy, the hypertrophy of the raw material sector, excessive financialization, and deindustrialization. We must *change Russia's economic* model and prioritize industrial development. Industrial production development trends indicate that the global need for raw materials, minerals, and energy is shrinking, both in the share of an individual product, and of (so to say) the global aggregate product, the world economy. Prices for many raw materials are falling, especially for energy resources, heralding the dawn of an era where traditional resources (the core of the Russian economy) are not as important as they once were in the global economy. What is becoming more and more important is industrial knowledge and technology, the pace of their acquisition, development, and implementation in the real sector. It is clear that the *economic leaders of the NIS.2 will be world's technological leaders*. So, what is there to do for Russia?

As I have stated more than once, we need to reindustrialize our economy and restore industry as its *basic component*. Industrial development should be our *first priority*, specifically *new industrialization*, by which I mean the intensive accumulation of industrial potential based on high-tech, knowledge-intensive production. To correct our economic trajectory, we must *change popular attitudes, government policies,* state programs, and the *relevant institutions.*

The development of high-tech material production and the ever-increasing share of knowledge in the product necessitate that we restore the systematic integration of production, science, and education, which was destroyed during the reform years. This reintegration must take place in fundamentally new economic forms that harness the potential of both the state and the market and private property. These new economic systems must address not only the development of production and technology, but also the fundamental development of the human personality, as well as other social and environmental problems.

Appendix 2

The New Industrial State: Production, Economy, Institutions[1] (10 Theses)

1. The study of the *product* in its capacity to fulfill human *needs*; human activity in the process of *production* (its many *components*); and the changes that humanity has gone through over the history of *conscious production* (its accumulated *knowledge* about the tools and methods of labor organization, leading to the industrial mode of production) demonstrate that: Despite the many changes that have taken place in material production over the last century, like its declining share in the GDP of various countries or the information revolution, *material production remains the basis of the economy*, of its very existence. And the dominant mode of production remains industrial production. On the basis of scientific and technological progress, industry makes it possible to *meet the ever-increasing needs of mankind more and more fully.*

2. It is undeniable that a society's given *mode of production determines the structure of that society.* As the technological application of scientific knowledge becomes more prevalent and important, this will generate more change within societies that are based on the industrial mode. This fact leads me to conclude that the transition to a new stage of

---

1 Based on a report from a meeting of the Economics Section of the Department of Social Sciences of the Russian Academy of Sciences on March 9, 2016.

human development, a *new generation of industrial society*, which I have termed *the second generation of the new industrial state* (NIS.2 for short), is inevitable. The NIS.2 and its economy will be a "negation of a negation," a dialectical sublation of both Galbraith's late industrial system and the post-industrial system of Bell and others.

3. In order to characterize the coming NIS.2, allow me to analyze some *important modern-day trends in the development of modern material production that alter both the process of industrial production itself* (its *materials, technology, organization, and labor*) and *its result* (the *product*).

    3.1 Any product that is the result of production contains within it, in addition to its material components, an intangible element: knowledge. Knowledge is present in all the components of the production process: its *materials, technology* (i.e., instruments), *organization*, and finally, the human *labor* that goes into the production process. Along with its material basis, knowledge constitutes an *integral part* of the product.

    3.2 Throughout society's historical development, the *relative share of knowledge* in all components of production and in the product itself has been *continuously increasing*, as the material share has been accordingly decreasing. It is this trend that determines the gradual *qualitative* change of both the *production process and the industrial product* that is its result, generating new possibilities in the satisfaction of human needs and forming new needs. This trend may also create the illusion of the possibility of their "non-material," "non-productive," or "non-industrial" satisfaction. But it is incorrect to conclude on the basis of this trend that the *defining role* of material production is itself dying out. Another conclusion seems all the more likely: namely, that the *knowledge-intensity of material production* is constantly growing, and that on this basis *a new type of material production is emerging*.

    3.3 The new material production will be based on technologies with an ever-increasing level of knowledge, leading to the *knowledge-intensive technologies* of material production in the NIS.2. In such production, operations and processes where the worker acts not as an appendage of a machine, but as a carrier of knowledge, begin to play a defining role. "Man grows closer to production" and "relates to the production process as its controller and regulator."[2]

---

2 Karl Marx and Friedrich Engels, *Collected Works*, vol. 46, pt. 2, 213.

3.4 On this basis, a fundamentally *new type of material production* is born: *knowledge-intensive production.* Knowledge-intensive production meets the needs of people in fundamentally different ways than traditional industrial production: it *prioritizes the intangible component* of the product, reduces the share of the material component, and can better meet the demands of the consumer (in terms of the product's content and the speed at which it can be produced.) In knowledge-intensive production we see a fundamental change in production technologies, the methods of production organization, the nature of industrial labor, and the assimilation of industrial knowledge.

3.5 At the same time, changes in the technologies of material production led to *changes in its product,* which becomes the *knowledge-intensive material product,* both the main resource and result of the new industrial economy. Of course, any product is, philosophically speaking, "objectified" human knowledge. But the specificity of the *knowledge-intensive product* lies in its *level of complexity.* Industrial production tends toward the *constant increase of the product's level of complexity.* In new industrial production, this trend is coupled with another: a product's knowledge content grows, while it requires less natural energy and fewer raw materials to produce.

4. The NIS.2 is characterized not only by the product's ever-growing complexity, the growing role of technological innovation, or the growing share of knowledge in the product. This new stage of industrial development is also characterized by its *ever-increasing rate of technological change,* an "acceleration of acceleration" that is *one of the most important features of the new economic system.* Consequently, *the rate at which scientific advances are directed into industrial production,* into its *processes* and *products,* is fundamentally important. Industrial production must undergo (and is, in some cases, already undergoing) *continuous innovation.*

5. All these changes will lead to *changes in the structure of the economy at large.* The classical industrial system (based on the dominance of industrial production) and today's "service society" (in which service industries replace material production) will both be replaced by the new industrial economy, the *second generation of the new industrial state.*

The NIS.2 will structure the main sectors of its economic differently than we do now. Sectors that produce knowledge-intensive products will come to dominate, as will those where knowledge itself is created, and where workers capable of acquiring and using that knowledge are trained.

6. The economy of the NIS.2 should be based (both at micro- and macro-levels) on the combination of: a) *knowledge-intensive high-tech material production*, which creates knowledge-intensive products; b) *science*, which creates the know-how; c) *education and culture*, which creates a person who not only possesses knowledge and is able to apply it in production, but is also able to generate it.

The *foundation* of these three basic spheres *of new social production* is *material production* itself. (My argument here follows the principles of classical political economy.) Science becomes a *direct productive force*, and education "throughout life" becomes an *indispensable condition for the efficiency* of production.

7. These changes in social production, particularly the ever-increasing acceleration of knowledge-intensive production, necessitate that production, science, and education *converge* and form new structures under the umbrella of material production. The *main production link* of the NIS.2 will the *new industrial complex, which integrates production, science, and education in a single production process* at both the macro- and micro-levels: for example, production enterprises, R&D centers, and educational organizations with a unified infra- and ultra-structure. At the macro-level, the main organizational structure will be *networks of cooperation between research and production*.

8. As the new industrial economy emerges and social production develops new content and new structures, *new economic relations and institutions are established*.

Changes in the technological basis of society lead to new needs in a society, to new social "players" (i.e., new social strata) with differing interests. Consequently, *tensions may grow between the different elements of an economic system*. This tension between different social groups intensifies as they attempt to satisfy their own interests; a confrontation that may be resolved either by a revolutionary breakdown or by a systemic transformation, both of which are avenues toward a new economic state. By using socio-economic *planning and forecasting methods* in our economic management practices, we can alleviate some of the dramatic social shocks caused by the radical transformation of economic systems. The new industrial economy recontextualizes the positive features of past systems and gives them new life. At the same time, it also presents new challenges to the development of *market self-regulation* and *private property*, on the one hand, and *state influence on the economy*, on the other.

The tasks at hand include: the development of complex integrated production units; the macroeconomic integration of production, science, and education; the major restructuring of the economy; and overhauling hypertrophied sectors of financial intermediation. These tasks demand an *active state industrial policy* and *long-term public-private investments*. The state regulation of the economy must be structured such that it supports these tasks (a process that is underway in many countries, especially in China).

9. The liberal monetary economic model has long dominated the Russian economy, leading to the distortion of the national economic structure, the hypertrophy of the raw material sector, excessive financialization, and deindustrialization. For this reason, the above-mentioned challenges of the transition to the NIS.2 are especially pronounced in Russia. We must *change Russia's economic* model and prioritize industrial development. Industrial production development trends indicate that the global need for raw materials, minerals, and energy is shrinking, both per unit and for the world economy as a whole. Prices for many raw materials are falling, especially for energy resources, heralding the dawn of an era where traditional resources (the core of the Russian economy) are not as important as they once were in the global economy. What is becoming more important is industrial knowledge and technology, the pace of their acquisition, development, and implementation in the real sector. A new technological revolution is not far off. It is clear that the *economic leaders of the NIS.2 will be world's technological leaders*.

We need to *reindustrialize our economy* and restore industry as its *basic component*. Industrial development should be our *first priority*, specifically *new industrialization*, by which I mean the *intensive accumulation of industrial potential based on high-tech, knowledge-intensive production*. To correct our economic trajectory, we must change popular attitudes, government policies, state programs, as well as relevant institutions.

10. To correct our path and redirect Russian economic development, which is still entirely possible, Russia requires certain *systemic changes*. Our priorities must include economic management based on *long-term programs* and medium-term *indicative planning* and *forecasting*; an *active industrial policy*; a system of institutions that guarantees state support

to private, *long-term* investment in R&D and *technological upgrading in production*; a tax and credit system favorable to the real sector, especially the high-tech sector; and other methods of stimulating the development of these industries and their industrial potential. The new economic system should allow for a *moderate level of social differentiation*: variations in income should depend manly on the worker's real contribution to economic development.

The suggestions that I have put forth here should be concretized in economic policy programs. The INID,[3] the Moscow Economic Forum,[4] and RAS economists under the supervision of Sergei Glazyev[5] have provided some guidelines toward this kind of policymaking.

3 S. D. Bodrunov. *Shaping Russia's Reindustrialization Strategy.* St. Petersburg: Institute for New Industrial Development (INID), 2013.
4 See *Russia's Economic System: Anatomy of the Present and Strategies for the Future (Reindustrialization and/or Advanced Development).* Moscow: LENAND, 2014.
5 S. Y. Glazyev. *Strategy of Russia's Advanced Development in the Context of Global Crisis.* Moscow: Ekonomika, 2010.

Appendix 3

Toward A New Material Production: Russia's Future in Eurasia[1]

It is not only the global economy that is on the threshold of major change, but human civilization at large. As different countries vie for a top spot in the future global economy, the question remains: which countries will retain, gain, or lose a competitive edge, moreover, which will become new centers of soft power and which will become subordinate? To better understand Russia's prospects in this new economic landscape, I will lay out some preliminary considerations and questions.

1. Economic and political cooperation can take place on an equal footing only if both parties have mutual interests and similar economic potential. For this reason, Russia must shed its role as a supplier of raw materials, which it can do only by transitioning to *a new stage of development*. Russia's *effective economic cooperation* with other economic players, especially with other Eurasian countries, is conditional upon this transition. The first step toward this goal is answering the question: what is the nature of this new stage of development and where is the modern economy heading?

---

1 Based on a presentation at the International Seminar on Conceptualizing Economic Development and Cooperation in Eurasia in Cambridge on May 2, 2016.

I will attempt to answer this question with some basic provisions. I have studied the *product* in its capacity to fulfill human *needs*; human activity in the process of *production* (its many *components*); and the changes that humanity has gone through over the history of *conscious production*. My studies show that *quantitative changes* in material production (accumulated *knowledge* about the tools and methods of labor organization) lead to *qualitative changes* in the **mode of material production**, specifically to the *industrial mode* of production. Despite the many changes that have taken place within it, *material production remains the basis of the economy*, of its very existence. And the dominant mode of production remains industrial production. On the basis of scientific and technological progress, industry makes it possible to *meet the ever-increasing needs of mankind more and more fully*.

2. A second question follows the first: what comes next in material production?

It is undeniable that a society's given *mode of production determines the structure of that society*. More specifically, as the technological application of scientific knowledge becomes more prevalent and important, and as new technologies enter into all spheres of both economic and social life, the more that a society based on the industrial mode changes. This fact leads me to conclude that the *transition* to a new stage of human development is *inevitable*.

Different visions of this future exist. If Russia is to effectively take the lead in the future economy, we must correctly assess its parameters and characteristics in preparation.

Thus, the third question is: what will the new society look like?

I argue that we are witnessing the birth of the next generation of industrial society, what I have termed the *second generation of the new industrial state* (NIS.2 for short). The NIS.2 and its economy will be a "negation of a negation," a dialectical sublation of both Galbraith's late industrial system and the post-industrial system of Bell and others.

3. Having established that this change is imminent, I will address the next question: what is the main factor of this development? This question demands an answer, if we are to make progress toward the future society.

I argue that the basic factor of this future development is **knowledge**.

3.1 Any product that is the result of production contains within it, in addition to its material components, an intangible element: *knowledge*. Knowledge is present in all the components of the production process: its *materials, technology* (i.e., instruments), *organization,* and finally, the human *labor* that goes into the production process. Along with its material basis, knowledge constitutes an *integral part* of the product.

3.2 Throughout society's historical development, the *relative share of knowledge* in all components of production and within the product itself has been *continuously increasing,* as the material share has been decreasing. It is this trend that determines the gradual *qualitative* change of both the *production process and the industrial product* that is its result, generating new possibilities in the satisfaction of human needs and forming new needs. This trend may also create the illusion of the possibility of their "non-material," "non-productive," or "non-industrial" satisfaction. But it is incorrect to conclude on the basis of this trend that the *defining role* of material production is itself dying out. Another conclusion seems all the more likely: namely, that the **knowledge-intensity** *of material production* is constantly growing, and that on this basis *a new type of material production is emerging.*

3.3 **The new material production** will be based on technologies with an ever-increasing level of knowledge, leading to the knowledge-intensive technologies of material production in the NIS.2. In such production, operations and processes where the worker acts not as an appendage of a machine, but as a carrier of knowledge, begin to play a defining role. As Marx said, "man grows *closer* to produc*tion" and* "relates to the production process as its controller and regulator."[2]

Having analyzed various trends in the development of modern material production, I argue that the most fundamental trend is that of the *accumulation of knowledge* in all components of production and, consequently, in the product itself. This trend is the basic factor that determines the direction and pace of the development of material production. It gives material production new and important features and ensures its transformation into a **new type** of production (in our time, industrial production).

On this basis, a fundamentally *new type of material production* is born: **knowledge-intensive production.** Knowledge-intensive production meets the needs of people in *fundamentally different* ways than traditional industrial production.

---

2   Karl Marx and Friedrich Engels, *Collected Works,* Vol. 46 (London: Lawrence Wishart, 1992), 213. (in Russ.)

[Some important features of this type of production, characteristic of the NIS.2, include:

- *the intangible component of the product* becomes more important and its share in the product grows; there is a continuous increase of information in the product and decrease of its material component; miniaturization, i.e., a tendency toward the reduction of energy, material and, capital that goes into production;

- production becomes both "broader" and "deeper" in its processes (individualization, optionality, etc., plus more flexibility, modularity, standardization, etc.), ensuring that the product maximally approximates the consumer's needs, can be delivered almost instantaneously, but at the same time requires less labor-intensity and lower production costs. These factors of the NIS.2 radically alter the possibilities of meeting people's growing needs, not through a return to the handmade production of individual products, but through the development of the *industrial mode of production;*

- *network-model industry structuring*, replacing vertically-integrated structuring;

- the use of *modern methods* of production and management (just-in-time, lean-production, etc.);

- the development of *new technologies* in material production, transport, and logistics (nanotechnologies, 3D-printing, etc.);

- the basic technological paradigm of industrial production is itself changing; the role of the traditional manufacturing industry is shrinking due to the spread of additive technologies (the process of combining materials to create an object from a 3D model, usually layer by layer, as opposed to traditional, subtractive manufacturing technologies: trimming, grinding, cutting, etc.;

- the nature of *industrial labor* is also changing toward *knowledge-intensive labor* (management control, high-tech labor, unmanned technologies, automatization, etc.);

- the way that workers assimilate the knowledge and skills necessary to carry out effective production in the new system is likewise changing: the use of gadgets,

> chips, the Internet, virtual and augmented reality technologies, etc.;
> - and other such changes.]

4. An in-depth analysis of knowledge-intensive production and its tendency toward acceleration leads me to conclude that one of the most important characteristics of the new economic system is this tendency to *continually increase the rate of technological change*: an "acceleration of acceleration." Industrial production must undergo (and is, in cases, already undergoing) *continuous innovation*. Consequently, *the rate at which scientific advances are directed into industrial production*, into its *processes* and *products*, is fundamentally important.

5. All these changes will lead to *changes in the economic macrostructure structure*. The classical industrial system (based on the dominance of industrial production) and today's "service society" (in which service industries replace material production) will both be replaced by the new industrial economy, the **second generation of the new industrial state**.

   In the NIS.2, sectors that produce knowledge-intensive products will come to dominate: those where these products are produced, as well as those where knowledge itself is created, and where workers capable of acquiring and using that knowledge are trained.

6. The economy of the NIS.2 should be based (both at micro- and macro-levels) on the combination of: a) *knowledge-intensive high-tech material production*, which creates knowledge-intensive products; b) *science*, which creates the know-how; c) *education and culture*, which creates a person who not only possesses knowledge and is able to apply it in production, but is also able to generate it.

7. These changes in the **content** of social production, particularly the ever-increasing acceleration of knowledge-intensive production, necessitate that production, science, and education *converge*, leading to fundamental changes in the **structure** of material production.

   The **main production link** of the NIS.2 will the *new industrial complex, which integrates production, science, and education in a single production process* at both the macro- and micro-levels: for example, production enterprises, R&D centers, and educational organizations with a unified infra- and ultra-structure. At the macro-level, the main organizational structure will be *networks of cooperation between research and production*.

8. As the new industrial economy emerges and social production develops new content and new structures, **new economic relations and institutions also pop up**.

[Changes in the technological basis of society lead to new needs in a society, to new social "players" (i.e., new social strata) with different interests. Consequently, *tensions may grow between the different elements of an economic system and in their links.* This tension between different social groups intensifies as they attempt to satisfy their own interests, a confrontation that may be resolved either by a revolutionary breakdown or by a systemic transformation, both of which are avenues toward a new economic state. By using socio-economic *planning and forecasting methods* in our economic management practices, we can alleviate some of the dramatic social shocks caused by the radical transformation of economic systems. The new industrial economy recontextualizes the positive features of past systems and gives them new life. At the same time, it also presents new challenges to the development of *market self-regulation* and *private property*, on the one hand, and *state influence on the economy*, on the other.]

9. Having outlined the basic contours of a future society, the question remains: what place will Russia occupy in it? Is it possible for Russia to succeed in this future, and what must be done to ensure its success?

The liberal monetary economic model has long dominated in the Russian economy, leading to the distortion of the national economic structure, the hypertrophy of the raw material sector, excessive financialization, and deindustrialization. For this reason, the above-mentioned challenges of the transition to the NIS.2 are especially pronounced in Russia.

We must *change Russia's economic* model and prioritize industrial development. Industrial production development trends indicate that the global need for raw materials, minerals, and energy is shrinking, both per unit and for the world economy as a whole. [Prices for many raw materials are falling, especially for energy resources, heralding the dawn of an era where traditional resources (the core of the Russian economy) are not as important as they once were in the global economy.] What is becoming more and more important is industrial knowledge and technology, the pace of their acquisition, development, and implementation in the real sector.

A new technological revolution is not far off. It is clear that the **economic leaders of the NIS.2** will be world's **technological leaders.**

How can Russia find its place in the new global economy? I argue that Russia cannot do so without cooperating with other players on the global economic stage. First and foremost, Russia must strengthen its cooperation with other

Eurasian states. And we can only meet this goal if we reduce the share of raw materials and increase the share of knowledge-intensive production in our economy.

[Note that our approach is not an original one: our closest economic partners, such as Kazakhstan, for example, are approaching the task of Eurasian integration in the same way. Some British economists have given their input on the situation. For example, Siddharth Saxena had this to say about the president of Kazakhstan on the topic of Eurasian integration:

"Nazarbayev's vision is driven by innovation and technology."[3] Stressing the need for equal partnership, Saxena also pointed to the similarity between Nazarbayev's and Putin's views, both of which support the Eurasian Union as pivotal to development, innovation, and modernization.[4]

Competition in the global high-tech market is very high, and no one is keen to allow a new, strong player into the mix. Even China, with a high-tech sector that already dwarfs Russia's, faces serious challenges in the global market, as Peter Nolan and others have demonstrated.[5]]

If Russia manages to make a technological breakthrough, it will open up real prospects for Eurasian economic cooperation. Eurasian cooperation may be the key that opens the door for its participants to the global market: for partners with high-tech economies, Russia will be an attractive partner for technological exchange and joint projects to develop new technologies; and for countries without a strong national scientific and technological core, Russia can be a supplier of high-tech developed on their productive base, as well as a place to train engineering and research personnel.

By forming a regional economic bloc, Russia can alleviate the negative impact of globalization, not by cutting itself off from the global economy, but by effectively participating in it. David Lane has the right idea on this topic.[6] Both

3 Prajakti Kalra and Siddharth S. Saxena. "Asiatic Roots and Rootedness of the Eurasian project." In *The Eurasian Project and Europe: Regional Discontinuities and Geopolitics*, ed. David Lane and Vsevolod Samokhvalov (New York: Palgrave Macmillan, 2015). https://www.researchgate.net/publication/281593568_Asiatic_ Roots_and_Rootedness_of_the_Eurasian_project, accessed April 12, 2016.

4 Ibid.

5 See Peter Nolan and Milan Hasecic. "China, the WTO and the third industrial revolution." *Cambridge Review of International Affairs* 13, no. 2 (2000), 164–180.

6 "The proposed Eurasian Union (formed by Russia, Kazakhstan and Belarus) favors a capitalist form of economy which is still part of the world economic system. It seeks to reverse in many ways the effects of globalisation, particularly to ensure the sovereignty of the nation state. The objective is to achieve these goals by forming regional blocs." David Lane, "Eurasian Integration as a Response to Neo-Liberal Globalisation,"

Russian and foreign experts, Lane included,[7] also argue that Eurasian integration is not enough. Broader cooperation is necessary, including with other BRICS countries and the Shanghai Cooperation Organization.

The Russian economy must first shed its twenty-year-long dependence on imports (especially of machinery and equipment). Import substitution is one part of the solution. A policy of import substitution is a good first step in modernizing the Russian economy.

By modernization, I mean production processes and products based on the latest technologies, continuously integrating and applying new knowledge in production. We need to *reindustrialize our economy* and restore industry as its *basic component.* Industrial development should be our *first priority,* specifically *new industrialization,* by which I mean the *intensive accumulation of industrial potential based on high-tech, knowledge-intensive production.* To correct our economic trajectory, we must change popular attitudes, government policies, state programs, and the relevant institutions.

To correct our path and redirect Russian economic development, which is still entirely possible, Russia requires certain *systemic changes.* Our priorities must include economic management based on *long-term programs* and medium-term *indicative planning* and *forecasting;* an *active industrial policy;* a system of institutions that guarantees state support to private, *long-term* investment in R&D and *technological upgrading in production*[; a tax and credit system favorable to the real sector, especially the high-tech sector; and other methods of stimulating the development of these industries and their industrial potential].

[The suggestions that I have put forth here should be concretized in economic policy programs. The INID,[8] the Moscow Economic Forum,[9] and RAS economists under the supervision of Sergei Glazyev have provided some guidelines toward this kind of policymaking.][10]

Valdai Discussion Club, May, 2, 2014. http://valdaiclub.com/opinion/highlights/eurasian_integration_as_a_response_to_neo_liberal_globalisation/.

7   "When combined, Russia, India and China have considerable manufacturing and military capacity and enormous internal markets. They already have considerable capacity for research and development." Ibid.

8   S. D. Bodrunov. *Shaping Russia's Reindustrialization Strategy.* St. Petersburg: Institute for New Industrial Development (INID), 2013.

9   See *Russia's Economic System: Anatomy of the Present and Strategies for the Future (Reindustrialization and/or Advanced Development).* Moscow: LENAND, 2014.

10 S. Y. Glazyev. *Strategy of Russia's Advanced Development in the Context of Global Crisis.* Moscow: Ekonomika, 2010.

Bibliography

Russian-Language Sources

Abachiev, S. K. "Machine and Non-Machine Technology: Essence, History, Prospects." *Naukovedenie* 3, no. 4 (2012): 3–6. http://naukove-denie.ru/sbornik12/12-34.pdf.

Abalkin, L. I. *Russia: The Search for Self-Determination: Essays.* 2nd ed. Moscow: n.p., 2005.

Aganbegyan, A. G. *Russia's Economy at the Crossroads . . . Choice of Post-Crisis Space.* Moscow: AST; Astrel, 2010.

———. "On the Acceleration of Russia's Socio-Economic Development." *Actual Problems of Economics and Management* 4, no. 4 (2014): 3–6.

———. "The Current Economic Situation in Russia: Trajectory of Development and Economic Policy." *Money and Credit* 11 (2014): 3–10.

Amosov A. I. "On the Possibility of Achieving the Target Indicators of New Industrial Development." *Bulletin of the RAS Institute of Economics* 4 (2014): 21–32.

Auzan, A. A. "We Are Approaching the Moment of Truth of Our Civilization." *Free World* (2011). http://www.liberty.ru/Themes/Aleksandr-Auzan-My-priblizhaemsya-k-momentu-istiny-nashej-civilizacii.

———. *The Economics of Everything: How Institutions Determine Our Lives.* Moscow: Mann, Ivanov, and Ferber, 2014. http://read.bizlib.org/ aleksandr-auzan-ekonomika-vsego.

———. "Alternative Strategies to Optimize State Regulation." *Journal of the New Economic Association* 23, no. 3 (2014): 154–57.

———. *The Economics of Everything: How Institutions Determine Our Lives.* Moscow: n.p., 2014. http://read.bizlib.org/ aleksandr-auzan-ekonomika-vsego.

Babkin, K. A. *Reasonable Industrial Policy, or How We Get out of the Crisis.* Moscow: n.p., 2008.

Barabaner, H. "Formation of New Ecological-Socio-Economic Paradigm of Higher Education in Conditions of Globalization and Global Poly-Systemic Crisis." *Economics and Management* 3 (2011): 10–13.

Baudrillard, J. *For a Critique of the Political Economy of the Sign.* Translated by D. Krachkin. Moscow: Academic Project, 2007.

Bell, Daniel. "Post-Industrial Society." In *"The American Model": In Conflict with the Future*, edited by G. K. Shakhnazarova, 16–24. Moscow, Progress, 1984.

———. "The Social Framework of the Information Society." *The New Technocratic Wave in the West.* Moscow: Progress, 1986.

Bernard, I. *Explanatory Dictionary of Economic.* Vol. 2. Edited by I. Bernard and J.-C. Collie. Moscow: International Relations, 1994.

Bilevskaya, E. "The Kremlin will assess risks." *Novaia Gazeta*, August 11, 2010.

Blaug, M. "I. A. Schumpeter." In *Great Economists before Keynes: An Introduction to the Lives & Works of One Hundred Great Economists of the Past*, 332-335. St. Petersburg: Economikus, 2008.

Blinov, A. O. "Innovative and Technological Modernization of Russian Industry—the Basis of State Security." *Economics of Sustainable Development* 13 (2013): 44–50.

Bodrunov, S. D., ed. *Administrative Systems and Administration in the Aviation Industry.* St. Petersburg: St. Petersburg GUAP, 2001.

———. *Analysis of the State of Domestic Machine Building and the Imperatives of New Industrial Development.* St. Petersburg: Institute for New Industrial Development (INID), 2012.

———. *An Investigation of Supply Operations.* 4 Parts. St. Petersburg: MFPG "Aerospace Equipment," 2004.

———. "Another Reincarnation of the Idea of Russian Modernization: The Choice of Model." *Economic Strategies* 89, no. 3 (2011): 24–31.

——. "Concept Concerning Machine-Building in Modern Conditions." *Russia's Aerospace Instrumentation*. Collection 1 of *Economics of Aircraft Instrument-Making* 10 (2009): 30–64.

——. "Corporate Structures in Science-Intensive Industries." *Problems of the Theory and Practice of Management* 6 (1999). http://vasilievaa.narod.ru/14_6_99.htm.

——. "Developments Remained on Paper. Domestic Manufacturers Are Poorly Controlling the Domestic Market." *Russian Business Newspaper. Innovations, Weekly Economic Supplement,* January 13, 2015. https://inir.ru/wp-content/uploads/2015/02/Разработки-остались-на-бумаге.pdf.

——. "Dualism of the Innovation Economy." In *Russia's Aerospace Instrumentation*. Collection 1 of *Economics of Aircraft Instrument-Making* 10, edited by S. D. Bodrunov, 55–59. St. Petersburg: NAAP, 2010.

——. "Modernization of Public Institutions: Russia's Basic Anti-Crisis Strategy." In *Russia's Aerospace Instrumentation*. Collection 1 of *Economics of Aircraft Instrument-Making* 9, 5–16. St. Petersburg: NAAP, 2009.

——. *Entrepreneurial and Commercial Activity in Russia's Aircraft Instrumentation Complex*. St. Petersburg: St. Petersburg GUAP, 2001.

——. *Foresight "Russia": Designing a New Industrial Policy: Proceedings of the St. Petersburg International Economic Congress* (SPEK-2015). Moscow: Cultural Revolution, 2015.

——. *Infomarketing*. Moscow: BelANTDI, 1995.

——. *Information Technologies in Department Work*. Edited by A. G. Stepanov. St. Petersburg: GUAP, 2014.

——. *Information Technologies of Corporate Management*. St. Petersburg: Aerospace Equipment Corporation, 2006.

——. *Innovative Development of Industry as the Basis of Technological Leadership and National Security of Russia*. St. Petersburg: Institute for New Industrial Development (INID), 2015. https://inir.ru/wp-content/uploads/2015/09/Инновационное-развитие-промышленности-2.pdf.

——. "Institutional Mechanisms of the Concept of Russia's New Industrial Development in the WTO Environment." *Russia's Economic Revival of Russia* 3, no. 33 (2012): 47–52.

——. *Intellectual Property Risks of Import Substitution in the Framework of the Reindustrialization of Russian Industry*. Edited by S. D. Bodrunov and V. N. Lopatin. St. Petersburg: Institute for New Industrial Development (INID), 2014.

———, ed. *International Sanctions: Threats, Challenges and Opportunities for the Modernization of Russia's Economy*. St. Petersburg: Polytechnic University Press, 2014.

———. "Labor Productivity as a Key Factor in the Development of Russia: Speech at the Meeting of the Scientific-Expert Council under the Chairman of the Federation Council of the Federal Assembly of the Russian Federation." In *Materials for Parliamentary Hearings on the "Reindustrialization of the Economy of the Russian Regions as a Basic Condition for the Implementation of Import Substitution Policy*," 152–56. Moscow: n.p., 2015.

———. "Labor Productivity as a Key Factor in the Development of Russia." *Labor Productivity as a Key Factor in the Development of Russia: Legal and Regional Aspects. Analytical Bulletin of the Federation Council of the Federal Assembly of the Russian Federation* 22, no. 540 (2014): 38–42.

———. *Methods of Risk Analysis and Assessment in the Problems of Security Management of Complex Technical Systems*. St. Petersburg: Corporation "Aerospace Equipment." 2007.

———. "Model of Russian Modernization—from State Support of Demand to Stimulation of Supply." In *Federal Handbook. Defense-Industrial Complex: Information-Analytical*. Vol. 7, 509–517. Moscow: Center for Strategic Programs, 2011.

———. *Modern Economic and Social Development: Problems and Prospects*. Vol. 17 St. Petersburg: Institute for New Industrial Development (INID), 2015.

———. "Modernization of Public Institutions as a Basic Strategy for the Modernization of the Russian Economy." In *Proceedings of the Delegate to the Jubilee Congress of the Free Economic Society of Russia (245 Years of FES Russia)*, 35–43. Moscow: n.p., 2010.

———. "Modernization of Public Institutions: Russia's Basic Anti-Crisis Strategy." In *Russia's Aerospace Instrumentation*. Collection 1 of *Economics of Aircraft Instrument-Making* (2009): 5–16.

———. "Modernization of the Economy and Fiscal Policy." *Russia's Economic Revival* 46, no. 4 (2015): 43–47.

———. *New Industrial Society: The Face of the New Industrial Era*. St. Petersburg: Institute for New Industrial Development (INID), 2015.

———. "New Industrial Society: The Structure and Content of Social Production, Economic Relations, Institutions." *Russia's Economic Revival* 46, no. 4 (2015): 9–23.

———. "On the Basic Principles of the Formation of Import-Substituting Industrial Policy in Russia." In *Current Economic Problems*, edited by S. D.

Bodrunov and E. M. Rogova, 7–12. St. Petersburg: St. Petersburg GUAP, 2014.

———. *On the Necessity and Possibility of the Reindustrialization of the Russian Economy*. St. Petersburg: Institute for New Industrial Development (INID), 2014.

———. "On the Reindustrialization of the Russian Economy in the WTO Environment." *Russia's Economic Revival* 33, no. 3 (2012): 47–52.

———. "Principles of Forming a New Economic Model: Report." In "On the Tasks of the Federation Council to Implement the Provisions of the RF President's Address to the Federal Assembly." Special issue, *Scientific-Methodical Seminar of the Analytical Department of the Federation Council of the Federal Assembly of the RF: Analytical Bulletin. Series: Development of Russia* 9, no. 562 (2015): 10–17.

———. "Problems of Military-Technical Cooperation at the Level of MTC Subjects." In *Collection of Materials from the Sixth St. Petersburg Economic Forum*. Vol. 2, 93–97. St. Petersburg: n.p., 2002.

———. *Problems, Principles, and Methods of the Corporatization of Aviation Industry in Russia*. St. Petersburg: Petrogradskii & Co, 2000.

———. "Production, Science, Education: Problems of Reintegration." In *Transcript of the Scientific Seminar in the State Duma of the Federal Assembly of the Russian Federation*, 39–63. St. Petersburg: Institute for New Industrial Development (INID), 2014.

———. "Reindustrialization and Modern Industrial Policy." In *Scientific Papers of the Institute for New Industrial Development (INID)*, edited by S. D. Bodrunov, 4–13. St. Petersburg: Institute for New Industrial Development (INID), 2015.

———. "Reindustrialization as the Basic Direction of Modernization of the Russian Economy." In *Proceedings of the Scientific Seminar of the Institute for New Industrial Development (INID)*, edited by S. D. Bodrunov, 51. St. Petersburg: Institute for New Industrial Development (INID), 2014.

———. "Reindustrialization of the Economy, Import-Substitution and Anti-Crisis Measures of the Russian Government: Proposals for the Correction of the Anti-Crisis Plan of the Russian Government." In *Proceedings of the Institute of New Industrial Development (INID)*, edited by S. D. Bodrunov et al., 4–13. St. Petersburg, Institute for New Industrial Development (INID), 2015.

———. "Reindustrialization of the Russian Economy and Import Substitution Based on the Integration of Production, Science, and Education." In *Integration* of Production, Science, and Education as a Basis for the Reindustrialization of Russian Economy: Proceedings of the Scientific Seminar "Modern Problems of Development," 26–51. St. Petersburg: Institute for New Industrial Development (INID), 2015.

———. "Reindustrialization: Roundtable at the Free Economic Society of Russia." New Economic World 1 (2014): 11–26.

———. Reindustrialization of the Russian Economy: Imperatives, Potential, Risks. Edited by S. D. Bodrunov and R. S. Grinberg. Moscow: RAS Institute of Economics; Institute for New Industrial Development (INID), 2013.

———. "Reindustrialization of the Russian economy: opportunities and limitations," Proceedings of the Free Economic Society of Russia 1 (Moscow, 2014):15–46.

———. Reindustrialization of the Russian Economy: Opportunities, Benchmarks, Imperatives, Constraints, Risks. St. Petersburg: Institute for New Industrial Development (INID), 2013.

———. "Resolution of St. Petersburg International Economic Congress 'Foresight 'Russia': Design of New Industrial Policy.'" In Proceedings of the St. Petersburg International Economic Congress (SPEK-2015), 735–744. Moscow: Cultural Revolution, 2015.

———. "Restructuring: A New Approach to an Old Problem." World of Avionics 4 (1998): 8–11.

———. Russia's Aviation-Industrial Complex of Russia at the Turn of the XXI Century: Problems of Effective Management: In 2 Parts. Edited by S. D. Bodrunov, O. N. Dmitriev, and Y. A. Kovalkov. St. Petersburg: Aerospace Equipment Corporation, 2002.

———. "Russia's Modernization: Demand Model or Supply Model?." World of Avionics 1 (2011): 14–18.

———. "Russia's Modernization: New Industrialization, a New Model of Economic Growth, a New Model of Social Development, New Ideology." In Current Problems of the Economy of Modern Russia: Collection of Scientific Works, edited by A. A. Ovodenko, 15–30. St. Petersburg: GUAP, 2013.

———. "Russia's Modernization: The Lessons of History and the Tasks of Public Administration." Management and Business Administration 2 (2011): 167–170.

———. Russia's Modernization: Through New Industrialization to a New Model of Economic Growth and a New Model of Society Development. St. Petersburg: Institute for New Industrial Development (INID), 2012.

———. *Shaping the Strategy of Russia's Reindustrialization.* 2nd ed. St. Petersburg: Institute for New Industrial Development (INID), 2015.

———. *Shaping the Strategy of Russia's Reindustrialization.* St. Petersburg: Institute for New Industrial Development (INID), 2013.

———. *Strategy and Politics of Reindustrialization for Russia's Innovative Development,* edited by S. D. Bodrunov and V. N. Lopatin. St. Petersburg: Institute for New Industrial Development (INID), 2014.

———. *Structural Assessment of the Consequences of Implementing Management Decisions Concerning Enterprises.* Edited by S. D. Bodrunov, O. N. Dmitriev, and Y. A. Kovalkov. Moscow: "Gnom I D" Publishing House, 2003.

———. *Technological Platforms: Opportunities for the Reindustrialization of Russia.* St. Petersburg: Institute for New Industrial Development (INID), 2013.

———. "The Complex Modernization of Social Institutions—the Strategy of the Socio-Economic Development of Russia." In *Institute for New Industrial Development (INID). Proceedings: Collected Scientific Articles,* edited by S. D. Bodrunov, 214–221. St. Petersburg: Institute for New Industrial Development (INID), 2012.

———. "The Integration of Production, Science and Education and Reindustrialization of Russian Economy." In *Proceedings of the International Congress "Revival of Production, Science and Education in Russia: Challenges and Solutions,"* 26-51. Moscow: LENAND, 2015.

———. "The Integration of Production, Science and Education as the Basis for Reindustrialization of the Russian Economy." *Russia's Economic Revival* 1 (2015): 7–22.

———. "The Integration of Science, Education, Production and the New Industrialization of Russia." *Vedomosti* 215 (November 19, 2014): 17.

———. "The modernization of the defense-industrial complex and the provision of economic security of the state." In *Year of the Planet: Politics, Economy, Business, Banks, Education,* 107–112. Moscow: IMEMO RAS; Ekonomika, 2005.

———. "The Modernization of the Russian Economy: From Demand Support to Supply Stimulation." In *Modern Economic and Social Development: Problems and Prospects; Collection of Scientific Works,* edited by S. D. Bodrunov, 23–36. St. Petersburg: SPAN Ltd, 2011.

———. *Theory and Practice of Import Substitution: Lessons and Problems.* St. Petersburg: Institute for New Industrial Development (INID), 2015.

———. "The Question of Reindustrialization of the Russian Economy." *Russia's Economic Revival* 38, no. 4 (2013): 5–27.

———. *The Role of Regional Clusters in the Reindustrialization of Russia*. St. Petersburg: Institute for New Industrial Development (INID), 2013.

———. "The Russian Economic System: The Future of High-Tech Material Production." In *Proceedings of the Meeting of the Scientific Council of Lomonosov Moscow State University on the Development of Modern Economic Theory and the Russian Model of Socio-Economic Development (June 5, 2014)*, edited by S. D. Bodrunov. St. Petersburg: Institute for New Industrial Development (INID), 2014.

———. "The Russian Economic System: The Future of High-Tech Material Production." *Russia's Economic Revival* 2 (2014): 5–16.

———. *The Russian Tragedy of the Deindustrialization of the Domestic Economy*. St. Petersburg: Institute for New Industrial Development (INID), 2013.

———. *The Valuation of Integrated Enterprises*. St. Petersburg: St. Petersburg AUE Press, 2009.

———. "Transfer of Innovations: Corporate Mechanism of Implementation." In *Proceedings: Collection of Scientific Articles*, edited by S. D. Bodrunov and A. V. Martynenko, 121–29. St. Petersburg: Institute for New Industrial Development (INID), 2012.

———. "What Is to Be Done? Imperatives, Opportunities and Problems of Reindustrialization." In *Collection of the Materials the Scientific and Expert Council under the Chairman of the Federation Council of the Russian Federation "Re-Industrialization: Opportunities and Limitations,"* edited by S. D. Bodrunov and R. S. Grinberg, 14–25. Moscow: Federation Council of the Russian Federation, 2013.

———. "What Kind of Industrialization Does Russia Need?" *Russia's Economic Revival* 44, no. 2 (2015): 6–17.

Bodrunov, S. D., A. E. Karlik, and V. E. Rokhchin. *Concept of the Strategic Development of City Industry: Scientific Support and Development Experience,* edited by A. E. Karlik and V. E. Rokhchin. St. Petersburg: St. Petersburg State University of Economics and Finance Press, 2011.

Bodrunov, S. D. and Y. A. Kovalkov. *The Economics and Organization of Aircraft Building*. St. Petersburg: "Aerospace Equipment" Corporation, 2001.

Bodrunov S. D. and V. N. Lopatin. *Intellectual Property: Distribution of Intellectual Rights between the Customer, Executor, and Author on the Protected Results of Intellectual Activity, Created and/or Used during Research, Development,*

Technological, and Industrial Work. St. Petersburg: Institute for New Industrial Development (INID), 2014.

———. *Institutional Modernization of Russian Industry in the WTO.* St. Petersburg: Institute for New Industrial Development (INID), 2012.

Bodrunov, S. D. and A. A. Porokhovsky, eds. *The Economic System of Modern Russia: Anatomy of the Present and Alternatives of the Future.* 2nd ed. Moscow: LENAND, 2015.

Bodrunov, S. D. and I. V. Maximei. *Marketing of Information Services: Management Models.* Moscow: Ekonomika, Luch, 1993.

Bodrunov, S. D., R. S. Grinberg, and D. E. Sorokin, "Reindustrialization of the Russian economy: imperatives, potential, risks," *Economic Revival of Russia 1,* no. 35 (2013): 19–49.

———. "Reindustrialization of the Russian Economy: Imperatives, Potential, Risks." *Russia's Economic Revival 1,* no. 35 (2013): 19–49.

Bodrunov, S. D., V. N. Lopatin, and V. V. Okrepilov, eds. *Russia's Reindustrialization: Improving Public Administration, Legal, and Technical Regulation.* St. Petersburg: Institute for New Industrial Development (INID), 2013.

Bodrunov, S. D. et al. *Corporate Management of Post-Industrial Society.* St. Petersburg: Aerospace Equipment Corporation, 2005.

Bodrunov, S. D. et al., "Scenarios of the Long-Term Development of the Scientific-Industrial Complex of St. Petersburg. Aerospace Instrumentation of Russia: Series 1. Special Issue, *Economics of Aerospace Instrument Engineering.* St. Petersburg: NAAP (2010): 19–29.

Böhm-Bawer, O. von, *Capital and Interest, 1884–1889.* In *Selected Works on Value, Interest, and Capital,* 365–445. Moscow: Eksmo, 2009.

Brandt, V. "Sergey Y. Witte (addition to article)." In *Encyclopedic Dictionary of F. A. Brockhaus and I. A. Efron.* Vol. I, edited by K. K. Arsenyev and F. F. Petrushevsky, 430–434. St. Petersburg: Brockhaus-Efron, 1905.

Burmenko, T. D. *The Sphere of Services in Modern Society: Economics, Management, Marketing; A Course of Lectures.* Edited by T. D. Burmenko, N. N. Danilenko, and T. A. Turenko. Irkutsk: BGU-EP, 2004.

Buzgalin, A. V. "Discussion on the Problems of Updating the Economic System of Russia and Reindustrialization." *Problems of Modern Economics 51,* no. 3 (2014): 46.

———. "Economics and 'Economic Imperialism': There Are Alternatives." *Questions of Political Economy 1,* no. 2 (2012): 19–35.

———. "Planning: Its Potential and Role in the Market Economy of the XXI Century." *Questions of Economics* 1 (2016): 63–80.

———. "Reindustrialization as Nostalgia? Theoretical Discourse." *Sociological Studies* 357, no. 1 (2014): 80–94.

———. "The Renewal of Russia's Economic System: The Need to Abandon Market Fundamentalism." *Problems of Modern Economics* 3 (2014): 53–55.

Buzgalin, A. V. and A. I. Kolganov. "The Russian Economic System: The Specificity of Property Relations and Intracorporate Management." *Problems of the Theory and Practice of Management* 10 (2014): 8–17.

———. "The Simulacrum Market: A View through the Prism of Classical Political Economy." *Philosophy of Economy* 2, no. 3 (2012): 153–165.

Castells, M. "Network Society." *The first of September*, no. 12 (2001). https://ps.1sept.ru/article.php?ID=200101210

———. "The Formation of Network Society." In *The New Post-Industrial Wave in the West: An Anthology*, edited by V. L. Inozemets, 496–510. Moscow: Academia, 1999.

———. *The Information Age: Economy, Societies, and Culture*. Translated and edited by O. I. Shkaratan. Moscow: MGU HSE, 2000.

Polyansky. F. Y., and V. A. Zhamin, eds. "Industrial Revolution in England." In *Economic History of Capitalist Countries*. Moscow: MGU, 1986. http://www.gumer.info/bibliotek_Buks/Econom/bubl/18.php

Eskindarov, M. A. "Economic Policy of Russia Under Conditions of Global Turbulence." *Bulletin of Finance University* 84, no. 6 (2014): 6–9.

Frolova, T. A. "Economics and Management in the Sphere of Social and Cultural Service and Tourism." Lecture at TTI SFU, Taganrog, 2010. http://www.aup.ru/books/m204/1_2.htm

Gasanov, E. "The Structure of the Information Economy and Its Main Functions." *Bulletin of Khabarovsk State Academy of Economics and Law* 1 (2005): 14–29.

Gerasimov, I. V. "Innovative development of machine building division of SC 'Rosatom' in WTO context (by the example of CJSC 'AEM-technology')." *Proceedings of St. Petersburg State Economic University* 3 (2014): 80–82.

Gide, S. and S. Rist, eds. *History of Economic Studies*. Moscow: Ekonomika, 1995.

Glazyev, S. "From Market Fundamentalism to a Convergent Model." In *New Integral Society: General Theoretical Aspects and World Practice*. Edited by G. N. Tsagolov, 69. Moscow: LENAND, 2016.

———. "New Course: A Breakthrough Strategy." *Economic Strategies* 117, no. 1 (2014): 6–15.

——. *On External and Internal Threats to Russia's Economic Security in the Context of American Aggression: Scientific Report.* Moscow: n.p, 2014. https://spkurdyumov.ru/uploads/2014/12/glaziev_o-vneshnix-i-vnutrennix-ugrozax-ekonomicheskoj-bezopasnosti-rossii.pdf

——. *Strategy for the Advanced Development of Russia in the Context of Global Crisis.* Moscow: Ekonomika, 2010.

——. "The Transition to a New, Humanitarian Techno-Economic Paradigm." In *Modernization of the Russian Economy: Lessons of the past, Opportunities, Risks.* Moscow: IKF, 2012.

Glazyev, S. Y., S. Kara-Murza, and S. A. Batchikov, eds. *The White Book: Economic Reforms in Russia, 1991–2001.* Moscow: Eksmo, 2004.

Glazyev, S. Y., and V. V. Kharitonov, eds. *Nanotechnology as a Key Factor of the New Techno-Economic Mode in the Economy.* Moscow: Trovant, 2009.

Grazhdankin, A. and S. Kara-Murza, eds. *The White Book of Russia: Construction, Perestroika and Reforms: 1950–2012.* Moscow: Librokom Book House, 2013.

Grinberg, R. S. *Freedom and Justice: Russian Temptations of False Choice.* Moscow: Magister: INFRA-M, 2012.

——. "Russia: Economic Success without Development and Democracy?." *Russia's Economic Revival* 2 (2005): 10–18.

——. "The Big Crisis: It's Time to Get Away from Radical Liberalism." In *The Main Book on the Crisis,* edited by A. V. Buzgalin, 59–72. Moscow: Iauza; Eksmo, 2009.

——. "Reindustrialization and Industrial Policy." *Proceedings of the Free Economic Society of Russia* (2014): 66–70.

——. "The Economy of Modern Russia: Condition, Problems, and Prospects." *Bulletin of the Institute of Economics of the Russian Academy of Sciences* 1 (2015): 10–29.

Grinberg, R.S. and A. Y. Rubinstein, eds., *Economic Socio-Dynamics.* Moscow: ISE press, 2000.

Grinberg, R. S., and A. Y. Rubinstein, eds. *The Individual & the State: An Economic Dilemma.* Moscow: The Whole World, 2013.

Grinberg, R. S., K. A. Babkin and A. V. Buzgalin, eds. "Myths about the Free Market We Should Leave in the Past: 'Economy for the People." In *Socially-Oriented Development Based on the Progress of the Real Sector: Materials of the Moscow Economic Forum,* 32–43. Moscow: Cultural Revolution, 2014.

Gubanov, S. S. *The Sovereign Impulse: Russia's Neo-Industrialization and Integration.* Moscow: Book World, 2012.

———. "Russia's Systemic Choice and the Standard of Living." *The Economist* 11 (2011).

Gurieva, L. K. "The Concept of Techno-Economic Paradigms." *Innovational Economics* 10 (2004): 70–75.

Hasanov, E. "Structure of the Information Economy and its Main Functions." *Bulletin of Khabarovsk State Academy of Economics and Law* 1 (2005): 14–29.

Inozemtsev, V. L. *Beyond Economic Society*. Moscow: Academia, 1998.

———. *At the Turn of Era: Economic Trends and Their Non-Economic Consequences*. Moscow: Ekonomika, 2003.

———. "It's not about technology, it's about production." *Vedomosti*, July 12, 2010. https://www.vedomosti.ru/opinion/articles/2010/07/12/delo-ne-v-tehnologiyah,-a-v-proizvodstve

———. *Modern Post-industrial Society: Nature, Contradictions, Prospects*. Moscow: Logos, 2000.

———. "Modernizatsia.ru: Made in Russia," *Vedomosti*, December 7, 2010.

———. "The Post-Industrial Economy and 'Post-Industrial" Society (on the Problem of Social Trends of the XXI Century)." *Social Sciences and Modernity* 3 (2001).

Institute for New Industrial Development. "The Russian Economic System: The Future of High-Tech Material Production." *Materials of the Meeting of the Scientific Council of Lomonosov Moscow State University on the Development of Modern Economic Theory and the Russian Model of Socio-Economic Development (June 5, 2014)*. St. Petersburg: Institute for New Industrial Development (INID), 2014.

Institute of Economics at the Russian Academy of Sciences. *The Situation in the Russian Economy in 2014 and Forecast of Its Development in 2015–2016*. 2015.

International Labor Organization. *Global Employment Trends*. Geneva: ILO, 2009.

Ivanter, V. V. *The innovative and technological development of the Russian economy*. Moscow: MAX Press, 2006.

———. "The new economic policy." *Russia's Economic Revival* 33, no. 2 (2013): 7–12.

———. "Policy of Economic Growth as the Main Anti-Crisis Measure." *Proceedings of the Free Economic Society of Russia* 190, no. 1 (2015): 46–52.

———. "The Main Tendencies of the Development of the Russian Economy and a Forecast of Macroeconomic Dynamics." *Economics and Management* 99, no. 1 (2014): 4–9.

Ivanter, V. V., et al. *Prospects for the Development of the Russian Economy. Forecast to 2030.* Edited by V. V. Ivanter and M. Y. Ksenofontov. Moscow: Ankil, 2013.

Lukash, Y. A. "Works (Services) of Industrial Character." In *Encyclopedic Dictionary-Handbook of the Head of the Enterprise,* 1504. Moscow: Book World, 2004.

Kalmatsky, M. "The Wrong Climate." *Novie Izvestiia,* September 15, 2010. https://newizv.ru/news/2010-09-15/ne-tot-klimat-125256.

Karlik, A. E. and M. A. Osipov, "The state and prospects of Russian macroeconomic development in the context of the theory of economic growth taking into account the crisis phenomena." *Economic Sciences* 57 (2009): 12–18.

Kashin, B. S. "The philosophy of innovation parasitism." *The Free Press,* December 13, 2011. http://commpart.livejournal. com/15221.html.

Khasbulatov, R. I. *The World Economy and International Economic Relations.* Moscow: Gardariki, 2006.

———. "The Russian Economy: Where is the Expected Growth?." *Bulletin of Russian University of Economics Named after G. V. Plekhanov* 1 (2014): 3–14.

Khoros, V. G., and D. B. Malysheva, eds. *The Third World: Half a Century Later.* Moscow: IMEMO RAS, 2013.

Kindzersky, Y. "Deformation of the institute of property in Ukraine and problems of forming an effective owner in an ineffective state." *Questions of Economics* 7 (2010): 123–134.

Kleiner, G. B. "Rhythms of Evolutionary Economics." *Questions of Economics* 4 (2014): 123–136.

———. "On Increasing the Efficiency of Russian Enterprises." *Economic Science of Modern Russia* 64, no. 1 (2014): 10–11.

———. "Strategic Planning: The Basis of the Systemic-Approach." *Modernization of Economy and Socio-Economic Development.* Book 2, 10-24. Moscow: GU-HSE Publishing House, 2008. http://www.kleiner.ru/skrepk/strategplan-2008.pdf.

———. "Systemic economics as a platform for the development of modern economic theory." *Questions of Economics* 6 (2013): 4–28.

———. "Systemic Management in Transforming the Economy." *Efficient Anti-Crisis Management* 5 (2014): 54–59.

———. "What kind of economy does Russia need and why?" *Questions of Economics* 10 (2013): 4–27.

Kleiner, G. B. et al. *Mesoeconomics of Development.* Moscow: Nauka, 2011.

Kokoshin, A. A. *Issues of the Long-Term Development of Eastern Siberia and the Russian Far East in the Context of Global Political and Economic Dynamics.* Moscow: LENAND, 2012.

———. *Methodological Problems of Forecasting in the Interest of Russia's National Security.* Moscow: Institute of Oriental Studies of the Russian Academy of Sciences, 2014.

Kolganov, A. I. "Institutional and Organizational Problems of Russian Universities' Participation in the Innovation Process." In *The University as a Link of the National Innovation System.* Moscow: MAX Press, 2011.

Kolganov, A. I., and A. V. Buzgalin, eds. *Comparative Economics: Comparative Analysis of Economic Systems: Textbook for University Students Majoring in Economics.* Moscow: INFRA-M, 2005.

Kolganov, A. I. "Project 'USSR': what could not be completed?." In *USSR: Incomplete project,* edited by A.V. Buzgalin and P. Linke, 171–179. Moscow: LENAND, 2012.

———."Reindustrialization as Nostalgia? Polemical Notes on Targets of an Alternative Socio-Economic Strategy." *Sotsis* 3 (2014): 120–130.

———. "Reindustrialization as Nostalgia? Theoretical Discourse," *Sotsis* 1 (2014): 80–94

Kornai, I. A. "The Systemic Paradigm." *Questions of Economics* 4 (2002): 4–22.

Korol, A. N. and S. A. Khlynov. "Services: Definition and Classification." *Scientific Notes of Taganrog State University* 5, no. 4 (2014): 1323–28. http://pnu.edu.ru/media/ejournal/articlec/2014/TGU_5_357.pdf.

Krasilshchikov, V. A. *Catching up with the Past Century: Russia's Development in the 20th Century from the Perspective of Global Modernization.* Moscow: Russian State Library, 2010.

———. "Modernization and Russia on the Threshold of the XXI Century." *Problems of Philosophy* 7 (1993): 40–56.

Kudymov, M. V. "Criteria for Identifying Outsourcing in Instrument-Making and Machine-Building Enterprises." *Russian Entrepreneurship* 10, no. 2 (2009): 43–47.

Kulkov, V. M. "Dominants of Russia's Economic System." *Russia Today.* Moscow: Volgograd, 2000.

Kuzyk, B. N. "On the Formation of a Strategic Management System for the Modernization and Development of the Russian Economy." *Economic Strategies,* Vol. 16, 118, no. 2 (2014): 24–29.

Kuzyk, B. N., and B. I. Kushlin, eds. *Forecasting, Strategic Planning, and National Programming: Textbook*. 4th ed. Rev. ed. Moscow: Ekonomika, 2011.

Kvint, V. L. *Business and Strategic Management*. St. Petersburg: St. Petersburg GUP, 2010.

———. "Strategizing in Russia and the World: Counting on Man." *Economics and Management* 109, no. 11 (2014): 15–17.

———. *Strategizing in the Modern World*. St. Petersburg: RANEPA, 2014.

Lopatnikov, L. I. *Economic and Mathematical Dictionary*. Moscow: Nauka, 1993.

Lukash, Y. A. "Works (Services) of Industrial Character." In *Encyclopedic Dictionary-Handbook of the Head of the Enterprise*, 1504. Moscow: Book World, 2004.

Lundvall, B., ed. *National System of Innovation*. London: Pinter, 1992.

Lvov, D. S. and S. Y. Glazyev. "Theoretical and Applied Aspects of STP Management." *Economics and Mathematical Methods* 22, no. 5 (1986): 793–804.

Ministry of Industry and Science of the RF. *Main Directions for State Scientific and Technical Policy for the Medium- and Long-Term Period: Report of the Ministry of Industry and Science of the RF*. Moscow, 2000.

Makarov, V. L. *Social Clustering: The Russian Challenge*. Moscow: Business Atlas, 2010.

Makarov, V. L., et al. *Horizons of Innovative Economy in Russia: Law, Institutions, Models*. Moscow: LENAND, 2010.

Mamishev, A. I. "The Development of the Sphere of Industrial Services in the Conditions of Modernization of the Economy." PhD diss., St. Petersburg, 2013. http://dlib.rsl.ru/viewer/01005555145#?page=33.

Marx, Karl, *Capital*. Vol 1. Moscow: Progress Publishers, 1977.

———. *Capital*. Vol. 3. New York: International Publishers, 1959.

———. *Theories of Surplus Value*. Moscow: Progress Publishers, 1969.

Mekhanik, A. "Machine tools for a new way of life." *Expert* 7 (2013): 50–56. http://expert.ru/expert/2013/07/stanok-dlya-novogo-uklada/.

Menshikov, S. M., and L. A. Klimenko. *Long Waves in Economics: When Society Changes Its Skin*. 2nd ed. Moscow: LENAND, 2014.

Mgoyan, R. P. "Financial Instruments of State Support for High-Tech Industries." *Proceedings of St. Petersburg State University of Economics* 84, no. 6 (2013): 122–125.

Minakir, P. A. *Essays on Spatial Economics*. Khabarovsk: IEI FEB RAS, 2014.

———. "On the Key Tasks of Russia's Economic Development (Based on the Conclusions of the RF President's Message to the Federal Assembly)." *Economic and Social Changes: Facts, Trends, Forecast* 31, no. 1 (2014): 22–25.

Minutes of the Speeches of the Minister of Finance S. Witte and Foreign Minister M. N. Muravyov at the Ministerial Meeting Chaired by Nicholas II on the Foundations of Russia's Trade and Industrial Policy. n.p., March 17, 1899.

Nechvolodov, A. *From Ruin to Prosperity.* St. Petersburg: Printing house of the Headquarters of the Guard Troops and the St. Petersburg Military District, 1906.

Nekipelov, A. D. "Reindustrialization in Russia." *Proceedings of the Free Economic Society of Russia* Vol. 180 (2014): 60–65.

Nureev, R. M. "Scientific and Production Associations and the Problems of Acceleration of Scientific and Technological Progress." *Questions of Economics* 1 (1985): 68–73.

Okrepilov, V. V. *Economics of Quality.* St. Petersburg: Nauka, 2011.

Osipenko, A. S. "Technological transfer in the system of industrial innovation development" *Russia's Economic Revival* 39, no. 1 (2014): 83–88.

Osipov, M. Y. "Centenary of S. N. Bulgakov's Philosophy of Economy—One Hundred Years of Economic Philosophy." *Sophia. One hundred years of Russian Sophian philosophy,* edited by Yu.M. Osipov, A.I. Ageev, and E.S. Zotova. Moscow: Teis (2012): 9–22.

Panasyuk, M. I., E. A. Romanovsky, and A. V. Kessenikh, eds. "Initial stage of nuclear physicist training at Moscow State University in the thirties to the fifties." In *History of the Atomic Project.* 2nd ed., 491–518. Moscow: Russian Christian Institute for Humanities, 2002.

Perepelkin, V. A. "The Concept of 'Service' in Economic Theory." *Vestnik of Samara State University* 69 (2009): 38–46. http://cyberleninka.ru/article/n/ponyatie-usluga-v-ekonomicheskoy-teorii.

Peres, C. *Technological Revolutions and Financial Capital: The Dynamics of Bubbles and Golden Ages.* Moscow: Delo, 2011.

Plotnikov, V. A. "Innovative Activity of Russian Industrial Enterprises as a Factor of Economic Security." *Bulletin of Belgorod State University; Series: History, Political Science, Economics, Informatics* 13 (2012): 5–10.

Polyansky, F. Y. and V. A. Zhamin, eds. *Economic History of Capitalist Countries.* Moscow: MGU, 1986.

Political Economy: An Economic Encyclopedia. Vol. 4. Moscow: Soviet Encyclopedia, 1980.

Polterovich, V. M. "Industrial Policy: Prescriptions or Institutions?." *Journal of the New Economic Association* 22, no. 2 (2014): 190–95.

———. *Elements of the Theory of Reforms.* Moscow: Ekonomika, 2007.

Popov A. I. and V. A. Plotnikov. "Choosing a New Model of Development and Modernization: The Basis for the Transition to the Innovation Economy." *Proceedings of St. Petersburg State Economic University* 74, no. 2 (2012): 197–209.

Popov, A. I. "Creating a New Model of Development: Modernization and Conditions for Transition to an Innovative Economy." *Proceedings of the St. Petersburg State Economic University* 4 (2012): 18–26.

———. "Neo- industrialization of the Russian economy as a condition for sustainable development." *Proceedings of St. Petersburg State University of Economics* 3 (2014): 7–12.

Porfiryev B. N "New Economic Policy: The Most Important Imperatives of the Financial Policy of Modern Russia." *Economics and Management* 2 (2014): 6–11.

———. *Nature and Economics: Risks of Impact.* Moscow: Ankil, 2011.

Porokhovsky, A. A. "A Discussion on the Problems of the Renewal of Russia's Economic System and Reindustrialization." *Problems of Modern Economics* 51, no. 3 (2014).

———. *Debt Problem as a Phenomenon of the XXI Century.* Moscow: MAX Press, 2014.

———. "Modern Development and Economic Interests." *Questions of Political Economy* 7, no. 2 (2013).

———. "Political Economy at the Turn of the Century." *Questions of Political Economy* 2, no. 1 (2012): 3–18.

———. *The Economic System of Modern Russia: Paths and Goals of Development.* Moscow: Faculty of Economics, Moscow State University, 2015.

———. "The Russian Market Model: The Path toward Its Realization." *Questions of Economy* 10, no. 35 (2002): 35–49.

Pososhkov, I. T. *Book on scarcity and wealth.* Moscow: "Economics Newspaper" Publishing House, 2001.

Povorina, V. "Approaches to Determining the Place and Structure of the Market of Services to Enterprises and Organizations." *Service Plus* 2 (2011): 9–10. http://cyberleninka.ru/article/n/podhody-k-opredeleniyu-mesta-i-struktury-rynka-uslug-predpriyatiyam-i-organizatsiyam#ixzz3wHscKtKJ.

Pride, V. "The phenomenon of the NBIC convergence: Reality and expectations." In *Problems of the Effective Integration of Russia's Scientific and Technological Potential into the World Economy*, edited by V. Pride and D. A. Medvedev, 97–116. Moscow: LKI Publishing House, 2008. http://transhumanism-russia.ru/content/view/498/110/.

Prosvirnov, A. "The New Technological Revolution Is Passing Us by." *ProAtom Agency*, December 11, 2012. http://www.proatom.ru/modules.php?name=News&file=article&sid=4189.

Pshenichnikova, S. N. "Investments and Economic Growth in Eurasian Countries." *Proceedings of the St. Petersburg State Economic University* 83, no. 5 (2013): 14–26.

Putin, V. V. "We Need a New Economy." *Vedomosti*, January 1, 2012. https://www.vedomosti.ru/politics/articles/2012/01/30/o_nashih_ekonomicheskih_zadachah

Radaev, V. V. and A. V. Buzgalin. *Economy of the Transition Period.* Moscow: n.p., 1995.

Raizberg, B. A., L. Sh. Lozovsky and E. V. Starodubtseva, eds. *Modern Economics Dictionary*, 2nd ed. Moscow: Infra-M, 1999.

"Rethinking the Future: Major American Economists and Sociologists on the Prospects and Contradictions of Modern Development." MEMO 11 (1998).

Rogov, S. "Lack of demand for science—a threat to the country's security." *Nezavisimaia Gazeta*, February 8, 2010. https://www.ng.ru/ideas/2010-0208/9_science.html

Rozanov, V. V. *Solitary Thoughts.* Moscow: Politizdat, 1990.

Ryazanov, V. T. "New Industrialization of Russia as a Real Goal and Post-Industrial Ideal." *Problems of Modern Economics* 52, no. 4 (2014): 32–34.

———. "New Industrialization of Russia: Strategic Objectives and Current Priorities." *Economic Revival of Russia* 40, no. 2 (2014): 17–25.

———. "The Neo-Industrialization of Russia and Opportunities to Overcome Economic Stagnation." *Economic Revival of Russia* 46, no. 4 (2015): 24–33.

Sakaiya, T. "Cost Created by Knowledge, or the History of the Future." In *The New Post-Industrial Wave in the West: An Anthology*, edited by V. L. Inozemtsev, 337–371. Moscow: Academia, 1999.

Sakharov, A. D. "Convergence, peaceful coexistence." http://www.sakharov-archive.ru/Raboty/Rabot_70.html.

Say, Jean-Baptiste. *Treatise on Political Economy.* http://ek-lit.narod.ru/saysod.htm.

Semyonov, V. S. *The Service Sphere and Its Workers*. Moscow: Politizdat, 1966.

Sergeeva, I. and V. Bykov. "Material and Non-Material Factors of Labor Motivation." *Man and Labor* 9 (2010): 43–46.

Schumpeter, I. A. *Theory of Economic Development*. Moscow: Progress, 1983.

Scientific Session of the General Meeting of RAS, Scientific and Technological Forecast: The Most Important Element of the Development Strategy of Russia, Bulletin of RAS 3 (2009): 195–260.

Sitdikova, B. "Theoretical Bases of Service under Russian Federation Legislation." *Law Education and Science* 1 (2008): 28–32.

Smith, Adam. *An Inquiry into the Nature and Causes of the Wealth of Nations*. Moscow: Sotsekgiz, 1962.

Smolin, O. N. "Development of Human Potential as the Basis for XXI Century Modernization." *Economic Revival of Russia* 44, no. 2 (2015): 34–37.

———. *Education for All*. Moscow: Prospect, 2006.

Sokolov, A. A. "Influence of rent-seeking behavior on investments of Russian state corporations." PhD diss., Russian Academy of Sciences, 2013. http://www.cemi.rssi.ru/news/cemi/sokolov.pdf.

Solodkov, M. V., T. D. Polyakova and L. N. Ovsyannikov, *Theoretical Problems of Services in the Non-Productive Sphere under Socialism*. Moscow: Moscow University Press, 1972.

Sorokin, D. E. "Political and Economic Guidelines for Institutional Transformation." In *China and Russia*. Moscow: Nauka, 2003.

———. "The State Should Act as a Driver of Entrepreneurial Initiative." *World of Change* 1 (2014): 79–81.

———. "Transformation of the Economic System of Russia." *Problems of Modern Economics* 51.3 (2014): 46–49.

Sorokin, P. A. "Mutual convergence of the United States and the U.S.S.R. to the mixed sociocultural type." *International Journal of Comparative Sociology* 1, no. 2 (1960): 143.

Soros, George. "The Crisis of World Capitalism: Open Society in Danger." Translated by S. K. Umrikhina and M. Z. Shterngarts. Moscow: INFRA-M, 1999.

Stalin, Joseph. "On Industrialization and the Bread Problem. Speech at the Plenum of the Central Committee of the VKP(b) on July 9, 1928." In *Essays*. Vol. 11, 171–172. Moscow: Gosgolitizdat, 1949.

Joseph Stalin, "On the shortcomings of Party work and measures to eliminate Trotskyist and other two-faced men." In *A Word to Comrade Stalin*. Edited by Richard Ivanovich Kosolapov, 121–22. Moscow: Paleia, 1995.

Tatarkin, A. I. "Sobering up after the market euphoria is delayed, but still happens," *Gorod 812* 32 (2014): 21–23

Théry, E. *Russia's Economic Transformation of Russia*. Translated by A. A. Peshkov. Moscow: The Russian Political Encyclopedia (ROSSPEN), 2008.

"The Netherlands in the second half of the seventeenth century and in the eighteenth century." In *New History*. Tiumen: Tiumen State Academy of Culture, Arts, and Social Technologies, 2005. http://www.studfiles.ru/preview/3493421/./

"The Strategy of Russia's Economic Development: Materials of the All-Russian Discussion Held by the State Duma Committee on Economic Policy and Entrepreneurship, the Economics Department of RAS, the Russian Trade and Financial Union, and the Russian Economic Journal: Reports at the Extended Sessions of the State Duma Committee on Economic Policy and Entrepreneurship." *Russian Economic Journal* 7 (2000).

Tiriakian, E. A. "Pitirim Sorokin: My Teacher and Prophet of Modernity." *Journal of Sociology and Social Anthropology* 2, no. 1 (1999): 23.

Titova, N. E. *The History of Economic Doctrines: A Course of Lectures*. Moscow: Humanities Publishing Center "VLADOS," 1997. http://www.gumer.info/bibliotek_Buks/Econom/Titova/10.php.

Toffler, A. *The Third Wave*. Moscow: AST, 1999.

Tolkachev, S. A. "The Impact of Neo-Industrialization on Changes in Supply Chain Management." *Logistic* 10 (2015): 48–54.

Tolkushkin, A. V. "Works and Services of a Productive Character." In *Encyclopedia of Russian and International Taxation*. Moscow: Iurist, 2003.

Toynbee, A. *Civilization before the Judgment of History*. Moscow: Iris-Press, 2006.

Tsagolov, G. N. "New Integral Society - Seventh Formation." In *New Integral Society: General Theoretical Aspects and World Practice*. Edited by G. N. Tsagolov, 126–130. Moscow: LENAND, 2016.

———. "The Russian Imperative: From Bureaucratic-Oligarchic Capitalism to a New Integral Society." *Economics and Property Management* 4 (2015): 20–26.

———. "What Kind of Economy Leads to Happiness?." *Scientific Proceedings of the Free Economic Society of Russia* 181 (2014): 26–39.

Tsagolov, N. A., ed. *A Course in Political Economy*. Moscow: Ekonomika, 1973.

Tsatsulin, A. N. "Approaches to the economic analysis of complex innovation activity." *Proceedings of St. Petersburg State Economic University* 80, no. 2 (2013): 12–21.

Tsvetkov, V. A. "Integration Processes in the CIS and the International Experience of Economic and Political Cooperation." *Regional Economy* 39, no. 3 (2014): 64–73.

———. "The Extraterritoriality of Capital." *The Regional Aspect Management* 2, no. 1 (2014): 73–77.

Vatutnina, O. O., Vertakova Y. V. "Creating a sectoral integrated structure to increase the investment attractiveness of industry." *Microeconomics* 1 (2010): 174–180.

Vorachek, Kh. O. "On the State of the 'Theory of Services Marketing.'" *Problems of the Theory and Practice of Management* 1 (2002): 99–103.

Voronina, Y. "A cure for addiction." *Rossiiskaia Gazeta*, August 5, 2014. http://www.rg.ru/2014/08/05/zameshenie.htm.

Witte, S. *Abstract of Lectures on the National and State Economy, Delivered to His Imperial Highness the Grand Duke Mikhail Alekseevich in 1900–1902.* St. Petersburg: n.p., 1912.

———. *The strategy of the advanced development of Russia in the context of global crisis.* Moscow: n.p., 2010.

World History: Encyclopedia, Vol. 5. Moscow: Socio-Economic Literature Publishing House, 1958.

Zadorina I. N. "Management of Organizational-Economic Development of Enterprises of Industrial Services in Transport." Thesis, Kostroma State University N. A. Nekrasov, 2010.

Zhirnov, E. "Time of Despair, Panic of Thought." *Kommersant Vlast* 49 (December 14, 2015): 35. http://www.kommersant.ru/doc/2861286.

Non-Russian-Language Sources

Amin, S. *Accumulation on a World Scale: A Critique of the Theory of Underdevelopment.* New York: Monthly Review Press, 1974.

———. *Capitalism in the Age of Globalization: The Management of Contemporary Society.* New York: Zed Books, 1997.

Bell, Daniel. *The Coming of Post-Industrial Society: A Venture of Social Forecasting.* New York: Basic Books, 1973.

Berle, Adolf A., and C. Gardiner. *Means: The Modern Corporation and Private Property*. New York: The Macmillan Company, 1932. http://www.unz.org/Pub/BerleAdolf-1932.

Brzezinski, Zbigniew. *Between Two Ages: America's Role in the Technetronic Era*. New York: The Viking Press, 1970.

Börner, Katy. "Mapping the Structure and Evolution of Science." Presentation at the Symposium on Knowledge Discovery and Knowledge Management Tools at NIH, Bethesda, MA, February 6, 2006. https://grants.nih.gov/grants/KM/OERRM/OER_KM_events/Borner.pdf

Cairncross, A. "What Is Deindustrialization?" In *Deindustrialisation*, edited by F. Blackaby, 5–17, London: Pergamon, 1982.

Callinicos, A. *Against Postmodernism: A Marxist Critique*. London: Palgrave MacMillan, 1989.

Chase, Stuart. *A New Deal*. New York: The Macmillan Company, 1932.

Chiesa, G., and R. Medvedev, *Time of Change: An Insider's View of Russia's Transformation*. New York: Pantheon Books, 1989.

Chiesa, G. *Transition to Democracy: Political Change in the Soviet Union, 1987–1991*. Hanover: Dartmouth College, University Press of New England, 1993.

Clark, C. *The Conditions of Economic Progress*. London: Macmillan, 1940.

Cooper, P. D., and R. W. Jackson, "Applying a Services Marketing Orientation to the Industrial Services Sector." *Journal of Business & Industrial Marketing* 3, no. 2 (1988): 51–54.

Crawford, R. *In the Era of Human Capital*. New York: Harper Business, 1991.

Delaunay, Jean-Claude and Jean Gadrey. *Services in Economic Thought: Three Centuries of Debate*. New York: Springer, 1992.

Dosi, G., C. Freeman, and R. Nelson. *Technical Change and Economic Theory*. London: Pinter, 1988.

Drucker, P. *The Age of Discontinuity; Guidelines to Our Changing Society*. New York: Harper and Row, 1969.

Dworczak, H. "Creating an Alternative." *Extract of International Viewpoint*. (Autumn 2004). http://internationalviewpoint.org/spip.php?article21.

Eick, Christoph, Jens Reichel, and Paul Schmidt. *Instandhaltung des Kapitalstocks in Deutschland: Rolle und volkswirtschaftliche Bedeutung*. Frankfurt am Main: VDI Forum IH, 2011. http://www.fokus-instandhaltung.de/fileadmin/betriebsrat_vdi_ev/redakteur/ringelmann/Dateien/20110309_Instandhaltungsvolumen_in_der_BRDx.pdf

Fine, B. "Economics Imperialism and the New Development Economics as Kuhnian Paradigm Shift?" *World Development* 30, no 12 (2002): 2057–2070. https://doi.org/10.1016/S0305-750X(02)00122-5

Fisher, A. *The Clash of Progress and Security.* London: Macmillan, 1935.

———. "Production, Primary, Secondary and Tertiary." *Economic Record* 15, no. 1 (1939): 24–38.

Fölster, S. J. Gr. Göran. "Industri Och Tjänster – Båda Behövs För Tillväxt, Svenskt Näringsliv (the Confederation of Swedish Enterprise)." *The Economist* 377, no. 8446 (2005): 69–70.

Galbraith, John Kenneth. *The New Industrial State.* London: Hamish Hamilton, 1967.

Gitzel, Ralph. "Industrial Service as a Research Discipline." *ABB Corporate Research Service Solutions,* slide 7, June 6, 2014. http://cbi2014.unige.ch/Documents/CBI2014.IndustrialServiceAs AResearchDiscipline. RalfGitzel.Pdf.

Gruchy, A. G. "Uncertainty, Indicative Planning and Industrial Policy." *Journal of Economic Issues* 18, no. 1 (1984): 159–180.

Harvey, D. "The "New" Imperialism: Accumulation by Dispossession." *Socialist Register,* no. 40 (2004): 63–87.

Heilbroner, R. *An Inquiry into the Human Prospect.* New York: Norton, 1974.

———. *Business Civilization in Decline.* New York: Norton, 1976.

———. "Economic Problems of 'Postindustrial' Society." In *Dimensions of Society,* edited by D. Potter and P. Sarre. London: Hodder & Stoughton Educational Division, 1974.

Herbert, R., and C. Paraskevas, *The Business Services Sector: Calculating the Market Size.* Report, Lloyds Bank, 2012. http://www.lloydsbankcommercial.com/Business-Services-Calculating-the-market-size.

Hill, Peter T. "On Goods and Services." *Review of Income and Wealth* 23, no. 4 (1977): 315–338.

Homburg, C. and B. Garbe, "Towards an Improved Understanding of Industrial Services: Quality Dimensions and Their Impact on Buyer-Seller Relationships." *Journal of Business-to-Business Marketing* 6, no. 2 (1999): 39–71.

International Labour Organization. *World Employment and Social Outlook 2015: The Changing Nature of Jobs.* Geneva: ILO, 2015.

The Economist. "Industrial Metamorphosis: Factory Jobs Are Becoming Scarce. It's Nothing to Worry about." September 29, 2005. https://www.economist.com/finance-and-economics/2005/09/29/industrial-metamorphosis

Judy, R. W., and C. D'amico, *Workforce 2020: Work and Workers in the 21st Century.* Indianapolis: Hudson Institute,1997.

Kotz, D., and F. Weir. *Russia's Path from Gorbachev to Putin: The Demise of the Soviet System and the New Russia.* New York: Routledge, 2007.

Kotz, D. M., T. McDonough and M. Reich, eds. *Contemporary Capitalism and its Crises: Social Structure of Accumulation Theory for the Twenty-First Century.* Cambridge: Cambridge University Press, 2010.

Kowalkowski, Ch. "Enhancing the Industrial Service Offering: New Requirements on Content and Processes." PhD diss., International Graduate School of Management and Industrial Engineering, Linköping University, 2006. http://www. diva-portal.org/smash/get/diva2:22258/ FULLTEXT01.pdf.

Lane, D., ed. *Russia in Transition: Politics and Inequalities.* London: Routledge, 1995.

———. *Soviet Society under Perestroika.* 2nd ed. London: Routledge, 1991.

Lapavitsas, C., and L. Levina. "Financial Profit: Profit from Production and Profit upon Alienation." *Research on Money and Science* 24 (2010). https:// marxismocritico.files.wordpress.com/2012/10/rmf-24-lapavitsas-levina.pdf

Machlup, Fritz. *The Production and Dissemination of Knowledge in the USA.* Princeton: Princeton University Press, 1962.

Malakooti, B. *Operations and Production Systems with Multiple Objectives.* New York: John Wiley & Sons, 2013.

Masuda, Y. *The Information Society as Post-industrial Society.* Washington: World Future Society, 1983.

Marx, Karl. "Economic Manuscript 1857–58." In Marx, Karl, and Friedrich Engels, *Collected Works.* Vols. 28–29. New York: International Publishers, 1975.

Marx, Karl and Friedrich Engels. *Collected Works,* Vol. 46. London: Lawrence Wishart, 1992.

Mulgan, G. J. *Communication and Control: Networks and the New Economics of Communication.* Oxford: Polity, 1991.

Naisbitt, M. J. *Megatrends: Ten New Directions Transforming Our Lives.* New York, Grand Central Publishing, 1984.

Ohno, T. *Just-In-Time for Today and Tomorrow.* New York: Productivity Press, 1988.

Portal, R. "The Industrialization of Russia" in *Cambridge Economic History of Europe.* Vol. VI, edited by J. Habakkuk and M. Postan, 801–874. Cambridge: Cambridge University Press, 1966.

Quinn, J. B., T. L. Doorley and P. C. Paquette "Beyond Products: Services-based Strategy." *Harvard Business Review* 68, no 2 (1990): 58–60.

Research Study Monitor Group. *Industrial Services Strategies. The Quest for Faster Growth and Higher Margins.* Zürich, 2004. http://skyadvisory.ch/wp-content/uploads/2015/03/2004-Monitor-Group_Industrial-Services-Strategies.pdf.

Rifkin, J. *The End of Work: The Decline of the Global Labor Force and the Dawn of the Post-Market Era.* New York: G. P. Putnam's Sons, 1995.

Roco, M., and W. Bainbridge, eds. *Converging Technologies for Improving Human Performance: Nanotechnology, Biotechnology, Information Technology and Cognitive Science.* Arlington: National Science Foundation, 2004.

Rogelio, O. and R. Kallenberg. "Managing the Transition from Products to Services." *International Journal of Service Industry Management* 14, no. 2 (2003): 160–172.

Sakaiya, T. *The Knowledge-Value Revolution or, a History of the Future.* Tokyo: Kodansha USA Inc., 1991.

Schulze, P. W. "Russische und ueropaische Energiepolitik im Zeichen der Krise." In *Die neue Rolle Russlands im Osten der EU,* 2–29. Vienna: Internationales Institut Liberale Politik Sozialwissenschaftliche Schriftenreihe, 2009.

———. "The End of Transformation and the Reshaping of European Security: Challenges, Contradictions and Prospects." *In World Public Forum—Dialogue of Civilizations Anthology,* 239–252. Berlin: Dialogue of Civilizations Research Institute gGmbH, 2010.

Saxena, Siddharth (Montu). "Asiatic Roots and Rootedness of the Eurasian Project." In *The Eurasian Project and Europe,* edited by David Lane and Vsevolod Samokhvalov, 38–52. London: Palgrave Macmillan, 2009.

Smith, K. *What is the 'Knowledge Economy'? Knowledge Intensive Industries and Distributed Knowledge Bases.* Oslo: United Nations University, 2000.

Sneider, E. *Das politische System der Russischen Föderation. Eine Einführung.* Berlin: Springer, 2011.

Spulber, N. *The American Economy: The Struggle for Supremacy in the 21st Century.* Cambridge: Cambridge University Press, 1995.

Tillema, S. and M. Steen. "Co-Existing Concepts of Management Control: The Containment of Tensions Due to the Implementation of Lean Production." *Management Accounting Research* 27 (2015): 67–83.

Toffler, A. *The Third Wave.* London: Pan Books Ltd.; William Collins Sons & Co. Ltd., 1980.

Truel, J.-L. "Soutien aux PME innovantes: le problème de l'accès à un financement pérenne." *Vie & sciences de l'entreprise* 3 (2007): 159–167.

Veblen, T. *The Engineers and the Price System.* Kitchener: Batoche Books, 2001. http://socserv2.mcmaster.ca/~econ/ugcm/3ll3/veblen/Engineers.pdf.

Wadell, W., and N. Bodek. *The Rebirth of American Industry.* Vancouver: PCS Press, 2005.

Woll, A. et al., *Wirtwschaftslexikon.* Munich: Oldenbourg, 1994.

Woodside, Arch G. and William. G Pearce, "Testing Market Segment Acceptance of New Designs of Industrial Services." *Journal of Product Innovation Management* 6, no. 3. (1989): 185–201.

World Trade Organization. *International Trade Statistics,* 2012. https://www.wto.org/english/res_e/statis_e/its2012_e/its2012_e.pdf

Internet Sources

http://economy.gov.ru/minec/main/ — Ministry of Economic Development of the Russian Federation.

http://prognoz2030.hse.ru/ — Materials concerning the long-term forecast of the scientific and technological development of the Russian Federation until 2030. Higher School of Economics.

http://ras.ru/ — Russian Academy of Sciences.

http://superjet100.info/ — Website dedicated to the Sukhoi Superjet 100 aircraft.

http://tass.ru/ — Russian News Agency TASS.

http://www.bea.gov/ — Bureau of Economic Analysis (BEA) of the United States Department of Commerce.

http://www.cbr.ru/ — Central Bank of the Russian Federation.

http://www.fas.gov.ru/ — Federal Antimonopoly Service of Russia.

http://www.ft.com/ — The Financial Times.

http://www.gks.ru/ — Federal State Statistics Service.

http://www.hse.ru/ — Higher School of Economics.

http://www.minfin.ru/ — Ministry of Finance of the Russian Federation.

http://www.oanda.com/ —Oanda Company.

http://www.raskruting.ru/ — Industrial Marketing. Marketing and marketing research organisation.

http://www.robotforum.ru/novosti-texnogologij/svezhaya-statistika-mirovyie-prodazhi-robotov.html — Robotforum. Public portal dedicated to industrial robots.

http://www.worldbank.org/ — World Bank.

https://minobrnauki.gov.ru/ — Ministry of Science and Higher Education of the Russian Federation.

Babkin, K. A. Speech at the Moscow Economic Forum-2014. URL: http://me-forum.ru/media/events/rt_4/.

Dynkin, A. A. Russia in the global economy 2012–2020. URL: http://russiancouncil.ru/inner/?id_4=1377#top-content.

List of critical technologies of the Russian Federation (PR-842 dated May 21, 2016). URL: http://ispu.ru/node/2680.

Primakov, E. M. New industrialization of the country: Report from the meeting of the Mercury Club on June 8, 2012. URL: http://www.tpp-inform.ru/official/2393.html.

Priority Directions for the Development of Science, Technology and Engineering in the Russian Federation (PR-843 dated May 21, 2006). URL: http://ispu.ru/node/2680.

Priority Directions for the Development of Science, Technology and Engineering in the Russian Federation (Decree of the President of the Russian Federation No. 899 of July 7, 2011). URL: http://static.kremlin.ru/media/events/files/41d38565372e1dc1d506.pdf.

Putin, V. V. Speech at the expanded meeting of the State Council "On the Development Strategy of Russia Until 2020" February 8, 2008. Website of the President of Russia. URL: http://kremlin.ru/events/president/transcripts/24825.

Putin, V.V. On our economic goals. 30 January, 2012. URL: http://pu.virmk.ru/aktual/interview/PUTIN/econom.htm/.

Putin, V. V. Speech at the plenary session of the St. Petersburg International Economic Forum. V. V. Putin: Verbatim report on the plenary session of the XVIII St. Petersburg International Economic Forum. URL: http://kremlin.ru/events/president/news/21080

Smolin, O. N. Speech at the Moscow Economic Forum-2014. URL: http://me-forum.ru/media/events/plenary_discuss_I/

Verbatim report of the meeting of the expert group of the Strategy-2020 No. 7 held on 2 April, 2011. URL: http://2020strategy.ru

Strategy for Innovative Development of the Russian Federation (Approved by Decree of the Government of the Russian Federation of December 8, 2011 No. 2227 - p.). URL: http://base. garant.ru/70106124/

FTP "Research and advancement in priority areas of development of the scientific and technological complex of Russia for 2007-2012". URL: http://fcp.economy.gov.ru/cgi-bin/cis/fcp.cgi/Fcp/Title/1/2007

"Sergei Bodrunov's lively book addresses one of the most controversial consequences of liberal globalization—the deindustrialisation of the advanced capitalist states. Following the line of thinking of writers such as Clark Kerr and J.K. Galbraith, Bodrunov insists on the revival of industrialization and in doing so he makes advances on earlier theorizing. He insists that the development of civilization calls for a higher level of material production predicated on human knowledge and he anticipates much of current theorizing about the effects of artificial intelligence. In a provocative discussion, predicated on the experience of post-socialist Russia, he calls for positive economic policies to enhance the capabilities of modern economies to advance to higher levels of industrial development. The book will appeal to readers seeking solutions to modern economic problems through state coordination."

— David Lane, Emeritus Professor of Sociology, University of Cambridge, UK

"As Marx, Veblen and John Kenneth Galbraith understood, human society co-evolves with its material and technological conditions, which fact has grave implications for those seduced by financialization or the post-industrial mirage. In *The Coming New Industrial State: Reloaded*, Sergey Bodrunov gives a fair—and sometimes harsh—portrait of modern Russia's fall into dependence on outside technologies, machines, and components. He advocates a path forward for Russia at the technical frontiers, with a mixed economy rooted in 'an authentic culture' without which, he writes, 'there can be no effective industrial development.' The war and sanctions may now catapult this analysis to the forefront."

— James K. Galbraith, The University of Texas at Austin, Member, Free Economic Society and Foreign Member, Russian Academy of Sciences

"Sergey Bodrunov's work is a major contribution to human knowledge, rooted both in his practical experience in Russian industry and government, and in revival of interest in the most profound issues in the philosophy of thought. It deserves the attention of everyone with an interest in innovation. But beyond that, anyone concerned with the rising challenge of new technologies should read it.

At the center of *The Coming New Industrial State* lies the following proposition: until now, technology has driven society. The 'information economy' calls for a different relationship; it is society that must drive technology. Innovation, therefore, henceforth constitutes social innovation; a different way of organizing society. Bodronov not only poses the question but provides much-needed answers."

— Alan Freeman, co-director of the Geopolitical Economy Research Group